Author's Dedication to Veterinarians

The Veterinary industry is one of the cleanest industries in the U.S. when it comes to percentage of bad actors. While police departments seem to average about 15% bad cops compared to the 85% who work zealously and honestly to protect society, the percentage of bad actors in the Veterinary medicine field is remarkably low, averaging 2-5%.

No one dislikes bad actor veterinarians more than the 95+% of the great veterinarians in the country dedicated to helping our pets and farm animals.

Joey's Legacy: Seeking Truth and Integrity in Veterinary Medicine is about the small percentage of bad actors (the Bad Guys) and the victims they leave behind, heartbroken and guilt-ridden that they chose the wrong veterinarian to treat their beloved pets.

As Big Pharma and the Pet Food Dynasty seek to overtake the veterinary industry, pushing drugs that often kill and toxic pet foods and flea collars, all in the cause of Big Money, the industry has changed over the past few decades.

How would you like to check your child out of the hospital only to be told you must pay the $10,000.00 bill before they release your child, like being held hostage until the ransom is paid? Thankfully, this does not happen in the field of human medicine but is common in the field of veterinary medicine.

Why do so many State Veterinary Boards never see a veterinarian they don't love regardless of stack-loads of complaints filed by innocent Pet Parents who lost Fido or KitKat due to a bad teeth cleaning.

Why is human medical malpractice insurance $100,000.00 dollars per year... or more, but veterinary malpractice insurance is less than $1,000.00 per year?

A message to the small percentage of bad actor vets and the State Veterinary Board Swamp: Joey's Legacy is coming after you.

THE GIG IS UP!

JOEY'S LEGACY

SEEKING TRUTH AND INTEGRITY IN VETERINARY MEDICINE
VOLUME TWO

AUTHOR JL ROBB

Copyright © 2022 J. L. ROBB Editing by Jacqueline Poolton and Lynn Thomay

All rights reserved. No part of this book may be used or reproduced by any means, graphic, electronic, or mechanical, including photocopying, recording, taping or by any information storage retrieval system without the written permission of the publisher except in the case of brief quotations embodied in critical articles and reviews.

Energy Concepts Productions books may be ordered through booksellers or by contacting: Energy Concepts Productions A Division of Energy Concepts 3328 E Whippoorwill Drive Duluth, Georgia 30096

Because of the dynamic nature of the Internet, any web addresses or links contained in this book may have changed since publication and may no longer be valid.

The views expressed in this work are solely those of the author and do not necessarily reflect the views of the publisher, and the publisher hereby disclaims any responsibility for them. The information provided in this book does not, and is not, intended to constitute legal advice. All content available within this book is for informational purposes only. Readers of this book should contact an attorney licensed in their respective state to obtain advice pertaining to with respect to any potential veterinary malpractice action. The content within this book is provided "as is, not edited" and is based upon my research of this particular topic. I make no guarantees or representations that this content is free from errors.

ISBN: 978-0-57831-393-1 Case

ISBN: 978-0-57831-392-4 Perfect

Printed in the United States of America.

<u>Dedication</u>

"This book series is dedicated to our shining star, Joseph Russell Fine, and all of his feline, canine and equine brothers and sisters that met an unexpected fate at the hands of another: veterinarians that committed acts of negligence that resulted in their untimely demise." Scott Fine

This book is also dedicated to the majority of veterinarians, the good, ethical and dedicated doctors who genuinely care for our pets, day-in and day-out. God bless them.

May we all see an end to veterinary negligence and the deceitful conduct of some veterinarians in the aftermath. Every industry has a few bad apples; but in this particular industry, years of heartbreak and guilt are often the result of bad-actor veterinarians.

This book is dedicated to changing the way our courts look at our pets. Pets are family, not a lawn mower. It is also our intent to clean the State Veterinary Board swamp, a Board that has never seen a veterinarian they did not love, no matter how many complaints are lodged.

No one dislikes the bad-actor veterinarian more than the good veterinarians.

Joey's Legacy: Seeking Truth and Integrity In Veterinary Medicine

Other Books by JL Robb

The End Part One: *And Then The End Will Come*

The End Part Two: *You Have Been Warned*

The End Part Three: *Visions and Dreams*

The End Part Four: *The Disappearance*

The End Part Five: *The Two Witnesses*

The End Part Six: *The Third Woe*

The End Part Seven: *The Ninth of Av*

Joey's Legacy Volumes One & Two
Seeking Truth and Integrity in Veterinary Medicine-Volume 1
Seeking Truth and Integrity in Veterinary Medicine-Volume 2

ENDORSEMENT

I cannot believe that it has been a few years since Scott Fine called on me during the very early stages of his founding of Joey's Legacy, and his nonprofit, ground up movement for justice, regarding those "bad actors" Scott refers to, and who are guilty of negligence, malpractice, and/or purposely doctoring and/or altering medical records, in order to hide errors in case workup, case management or clinical judgement. And while I have stated to both grieving clients, and those other professionals involved with Scott's movement, we all are human and make mistakes, and forgiveness is indeed a very important part of the healing process, even in the face of such tragic loss. But when medical professionals go to such extreme measures as to lying, hiding mistakes or altering medical records, then it is my strong view that the tragic passing of these victimized animals does deserve justice. One of the biggest areas of frustrating negligence and malpractice I have seen over many decades of clinical veterinary practice has been the wanton overuse, or inappropriate use of both core and noncore vaccinations in our animal companions. Very often their use provides absolutely no clinical benefit to the animal, and in many cases does both short- and long term immune system damage. Every medical and veterinary physician has taken an oath on graduation from medical or veterinary school that states, "Above all, do no harm". In my experience, this specific issue is one of the most often overlooked areas of negligence and malpractice in the conventional veterinary profession, especially when administering these vaccinations to chronically ill animals with immune mediated disorders and/or cancers. There is plain and simply no excuse for such practices. In my work with Scott and the grieving clients over the years, I have often found that while the client was pursuing negligence or malpractice for different reasons, that the widespread clinical practice of over vaccination was often the key component in the timeline history of these cases that often triggered or accelerated patient decline. I am proud to be part of Joey's Legacy, both in their quest for accountability of the "bad actors", as well as hopefully working with state legislative bodies in legal reform, relative to characterization of animals as much more than property, in addition to allowing for recovery of more than just property value damage when an animal companion falls victim to negligent or poor medical practice. Ultimately, the goal for all of us in this movement, as well as the ix entire veterinary profession, should be for all of us to work as hard as we can together, while learning from our errors or mistakes, in providing the most competent and skilled medical care possible. After all, it always should have been about, and hopefully always will be about the health and wellbeing of the animals FIRST.

Michael Dym, VMD. Dr. Michael Dym is a Presidential Scholar graduate of Cornell University where he earned his Bachelor of Science in Animal Science in 1986.

Dr. Dym received his veterinary degree from the University of Pennsylvania where he was a top graduate. His veterinary degree came from the prestigious University of Pennsylvania where he was a top graduate. Dr. Dym has been treating pets since 1991. Dr. Dym is one of 250 veterinarians in the United States trained in classical veterinary homeopathy by Richard Pitcairn, DVM, PhD. He is an active member of the Academy of Veterinary Homeopathy and the American Holistic Veterinary Medical Association. He also offers progressive integrative conventional veterinary medicine.

A message from Thomas Nicholl, attorney and veterinarian

I have had the benefit of seeing veterinarian interactions with animals and clients from two different perspectives. The reason for this is that I practiced as a Veterinarian for over 20 years in both the companion animal and equine areas. Then someone I didn't know decided to run a stop sign at about 50 m.p.h. while drunk and try to put his car where mine was. When I came out of hospital about a week later, I was advised to "find something different to do." Therefore, I went to Law School, and have been in practice as an attorney for 16 years.

As an attorney, I see a lot of Veterinary malpractice cases (all for the owner of the animal, as all veterinarians are required to carry malpractice insurance, and the respective companies defend them, either by attorneys on staff, or given to a few regularly used outside firms). In SOME cases, there has, indeed, been malpractice – the vet did something below the standard of care which also caused the injury. In ALL cases, the owner is at the very least upset, and perhaps distraught. Even in the cases where there actually was malpractice, a few of these may never progress, but a vast majority of those where there was not malpractice, but the owner is nevertheless (and quite understandably) upset, would not progress if the veterinarian was caring and sympathetic.

Now putting on my Veterinarian hat, I have said, and I know many of my friends have said something similar, "I am sorry about……. I know he/she meant a lot to you. We did everything we could, but unfortunately it just didn't work. Is there anything I can do to help out" Also, when something did go wrong, hopefully not my fault, I would continue to see the animal without charge for that problem, until it was resolved. I'm not making myself to be a saint – I know of many others who do the same. I do know veterinarians who 1) are not perceived to be sympathetic 2) continue to charge full amounts for any conceivable treatment as long as the animal is still alive 3) make a bill dauntingly large (whether intentionally or not), and make a priority of getting paid, sometimes to the detriment of the animal. Although there are some veterinarians who manage well enough on their own, there are their malpractice carriers, who strongly advocate to their client veterinarians 1) admit nothing 2) never apologize 3) never refund any money 4) as soon as you get wind of anything, tell us first, and we will handle it. There is an overwhelming majority of veterinarians who are caring and sympathetic but are also somewhat under the repeated warnings similar to "failure to follow advice may result in us refusing to cover you." I find this a totally unacceptable mandate. Furthermore, some of the adjusters are so obnoxious, any settlement is rendered impossible. Back to being an attorney. I had one case where the vet. really did mess up, and left the dog on a heating pad, which caused burns so severe that the dog needed many skin grafts.

The veterinarian contacted his malpractice carrier, who I spoke to. When I explained the situation, he said "We are denying the claim because without a skin biopsy, there is no proof that the heating pad caused the burn." I couldn't resist but ask that if the paramedics came to a burning house and pulled out a person in need of treatment, they would not do anything without the results of a biopsy. I had another case where the vet. was a total jerk. However, he was not guilty of malpractice.

Wearing both hats, I see a much greater proliferation of young veterinarians who have a huge student loan debt. (In 1975 there were 13 vet schools in the country – now nearly every state has one, and they usually have over 200 students per year graduating). Because of the plethora of graduates, many of these veterinarians have spent minimal time with an older "mentor," and have set up their own practices. These veterinarians are not like the "old school" vet. many are used to, but instead are younger looking (hey anybody under 40 looks young to me,) are crippled with a vast debt which they must recover to pay both themselves, their loans, and their overhead. As a result, they are stressed, often perceived to be uncaring and money-hungry, and not spending enough time or interacting with patient. Of course., there are some clients who will be dissatisfied regardless of anything.

It's probably hopelessly optimistic, but where possible, it would be helpful to reduce the cost of veterinary education. It is, however, very easy to provide a course (even 1-2 lectures) about client relations. In addition, a letter from the AVMA to the veterinarian insurance carriers explaining to them how difficult their CYA policy makes for good client / veterinarian relationships. You don't have to say, "I'm sorry, I messed up, and as a result your pet died and I'm not going to charge you." But you can say "I'm sorry, I know they meant a lot to you, we did everything we could, but it wasn't enough I know you're upset, but we will take care of the cremation (or something else) as a humanitarian gesture for you. If veterinarians would start to behave like normal people, then I think their previous perception in the public eye can be recovered.

Thomas Nicholl is both an attorney and a Doctor of Veterinary Medicine.

He graduated from Veterinary Orlando School in 1975 and has practiced for over 20 years. He also holds a law degree and practices in the Central Florida area. He is a former State of Florida Prosecutor with extensive trial experience and is licensed with the Florida Bar Association as well as being a member of the American Veterinary Medical Association. Dr. Nicholl is originally from Ireland and has resided in the United States since 1975. He enjoys playing golf and has a Black Belt in Martial Arts. His office is located in Orlando, Florida.

FOREWARD

Scott and Debbie Fine
Joey's Legacy
JoeysLegacy.org

THE FIRST 60 YEARS OF MY LIFE were uneventful with all of my pet companions. All of the veterinarians were caring and compassionate people. Some visits were for vaccinations, some were sick visits, but none were as a result of life-threatening illness or injury. They all lived healthy, happy lives.

It was a different time.

I never experienced, nor heard any others talk about, the subject which is the basis for this book. It was never an issue brought into the public light, as far as I can recall.

The majority of veterinary practitioners today are loving, gentle professionals who entered the profession for the right reasons. They genuinely care about their patients. They want to make sure their patients live happy, healthy lives. They treat their patients like they treat their own loved ones, both human and animal.

There is a minority of veterinary practitioners that choose to follow a different path. Perhaps their practices have been bought by large conglomerates; entities whose bottom line is more important than the proper care of our loved ones. The practitioners, who are now controlled by others, must abide by the demands of their corporate bosses' new policies which often do not consider the welfare of their patients.

Part of this book will contain actual victim stories and photos. Nothing here is enhanced, embellished, or exaggerated for effect. It doesn't have to be. The reality of veterinary malpractice is that it exists. It will always exist because veterinarians are human, just like the rest of us. We accept that. Unexpected things happen to everyone in life. It's part of life.

We want to stop all the lying and deceit these "bad actors" feel is necessary to escape accountability. Ironically, 73% of the members of my Facebook group, Joey's Legacy-VetMal Victims, said that if the practitioner had only been honest with them about the events that led to the death of their pet companions, they could have eventually found a path to forgiveness, and they wouldn't feel the need for "revenge" by seeking justice through legal action and exposure of the bad actor through social, print and television media. What creates the need for a Joey's Legacy is all of the duplicity and dishonesty these otherwise revered members of a very beloved profession feel compelled to engage in. Maybe one day, there will be a change. I pray...

JOEY'S LEGACY

It was the summer of 2017 when we lost our shining star, our boy Joey, to whom this book is dedicated. He didn't die as a result of injury or natural causes, like the majority of his sisters and brothers. Joey, our dachshund, was given a drug that was contraindicated for his condition, according to its manufacturer. His condition was unknown at the time because no blood tests were performed to determine organ health. Two days later, we made the impossible decision to put an end to Joey's suffering, and so he was euthanized. We soon learned how many others were lost due to negligence, and so we decided to turn the worst experience of our lives into a place of comfort and solace for other victims of negligence. Joey's Legacy was born.

My vision was to form a non-profit organization that would include veterinary experts and animal law attorneys from around the country. The vets would review medical records and determine if veterinary malpractice occurred. If so, the vet would write an opinion letter that would be forwarded, along with all medical records, to an attorney in the state where the malpractice occurred to pursue legal action. Simple, right?

Not so fast.

I contacted a number of vet experts around the country. Most were unwilling to call out their unprincipled colleagues in writing. They contribute to the problem. The "sin of silence". Eventually, I found several vets who liked the idea of a "Joey's Legacy" because they, too, were disgruntled and frustrated with the actions of those practitioners who lacked an ethical and moral compass. They agreed to join our team, on a trial basis. So now I have the first part in place: the vet experts. What about the attorneys?

I contacted a number of animal law attorneys in different states to see what kind of spin they put on my idea. As you might imagine, their responses were similar citing the "pets are property" laws and it wouldn't be economically feasible for them to handle such cases.

Getting nowhere…shot down, over and over again. I wasn't done yet. One of the victims in our group told me about an attorney that might be interested in what I wanted to do. I contacted her, and she was on board with the idea within a few minutes.

Finally, attorney #1 was on board.

Slowly, we added one attorney after the other and we now have 31 attorneys that can assist members in all 50 states, who work with our 10 veterinary experts to assist our member victims seek justice.

Part of the age-old philosophy of convoluted thinkers like the AVMA and other vet-friendly organizations is trying to convince you that your dog or cat is only worth $100 in court, so suing your vet doesn't make sense. We now know that was part of the indoctrination we all fell for. That's why there were very few attempts to sue veterinarians for negligence. After all, if your potential damages are $100 in court it wouldn't make sense to proceed against a vet.

But Joey's Legacy found a better way in the last three years.

Not only do our attorneys sue for out-of-pocket costs and "replacement value" of your pet companion (still don't know what "replacement value" really means), our attorneys now also may sue for violations of consumer law, deceptive practices and common law fraud . This may include instances like when your veterinarian tells you that there will be someone at the clinic overnight to monitor your pet companion, who just had surgery and……guess what…..nobody will actually be there. Happens more than you know.

Some victims damage awards have since increased substantially from the $100 promised by the veterinary propaganda machine. In fact, some damage awards have reached into the thousands are commonplace. Joey's Legacy has demonstrated, over and over, that if you're a veterinary professional it doesn't pay to lie to one of our members.

THE "GOOD GUYS" IN VETERINARY MEDICINE

All professions have members that are competent at what they do. Let's call them the "good guys". They are ethical, professional, honest, and true. They don't lie, they don't deceive, and they don't play games with their clients. If something goes wrong, they tell the truth. They tell it like it is. They take their medicine, learn from it, and move on. They are professionals in every sense of the word.

The same applies to veterinarians. There are 60,000+ veterinarians in small animal practice in the United States. This paragraph applies to most of them. They provide compassionate care for their patients. Pet parents rely on their expertise to ensure a great outcome during a pet visit to the animal hospital.

Once in a great while, something unexpected occurs as a result of negligence. Sometimes the vet tech was negligent; perhaps the anesthesia dial was on "5" when it should have been on "2". The patient is overdosed with anesthesia, goes into cardiac arrest, and dies. Nothing done intentionally: just pure negligence. The vet was not present, but he must take the "hit", in most cases; because he is responsible for the actions of his employees.

The good guy confronts the pet parent, in what will be a difficult conversation. He/she knows how this situation must be handled: be straightforward, truthful, and transparent no matter how difficult it is. Remorse and contrition must be conveyed in a genuine fashion. Assistance to the pet parent must be offered in the aftermath.

The good guy has executed his responsibilities appropriately. The pet parent is now left to deal with grief, despair, shock and presumably anger at the loss of the loved one. If the pet parent decides to take legal action against the vet, the vet must consider it as part of the aftermath that he/she must endure: a relatively small price to pay in light of the emotional turmoil and unnecessary mayhem caused by his animal hospital.

However, my experience is that most pet parents in this situation are willing to find a path to forgiveness if the veterinarian was honest about what happened.

THE "BAD ACTORS" AND THEIR PLAYBOOK

Enter the bad actor.

In our group, a bad actor is a veterinarian who is super-motivated by the almighty dollar, someone who is usually a narcissist, is disinterested and insensitive to the needs of his/her clients and their pets and will lie in a heartbeat to protect himself/herself. This is the same misfit that would throw a staff member under the bus to save his/her own ass.

Bad actors are unprincipled misfits. Their depravity knows no bounds. They are trained to admit nothing if they commit negligence. Accountability, responsibility, and liability are words that are non-existent in their vocabularies. They won't think twice about altering medical records, if the pet parent files a complaint with the state board of veterinary medicine, in order to cover up their negligence. Serial offenders, some with a history of disciplinary action that dates back 10 years or more, are sharp enough to begin the process of scrubbing the records right away. The amateurs, those who haven't had an experience with the vet board tend to do nothing, expecting that they are in the clear. Then comes the letter from the vet board, and the race to scrub records begins. Scrubbing records can be done in a variety of ways, like changing lab results to reflect normal values or adding fictitious vital signs to present the appearance of a healthy patient. Just part of their playbook. It is stunning what levels the bad actor will go to in order to protect himself/herself. Nobody is safe, nothing is sacred. The irony of their conduct is that when a death occurs in their care as a result of negligence, they really have little to be concerned about. Here's why:

1. If the pet parent decides to file a complaint with the vet board, the investigation begins with the vet board sending the veterinarian a letter notifying him/her that the pet parent filed a complaint alleging negligence in the death of their pet companion. The good guy will respond with truth and integrity, sending copies of the deceased's medical records, untouched, unaltered, and appearing as it did after the original vet visit. The good guy responds promptly to any correspondence from the vet board and accepts his punishment. Case closed.

2. The bad actor will typically scrub records after receiving word of the complaint, then respond to the state's request. They contact a defense lawyer, in most cases, to represent them. In reality, they could handle their cases pro-bono since the final order is almost always a joke of a plea deal, constructed well in advance of the final hearing date. For the second and subsequent offenses, while you may think the level of disciplinary action would escalate, in most cases it is the same ineffective discipline as was imposed the first time.

3. Many victims are threatened by the bad actors and their staff, telling them that if they go to the media about what happened, they will be sued. In my experience and opinion, the best defense against being sued is to provide irrefutable facts and pure opinions.

Nevertheless, the victims heed the threat and are forced to suffer in silence.

AMERICA'S BOARDS OF VETERINARY MEDICINE-THE ACCOMPLICES THAT DRIVE THE GETAWAY CARS

Let's recap.

We have the good guys: veterinarians who entered the profession for the right reasons…NOT for money, but because of a genuine love for animals. These good guys provide great care and compassion for their patients and are truthful and transparent with their clients at all times, regardless of the situation. These are true professionals in every sense of the word. And then, of course, there are the bad actors. If something goes wrong and the patient suffers permanent injury or death, job one is to cover the negligence, deceive the pet parent about what happened, and scrub the medical records to make sure there are no signs of wrongdoing in case the pet caregiver files a complaint with the state veterinary board.

Most complaints are seemingly dismissed by vet boards… statistics show up to 80%. In contrast, Joey's vet team finds malpractice in 70% of the records that are submitted to them by our members.

Why is that?

There is an inherent bias toward forgiveness and leniency by the vet boards toward their "falsely accused" colleagues, so that could explain the massive number dismissals of complaints. A few complaints make it to the probable cause panels of the vet boards, which usually consists of 2-3 board members who screen cases and decide if there is reason to move the case to the next level, which in Florida is the Office of General Counsel. The case then proceeds to a final hearing, although the plea deal outcome is already known. The vet board does have discretion to modify the plea deal and I have seen boards either reduce the recommended sentence or enhance it. First time offenders receive a fine, perhaps a reprimand, continuing education requirements and a period of probation, none of which fazes the average veterinarian:

1. The fine usually isn't much more than an upscale Saturday night out.

2. The reprimand appears on the vet board's public website which most people, even vet mal victims, don't even know exists. It's just a formal description of what the pet parent writes on Yelp or Google. The difference is they can say whatever they want without fear of reprisal, as opposed to the pet parent who must stick with facts and pure opinions in order to mitigate the risk of being sued for defamation. Of course, any animal hospital that is dumb enough to sue for defamation exposes themselves to a very public lawsuit, which the astute pet parent will exploit to the max by providing all of the tragic details, many of which will not endear the public to the animal hospital. In addition, what pet parent would bring their loved one to a vet that might, one day, sue them?

3. CEUs (continuing education units) are perhaps the most valuable part of the disciplinary action because, as it turns out, education is greatly needed in some cases especially with the vets that have been practicing for 30-40 years who are not up to date on modern veterinary techniques.

4. Probation doesn't impede the vet's ability to generate income. He may practice "under supervision".

Disciplinary action for serial offenders is often the same, or similar, to first time offenders.

Why, you ask?

Think of the vet board members as the drivers of the getaway cars for the bad actors, who commit the negligence and count on the accomplices to help them "escape". Rarely will a veterinarian's license be suspended or revoked. Being that the vet board member is complicit, the act of suspending or revoking a license for something as "insignificant" as negligently causing the death of a pet companion is almost unheard of. They recognize that they can't suspend or revoke on a consistent basis for the same thing because they would be suspending the licenses of dozens of colleagues in their jurisdiction and, you know, that wouldn't do good things for their reputations in the community. However, if you want the reason given to me by one of the consumer advocates on the Florida Board of Veterinary Medicine…this is the official reason: "Who would take care of the dogs and cats if we suspended all of those licenses?" Spineless cowards.

Even if a pet caregiver proves fraud and deceit to the board, they typically ignore the fact that the bad actor altered medical records to erase the appearance of negligence. Recordkeeping violations by vets, along with practice below the standard of care, are the two most commonly charged violations by the board and the two least deterred by disciplinary action. The outrageous lack of morals and ethics will continue. The vet boards enact laws to insulate them from legal jeopardy. The veterinary justice system is broken, it's corrupt and is in massive need of reform.

One of the reasons for this book is to educate and enlighten you that vet board exists, the maltreatment of bereaved caregivers is an old story and will sadly continue on and without meaningful, impactful changes I believe this level of injustice will continue. The vet boards allow serial offenders to continue to offend.

It's more than enough to make you vomit.

A Message from Peggy R Hoyt, J.D., M.B.A., B.C.S.
The Law Offices of Hoyt & Bryan
Oviedo, Florida

I did not know my life was about to change the day I received a call from Scott Fine, founder of Joey's Legacy, Inc. He had been doing some research on Florida attorneys and discovered I had been the past chair of the Florida Bar Animal Law Section and adjunct professor of Animal Law. After we met, he learned about the depth and width of my true passion for animals.

I was born loving animals. I asked for my first horse before I turned one! Thanks to my mom, I've always had cats. Thanks to both my father and grandfather, I've always loved both horses and dogs. I got my first puppy as a toddler, a golden cocker spaniel, named Suzy. I'm happy to report I did finally get my first horse at age 10, an unbroke Arabian filly named Mint Julep. Since then, my life and heart has been filled with many meows, barks and neighs. For me, my trajectory was set.

Lucky for me, my formative years were spent surrounded by issues important to the emerging animal welfare movement in the United States. I am the eldest daughter of John A. Hoyt, the President and CEO of The Humane Society of the United States who served from 1970 to 1997. He assumed leadership of this now worldwide education and legislation organization just as the animal welfare movement in the United States was gaining steam. My dad was my mentor, my role model and my heart. He set the example for what was to become not only my passion, but an integral part of my profession.

Today, I am pet mom to seven (7) dogs, two (2) cats and three (3) horses: all rescued either from shelters and rescue organizations, as an unexpected gift from a deceased friend and through the Bureau of Land Management wild horse adoption program. They inspire me daily to promote, in both my personal and professional life, the importance of pets as family members that need to be protected, loved and revered. No loved pet ever deserves to end up scared, alone and frightened in a shelter or lost on the streets. Worse, they don't deserve to die because their pet parent didn't have a plan for their lifetime care.

I didn't always want to be a lawyer. As is true for many little girls, I thought I was going to be a veterinarian, and specifically, a horse vet. But since life doesn't always take us exactly where we think we might go, I got an undergraduate business degree in marketing and management, then an MBA in finance and eventually ended up in law school. For me, this was the natural progression of my professional career in finance and financial services. I spent a couple of years working as a financial consultant for a major brokerage house and then as CFO for a group of family owned companies. As a law student, I knew I wanted to work in the field of estate planning including wills, trusts, estate taxes and estate administration. Most of my classmates would roll their eyes and say, "boring, that's not for me."

I love the counselling aspect of an estate planning practice. Every day, as the founding partner of [The Law Offices of Hoyt & Bryan](), I get the opportunity to meet new friends who tell me stories about the people, pets, places, careers, and things they love. Since I am naturally, insatiably curious I'm never bored. In fact, I'm energized to be able to help someone custom craft an estate plan that is going to provide their loved ones with the resources and protections they deserve.

I always wanted to write a book. I know this is true for a lot of people; we all have something inside dying to get out in the form of the written word. My dad, also said he wanted to write a book, so I challenged him to a race – who can write their book first. Well, I won with the publication of my first book, [*All My Children Wear Fur Coats – How to Leave a Legacy for Your Pet*](). This book was the perfect marriage between my passion – pets – and my profession – law. It made complete sense to me. if you were going to create an estate plan for your human family, then you should also have an estate plan for your kids in fur coats! Today, the book is in its third edition (and I've published many more books since my first), I have a weekly "pawcast" titled [*All My Children Wear Fur Coats*]() and I founded [Animal Care Trust USA, Inc.](), a 501c3 not for profit whose mission is to keep loved pets in loving homes. We offer ongoing education for pet parents about the benefits of Pet Trusts, Forever Loved options for lifetime care and Pet Trustee services to provide fiscal management and oversight to ensure pets live long, happy, and healthy lives.

Not a single day goes by that I don't live my passion; loving my pets and educating pet parents about the importance of creating an estate plan that will 100% guarantee their pets receive lifetime love and care. Could it get any better than that? Yes!

And to bring my story full circle, after meeting Scott Fine and appearing on his podcast, he has included me as one of his trusted attorneys to support the mission of Joey's Legacy, Inc. Every day a loved pet loses its life due to the negligence of our veterinary community. Like lawyers, most veterinarians do an excellent job and always have the best interests of their clients and their pets at heart. But when they don't and when that mistake results in the loss of a loved family member, Joey's Legacy gives us the ability to take the steps necessary to make sure the loss of that precious life was not in vain.

Together we are working to develop a nationwide network of attorneys and trusted professionals who share these passions – keeping pets safe from veterinary harm AND keeping our loved pets in loving homes after the disability or death of their pet parent. If you are passionate about pets and our causes, we hope you will join us in this effort to assimilate the best and the brightest minds from across the country. We need eager young attorneys and seasoned veterans who can provide guidance and mentorship. We need supporting professions who can provide the resources and talent to help us accomplish some very big goals. We need loyal supporters and donors who can help us make a difference. We hope you'll join us.

PREFACE

Dear Bad Actor Veterinarian,

Perhaps you have already heard of Joey's Legacy: you may be one of the defendants involved in civil litigation as a result of the groundbreaking work of our animal law team. If you are, you've made mistakes that caused the permanent injury or death of the loved one that lived with our member. You've profoundly impacted a life. The bereaved animal guardian is now overwhelmed with intractable grief, anger and despair caused by your slipshod, "shotgun-style" practice of veterinary medicine. The legal costs that you (your insurance company) incur as a result of your negligence is considered by many bad actors to be just "a cost of doing business", like the electric bill or payroll expenses.

Were your ethics and morals ever respected? If so, what changed you? When did you abandon your professional conduct? Or were you always amoral, devoid of ethics, motivated by the great motivator: the almighty dollar? Was it the influence of a large corporation purchasing your practice, whose primary focus is the bottom line and who has little concern about providing great care for your patients? Do you have a monthly quota to perform 20 ultrasounds or 20 dental cleanings? Maybe you don't have the time to perform these types of procedures yourself, but want to meet such quotas, so you engage your unskilled, untrained office staff to perform veterinary care, many times leading to unexpected, dire consequences. Did you ever stop to think that providing great care for all your patients would enhance your bottom line, if money is your guiding light, because your satisfied clients would brag about your services to others, who would do the same. Maltreating a patient by engaging unqualified, uneducated staff members invites bad outcomes, and it is your name and reputation that will be sullied by their actions.

Lying about the facts that lead to death is not only unethical and unprincipled, but it also flies in the face of what we all learn as children: that honesty is the best policy. In a recent poll I conducted, 83% of our members declared that if the bad actor involved in the death of their loved one had just been forthcoming about what happened they would not have acted as they did in the aftermath (filing complaints, publicly exposing the bad actor and legal action) and actually would have forgiven practitioner. You alter medical records to try to exonerate yourself. What concerns do you have?

Your friends at the Board of Veterinary Medicine will protect you from meaningful disciplinary action. American courts do not provide appropriate justice in veterinary malpractice cases. The nominal settlements, which are typical in these cases, are paid by your insurance company. Even if they increase your malpractice insurance premiums from the average cost of $300 per year by a factor of 10, you can easily absorb the increase by raising your already exorbitant medical fees, which many do. Paying inflated costs for quality veterinary care is one thing; gouging a bereaved pet guardian for euthanasia and cremation costs is outrageous and contemptible. You are no different than retailers that charge $8.00 for a bottle of water when a hurricane approaches, due to short supply. Florida imposes stiff civil penalties for those that gouge the public. As a price gouger, you should be subject to the same treatment.

Are you wondering if I have anything good to say about you? Let not your heart be troubled; here it is:

There is still time to change your shoddy, insensitive behavior. Imagine becoming an ethical professional who is revered by the veterinary community, like the ethical majority of veterinarians in the world: veterinarians who put their patients care first; veterinarians who don't charge for certain services and demonstrate their kindness and consideration for animal guardians and the dire predicaments many find themselves in; veterinarians that cry genuine tears along with the family when the time comes to say good-bye to the family's loved one. Wouldn't you like to join, or rejoin, that highly esteemed, well-regarded part of your industry?

Sadly, most of you will continue your misguided, foolish ways that are motivated by your insatiable greed and sustained by your lack of integrity and conscience.

We don't want to meet you, and you certainly do not want to hear from us. If we hear about you in an unkind way, as a result of alleged mistakes made resulting in permanent injury or death of a beloved family member, rest assured we will investigate and, if warranted, pursue with great vigor and explore any and all legal remedies. Regardless of the outcome, we will become part of your life for a while.

In the past two years, we have assisted over 50 bereaved pet guardians. Our mission and our message continue to be heard all over the world, our membership continues to grow quickly, and with that growth more and more of you will be held accountable for mistakes made. The days of sailing along with no concern about accountability, responsibility and liability will now be replaced with accountability, responsibility and liability.

All we ask is that you treat your patients, our loved ones, with the same dignity and respect that you would hopefully treat your own pet companions, and your human family.

We fight bullies all the time, and we prevail most of the time. Don't be one of those bullies. ABOVE ALL, DO NO HARM. Make $1MM per week if you can, but do it ethically, honestly and professionally, and DO NO HARM.

DO NO HARM

We Can Help

Most veterinarians are caring and compassionate individuals, well-suited for their profession. There is a minority of veterinarians that places profits before quality care for their patients. Joey's Legacy has assembled America's first nationwide network of veterinary experts and animal law attorneys whose mission is to hold practitioners of veterinary medicine accountable for negligence that results in the permanent injuries and deaths of our pet companions.

A Word from the Author

I first learned of Joey's Legacy in July 2020. I was unaware of the veterinary malpractice issue.

When Scott Fine, the founder of Joey's Legacy, contacted me about his non-profit group, I was in the middle of writing a 3-part trilogy about Abe the Bartender, one of the characters in my series about the last days described by biblical prophets 2000 to 2700 years ago. Abe was the most favorite character. I told Scott I would have to finish the series' first. I am the proud owner of my sixth Great Dane since 1976. I have had pets my entire life: dogs, cats, rabbits, skunks. My mind started working on me, and Scott was pleasantly persistent.

I have used the same veterinary clinic, Duluth Animal Hospital, since 1985; and they have taken care of all my Great Danes. I have never experienced the loss that the stories in this book series lay out. They are heart-wrenching to say the least, and the tragedy lives on through the poor victims who took their pets to the veterinarian for routine procedures and never saw them alive again. Then the veterinarian doctors the notes and the coverup begins. I am convinced that God made all the animals, domestic and wild, for a purpose; and he classified the animals as domestic and wild in the very first book of the Bible.

On the very same day Noah with his sons, Shem and Ham and Japheth, and Noah's wife and the three wives of his sons entered the ark, they and every wild animal of every kind, and all domestic animals of every kind, and every creeping thing that creeps on the earth, and every bird of every kind—every bird, every winged creature.

Genesis 7:13-14

It was my honor to have a part in Joey's Legacy and this book! *Joey's Legacy-Seeking Truth and Integrity in Veterinary Medicine*

www.The-End-The-Book-The-Series.com/joeys-legacy

"A CRY FROM THE HEART"
Carol Morris 2020

Dedicated to Silver Puff
Nikki Wharton-Eby

I miss your sweet angelic face, your warm presence, dignity and grace.

It wasn't your time...

I miss a snuggle, purring delight, and frisky playfulness at night.

It wasn't your time...

I miss you nestled close to me. My joy and love, dear Silver Puff

It wasn't your time.

I feel your paw upon my face with compelling memory of our spirits' embrace…

When I saw you soon after you were born…so tiny, cold, so forlorn. I warmed you with my hands and breath… gave you sustenance and became your Mom.

Time pushed us along a curving path of sun-splashed days and stormy nights,… whether I was happy or depressed I always found you there…my loyal loving Silver Puff.

I think you know I loved you best!

In the arms of an angel…

Rest in peace, precious one

Chapter I

The United States is unique when it comes to Veterinary care:

1. US veterinary care is the most expensive on the planet.

2. Veterinary malpractice in the US is significant and occurs more often than in any other civilized country.

Unfortunately, the veterinary industry of today is hardly ever held accountable because:

*Veterinarians often run the state Veterinary Boards, which offer *oversight*.

*The US court system considers your pet, domestic and non, to be personal property, not part of the family. In other words, your pet is considered similar to a lawnmower, hedge trimmer or shed.

It does not matter if your pet is a service animal/companion. If you are blind and have a dog that assists you, if he dies from veterinary negligence, you just lost your lawnmower.

Medical and veterinary malpractice is not new, but medical malpractice has usually been the most prevalent of the two; because people are people and family pets and support animals are... well, just a lawnmower.

For the owner of pets, from furbabies to the equine community, from cockatoos to hedgehogs, these pets are definitely *family*. They have animal DNA and can replicate themselves, unlike the lawnmower.

Human medical malpractice has large settlements, the only repercussion available, often in the millions of dollars.

Until recently, until groups like Joey's Legacy (JoeysLegacy.org) brought this travesty to the forefront, the deterrent for Veterinarians was laughable, a hundred bucks for your pet or replacement value at the most. The courts, as a rule, do not award the price of your

$2,500.00 John Deere lawnmower but more of an award for killing your pet, valued in the range of a crockpot.

"I'm sorry I accidently killed your pet- and I am not acknowledging that I did- how about $100.00? Will that work?"

No, that will not work, not any longer.

Like the Police Unions protect the police at all costs, even when they know the police in question are bad apples, state Veterinary Boards do the same for their members. And often their members own and operate the Veterinarian Boards. No conflict here! Move on.

JoeysLegacy.org and the Joey's Legacy Vet-Mal Facebook page, have worked zealously to change this injustice, while educating the masses of pet owners who do not know this phenomenon occurs.

Soon, a documentary will expose this travesty for the world to see.

How it all began:

The fight back began with an adorable dachshund named Joey. The veterinarian clinic technicians neglected to conduct the necessary blood work and later claimed that Joey's owner wanted to save money, casting the blame on the victim and doctoring the records.

Most victims of this man-made tragedy understand that doctors sometimes make mistakes. Most veterinarians own up to it, try to console as best they are able and offer assistance, whether monetary or pet-replacement, as though their pet could be *replaced*.

It is not the malpractice or the negligence; it is the coverup by the bad-actor veterinarians and their defenders et al, the state Veterinary Boards.

The Veterinary Boards seemingly never saw a veterinarian they did not love, no matter how many accusations of incompetence or complaints have been filed. They are also a provider of the malpractice insurance the veterinarian buys. No conflict; no foul.

But now, "The gig is up!"

Joey's Legacy and similar groups are rapidly making changes in the current, very-flawed process of veterinary oversight by:

1. Changing the way the courts view a pet.

2. Cleaning of some veterinary board swamps. They are not all swamps, but too many truly are.

3. Upping the penalty for bad-actor vets and enforcing that penalty.

4. Increase monetary awards for the victims.

The reason Veterinary Malpractice Insurance is so inexpensive is because of the meager dollar-penalty awarded. While malpractice insurance for physicians ranges from $4,000-$12,000 per year and as much as $200,000.00 per year for obstetricians, veterinary liability insurance is about $400.00 per year.

This is changing, however, because of Joey's Legacy and animal rights activists across the land. The idea that our pets are more lawnmower than animal is evolving as courts begin to recognize them as *family or sentient beings*. Sentient references things that are alive, are aware of its surroundings and experience emotions. Anyone who is a pet lover considers the pet to be family.

Joey's Legacy works 24/7 to prevent stories like the one below:

Cape Breton veterinarian who mistakenly euthanized dog loses license, must sell practice

Dr. Sietse VanZwol will no longer have a licence to practise veterinary medicine after 5 p.m. on Friday

MEAT COVE, Nova Scotia (July 8, 2021 update)
By: Sharon Montgomery

A veterinarian who mistakenly euthanized a dog last year has been forced to surrender his licence and sell his animal clinic. Dr. Frank

Richardson, registrar of the Nova Scotia Veterinary Medical Association, said Dr. Sietse VanZwol, owner of Highland Animal Hospital in Port Hawkesbury, will no longer have a licence to practise veterinary medicine after 5 p.m. on Friday, July 9. "He's no longer allowed to practise anywhere," Richardson said.

"Not just Nova Scotia but anywhere." Richardson said. They don't believe VanZwol intends to try to get a licence elsewhere but if he does he will notify the licencing body of the jurisdiction in question and make them aware of this complaint.

As well, Richardson said according to their legislation, because VanZwol is not a licensed veterinarian anymore, he has one year from July 9 to sell his practice.

Highland Animal Hospital also has offices in Guysborough, Inverness, Chéticamp and Ingonish.

"He has to sell it," Richardson said. "Because of not being a veterinarian anymore, he cannot stay as an owner. I'm under the understanding the process is already underway."

Meanwhile, after waiting almost an entire grief-stricken year for the decision, Arlene Fougere of Meat Cove was extremely emotional while relaying she finally got justice for her beloved eight-year-old husky Cooper.

Fougere said her lawyer sent her a copy of the decision and admits it was difficult to open it at first.

"When I got to the final decision I just started bawling," she said. "I couldn't even read anymore at one point. I had to keep wiping away my tears to keep reading. I kept saying, 'omg Cooper won. He's going to save other animals. Cooper fought for justice for a whole year not just for himself but for other animals and he won, he did it.'"

On Aug. 4, 2020, Fougere took Cooper to a walk-in clinic held in Ingonish by the Highland Animal Hospital in Port Hawkesbury to have the dog's sore leg checked.

In an earlier story in the *Post*, Fougere said her dog was very healthy and that she had spoken to the veterinary assistant on several occasions regarding her dog's leg.

Due to COVID-19 restrictions at the time, Dr. Sietse Vanzwol came out to the parking lot. Seeing the doctor carrying a rubber band, Fougere assumed he was going to draw blood for testing.

Without carrying a chart or saying a word, the veterinarian gave her dog a needle euthanizing him. Fougere was extremely distraught.

"I screamed, "You killed my dog," she said.

Fougere was so distraught, RCMP responded to the scene to assist.

The veterinarian told her there were three dogs there to be put down and he made a mistake.

Fougere filed a complaint with the provincial veterinarian authority.

Richardson said it did take time for the panel to reach a decision as it was a serious allegation against a member. He said their mandate is what's in the public's best interest. The panel also did an extensive audit of VanZwol's medical records, which added to the time but also helped in making the final decision.

Richardson said even in the weeks leading up to this decision, Dr. VanZwol has only been allowed to practise under certain restrictions including not permitted to do euthanasia and only permitted to work under the direct supervision of two veterinarians.

"Every case he sees has been scrutinized by two veterinarians to see that he is practising in accordance to standards," he said. "That supervision will end Friday at 5 p.m. He's done."

In asking about deficiencies uncovered during the audit and listed in the decision of the panel, Richardson said medical records are an integral part of any medical practice and they take record keeping very seriously.

He said it disappoints him that the member did not have complete medical records as he should have had on his cases.

When asked if during the dealings the NSVMA and complaints panel had with this case if there's been any remorse expressed by VanZwol, Dr. Richardson said he can't answer that as he hasn't had any direct communication with the member since the complaint was lodged last year. However, he said the panel didn't indicate that in their decision.

Richardson agreed it was a heartbreaking situation for the family involved. He feels the complaints committee made the right decision based upon all the factors they had.

"Their intention is to minimize any further harm and risk to the public," he said. "In considering Dr. VanZwol's age and all of the factors playing in, I think to offer him an end date to get out of practice was the right thing and that end date is July 9."

Emotional year

Fougere said it was an emotional year waiting for this decision. Overcome with grief daily, she was unable to concentrate or be motivated to do much of anything, missing her best friend every single day. Fougere said she felt she let Cooper down by taking him to that clinic that day. A lobster fisher, she no longer went out during the year other than when fishing season was on. She has never even been able to bring herself to put her dog's things away. Cooper's treats, stuffed toys and dishes are still where they always were.

"I haven't been on a walk since August," she said, through sobs. "I can't without Cooper. It turned my life upside down. I couldn't function."

However, after the 11 painful months waiting for the decision, Fougere said she understands now why it took the NSVMA so long, she realizes the extent of their audit and is grateful to them for putting that effort into it and for their conclusion.

"I haven't been on a walk since August. I can't without Cooper. It turned my life upside down. I couldn't function." — Arlene Fougere

Throughout the year she has tried to accept the fact she can't change things, she can't go back and redo that day but knows no one else will have to go through the pain she experienced, as the veterinarian responsible can never practise again.

"It's Cooper that did it," she said, "My dog can finally rest in peace."

General deficiencies the NSVMA complaint's panel uncovered in regard to Dr. Sietse VanZwol treatment of patients during an audit as part of their investigation into Arlene Fougere's complaint:
All records audited demonstrated examples of illegible writing.

- There is often minimal variability in patient vital parameters suggesting the parameters may have not been measured.
- Species identification is frequently lacking.
- No record of justification for diagnoses and treatment plans.
- Minimal diagnostics recommended or performed.
- Surgical procedures performed in a practice without accreditation to do so.
- Diagnoses are often made presumptively without appropriate diagnostics where indicated.
- Numerous examples of inappropriate use of antibiotics.
- Lack of administration of analgesics following surgical procedures, or where patients may have been in pain.
- No review of any current medications that patients are taking.
- No progress or hospitalization notes.
- No follow-up of patients where required.
- No record of dose or duration of medications prescribed.
- No record of client communications.
- Where surgeries are performed, there is no indication of the location where the surgery took place. Additionally, anesthetic drugs used are poorly defined, anesthetic monitoring is not recorded, inhalant anesthesia is often not used or recorded where it would otherwise have been indicated, and post-op pain management is not.

Sharon-Montgomery-Dupeis a health and breaking news reporter at the Cape Breton Post.

Chapter II

Joey's Legacy: The Beginning

Death of Fort Myers family's dachshund leads to state complaint against Alva veterinarian

From News-Press.com, part of USA Today network, July 2, 2018 article by Michael Braun:

Who killed Joey the dachshund?

That question is at the heart of a dispute over the treatment of the 12-year-old animal between the dog's owners and an Alva veterinarian that resulted in a complaint the doctor violated state law.

The complaint filed with the Florida Veterinary Medicine Board on June 4 alleges that Dr. Gene Rinderknecht's treatment of Joey for intestinal bleeding, diarrhea and vomiting ultimately lead to the dog being put to sleep.

The complaint came after a two-month investigation by the Florida Department of Business and Professional Regulation in late 2017 prompted by Joey's owners, Scott and Debbie Fine of Fort Myers.

The complaint claims Rinderknecht failed to recommend blood work, failed to address the dog's vomiting and had medicine given that was not recommended for dogs with kidney issues without verifying the dog's kidney function.

The complaint also claims that up-to-date written medical records were not kept on the dog.

The complaint asks the seven-member veterinary board, which next meets Sept. 7, to suspend or permanently revoke Rinderknect's license, restrict his practice, impose a $5,000 fine on each count or place him on probation.

The last entry on the department's online complaint records listing shows Rinderknecht's complaint is in settlement negotiations.

The doctor, a contract vet at the Daniels Parkway Animal Hospital where he saw Joey, was already on state-imposed probation for an issue when he treated the dog. That probation was the second he has been issued by the state for veterinary work since 2011 and doesn't expire until October.

In the complaint, Scott Fine said Rinderknecht examined and treated Joey in October 2016 and again in June 2017.

The dog recovered after treatment in 2016. The complaint said Rinderknecht failed to note respiration, pulse and outcome of the blood work from this visit.

The complaint said that when Joey was seen by Rinderknecht on June 19, 2017, the doctor prescribed the antibiotic metronidazole but failed to offer blood work and did not note some of the dog's vitals in medical records. Joey was given a shot of Convenia, an antibiotic normally used to treat common bacterial skin infections in dogs and cats.

Fine found Joey later that day lying on the floor with his ear in the water bowl, the complaint said.

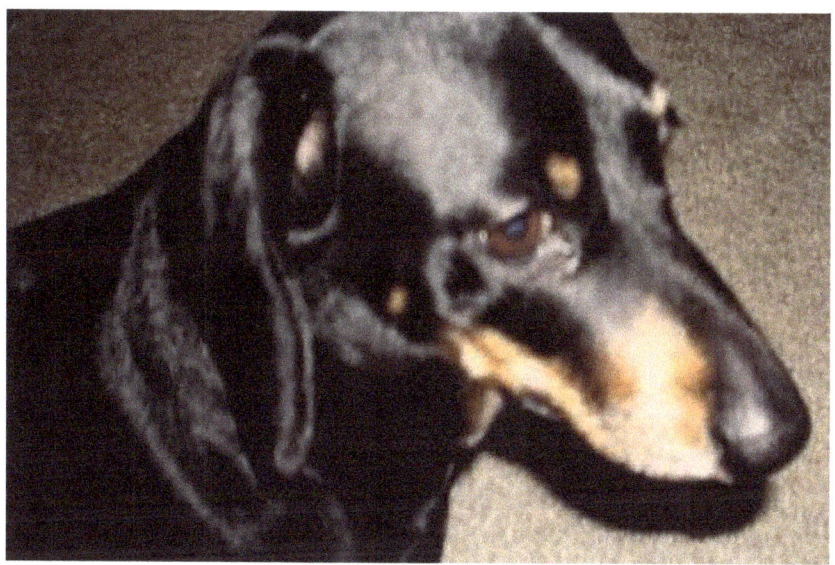

Joey was taken back to the veterinarian's office the next day and seen by Dr. Barry Hendon who performed blood tests. The outcome was that Joey was in kidney failure.

The complaint also said that Convenia, which had been given to Joey on June 19, is not recommended for dogs in kidney failure.
However, Hendon disputes that assertion and said Convenia is a good antibiotic that is commonly given to puppies and older dogs.

"I can see how he wants to blame the shot," Hendon said of Fine, adding, "The pet did not die because of a toxic medicine shot."

As for the completeness of Joey's medical records, Hendon agreed that the more complete they are, the better they are. "You try to document as you go," he said.

Joey's condition worsened on June 21, the complaint said, and the Fines agreed to have him put to sleep.

Rinderknecht, who received his veterinary degree from Iowa State University in 1972 and has been a practicing veterinarian for 45 years, declined comment about the complaint.

"When the situation is resolved, I will be able to issue a comment," he said.

However, in a formal written response to the complaint, Rinderknecht disavowed responsibility.

"I am sorry the Fines lost their little friend, Joey, but I do not feel I should shoulder the blame for his demise," Rinderknecht said. "The Fines were told about his severe periodontal disease and did not address the issue. Had they taken the necessary steps in October 2016 his renal disease may have been postponed."

Handwritten medical notes from the practice say that on June 19 the Fines were advised to have dental work done and a growth on the dog's tail removed.
Scott Fine said that never happened and that the doctor's claims that periodontal (tooth and gum) disease caused Joey's demise are wrong because that was addressed prior to the June 19 visit.
"Since he didn't suggest any treatment, we took it upon ourselves to investigate holistic methods of dealing with gum disease, and Joey was taking oral meds to help combat what was a very minor degree (Stage 1 or 2) of gum disease," Fine said. "This took place between the October 2016 and June 2017 visits. We didn't discuss Joey's gums on June 19."

Scott Fine added that claims of money issues raised by the doctor were also false.

"The other thing he told my attorney is that we claimed money was a problem for us. Absolutely not true...we had an agreement with Dr. Hendon to make payments every Thursday for any bills we could not pay all at once," he said.

A notation also says blood work would need to be done and that financial issues were raised. A similar note in the dog's medical files on June 20 said, "owners have financial concerns."

Hendon was sorry for the Fines' loss and agreed he worked with the Fines on financial issues related to Joey. He added that his practice is not adverse to doing blood tests.

"When an owner wants to do blood work," Hendon said, "there's no motivation not to do it."

Fine said he feels that Hendon is a victim in the dispute and that the contract veterinarian did not follow the practice standards.

"It may be the practice's policy to always ask to do blood work," Fine said, "but it's definitely not Rinderknect's."

***

Unfortunately, Veterinary Boards always defend the veterinarian involved and seem to provide the liability insurance in many cases.

There are many other stories:

A Long Island family is blaming a Plainview veterinarian at Long Island Veterinary Specialists for the death of their pet, a terrier and family member named Sydney.

The claim:

The clinic utilized improperly trained and unqualified technicians for the MRI procedure.

The veterinary clinic claimed their technicians were well-qualified, properly trained and apparently met all state veterinary requirements. A lawsuit was filed by the family's attorney after learning another dog suffered paralysis and had to be put to death after the same clinic allegedly botched another *non-invasive* procedure.

According to the attorney, "There is a pattern coming out of LIVS, from the facts the clients give me, and I believe in this case there was gross negligence."

According to a *New York Post* article July 31, 2019, a man from Manhattan took his arthritic dog, a 14-year-old rescue dog, Oscar, to

Long Island Veterinary Specialists. Oscar had been limping, so the pet's owner took him to the clinic for treatment and the veterinarian "gave him two risky MRIs that paralyzed Oscar" according to the suit, "after the dog was put under anesthesia for hours and the techs forced his body into positions that damaged his spine."

Court papers in the Oscar suit state that one technician at the facility "has seen this happen before and it is because of how they twist and position the dog for the MTI that causes the problems.

According to the story:

Then the vet - who originally said the MRI would be used to check for a slipped disc or cancer - tried to cover it up by saying the paralysis was temporary and would wear off in a few days and the dog's incontinence was due to the medications he was taking, "when in fact it was from spinal injury," the court documents allege.

A lawyer for LIVS, Alexander Bateman Jr., said, "Nobody at LIVS recommends or renders treatment unless it is medically necessary and fully explained to pet owners."

And another:

Beloved pet's death leads to suit, in trend
New Haven Register
July 28, 2017 update on story from May 4, 2009
By: William Kaempffer

NEW HAVEN -- Seventeen-year-old Brandy Broderick was diagnosed with a mass in her left adrenal gland and, in 2007, underwent surgery to have it removed. After the procedure, fluid was detected in her lungs -- an indication of over-hydration -- and she subsequently died from over-hydration and a pulmonary edema.

Those negligence claims alleged in a malpractice lawsuit filed this year are perhaps no more or less egregious than those made in thousands of wrongful death cases across the country.

One could argue, however, that Brandy's identity does.

She was a dog, a purebred Shetland sheepdog, owned by a Woodbridge man who is suing the animal hospital and surgeon for damages.

Animal law attorneys and legal experts say it's part of a growing trend nationwide of grieving pet owners turning to the legal system for justice because they believe veterinary errors killed their beloved pet. Even so, comparatively, veterinary malpractice suits remain much less common than cases against medical doctors, in large part because of how century-old laws classify animals.

"If you were my wife and you got killed, I could get millions and millions of dollars for pain and suffering, loss of consortium, lost future income," said Bruce Wagman, a California lawyer who specializes in animal law.

That's not allowed in veterinary cases, however. Though society increasingly views pets as irreplaceable family members, animal laws across the country identify them as personal property, not kin, and not much different than furniture or a Buick, which Wagman says is fundamentally unjust.

"People treat their companion animals and feel about them a lot differently than they feel about their sofa," he said.

The Broderick case was filed last month in Superior Court in New Haven by Michael Broderick, Brandy's owner, against the New Haven Central Hospital for Veterinary Medicine and veterinarian Melvyn Pond. The central claim is that Broderick, a licensed veterinarian, issued instructions before the procedure to avoid administering certain induction drugs that would be excreted through the kidneys because Brandy had chronic renal disease and was 17.

The suit claims the procedure was performed in a "hurried or careless manner" such that a surgical sponge was left in the dog's abdominal cavity, that an IV was left in despite detection of fluid in her lungs and the defendants disregarded his presurgical instructions.

Through his attorney, Michael Stone, Broderick declined comment. George Holmes, the attorney for the defendants, did not return phone calls seeking comment. Common law that governs animals generally was written centuries ago, evolving from a more agrarian era to address claims involving farm animals and livestock that were bought and sold with regularity.

While noneconomic damages in human malpractice cases can include awards for pain and suffering and emotional distress, those are rare in veterinary cases. Economic damages generally are limited to the fair market value of the animal, which with a mixed breed might be as low as $10, and vet costs.

TURNING TO THE COURTS

Courts, however, have started to take animal law more seriously. In Illinois, an appellate court overturned a lower court decision involving veterinary costs for treatment of an injured dachshund. The owner had sued and won a $5,000 verdict for the dog's treatment but the lower court capped damages at $200, the prorated replacement cost of the dog. The appellate court concluded she was entitled to the higher amount.

Some juries have concluded family pets have a "unique value" to the owner beyond market value or replacement cost. In California, a jury awarded a dog owner $39,000 in a veterinary malpractice suit, concluding the mixed breed's special value far exceeded its $10 market value. The jury awarded $9,000 for veterinary costs and a special value of $30,000 for the 3-year-old dog.
But lawyers say that remains the exception. Most successful malpractice suits might net at most $5,000 or $10,000, in some cases barely covering litigation costs.

Even so, according to Adam P. Karp, an animal law attorney in Washington state, people will turn to courts because veterinary boards and departments rarely discipline vets except in the most egregious cases.

"Most people bring animal cases out of principle and not out of a desire for money," he said.

Even as animal advocates make headway in the judicial system, legislators in some states have started introducing laws that seem to recognize pets' special value. In Connecticut, a 2004 public act makes a person liable for economic damages to a pet owner if he intentionally and unlawfully kills a cat or a dog. The damages include veterinary care, the animal's fair monetary value and burial expenses, if applicable.

A similar law was passed in Tennessee.

Critics say attempts by advocates to alter the legal status of animals could ultimately result in staggering malpractice awards and skyrocketing veterinary care costs. Estimates of premiums for veterinary malpractice insurance range from $500 to $2,500, while medical doctors in some specialties can pay more than $50,000 a year for malpractice insurance.

"One of our concerns is if these insurance rates are going to rise, what's that going to do to medical care?" said Duane Flemming, a lawyer, animal ophthalmologist and past president of the American Veterinary Medical Law Center. One theory, he said, is that the resulting increased cost of veterinary care will drive down its availability as it becomes less affordable.

At the same time, he noted, veterinarians who promote -- and profit from -- emotional bonds between humans and pets will have a difficult time in court claiming the animal had little value.

An Internet search on Veterinary Malpractice is an eye-opener and a black eye on an industry that once had the fewest members that were bad apples and bad actors, of all industries.

Though things are changing, thanks to Joey's Legacy and a few other groups who tirelessly fight for our pets, the courts still seem to think a dog, cat or horse is no different than a lawnmower, dishwasher or motorcycle.

Chapter III

Beware a scorned Veterinary Board

While bad-actor veterinarians are rare, bad actor Vet Boards (There are 50) seem to be abundant. They appear to be far from fair and balanced; and if you file a complaint, it is unlikely you will win.

This bit of news from the Aligus, established in 2002 to advocate against veterinary malpractice, incompetence, negligence and as a method to educate the public about state veterinary boards' handling of citizen complaints:

http://www.aligus.com/AboutVetBoards.html

Each state veterinary board is responsible for licensing veterinarians and regulating the practice of veterinary medicine for the State.

Their mission is to safeguard against unqualified practitioners and to protect the public against veterinary malpractice, incompetence and negligence by carrying out their regulatory duties.

State statutes and rules, generally called the Veterinary Practice Act, stipulate the regulation and enforcement of veterinary medicine.

A performance audit of the Arizona Veterinary Medical Examining Board conducted by The Office of the Auditor General pursuant to a May 29, 1995, resolution of the Joint Legislative Audit Committee detailed deficiencies so serious as to jeopardize the continued existence of the Board. The audit stated that if the Board did not rectify these problems after a five-year time period, the Legislature should consider other alternatives to ensure that the State's regulatory (missing)

Sources: http://www.auditorgen.state.az.us/PAD/97-7s.htm; http://www.auditorgen.state.az.us/Reports/State_Agencies/Agencies /Veterinary_Examining_State_Board_of/Performance/97-07/97-7.pdf

THESE DEFICIENCIES RAISE QUESTIONS ABOUT ALL STATE BOARDS.

1. Do Boards discipline when warranted?
2. Do Boards adequately investigate most complaints?
3. <u>Are disciplinary hearings conducted in a timely manner?</u>
4. Is there a need for uniform disciplinary guidelines?
5. Do Boards need to increase public access to information?
6. Do Boards adequately inspect veterinary facilities?
7. Is there adequate public representation?
8. What is the influence of Veterinary Medical Associations?
9. Are disciplinary actions reported to the national database?
10. Do state performance audits need conducted?

From *JoeysLegacy.org*:

LET'S BE CLEAR ABOUT VET BOARDS

For those that have just filed their complaints with their state's vet boards, here are some things you may not already know:

1. Vet boards are set up for success. Not yours, their success and your veterinarian's success, the one that committed the negligence or malpractice. Their mandate is supposed to be to protect your rights as a pet parent as well as the rights of their colleagues in a fair and equitable way. Forget about it. They will, by and large, protect the rights of their colleagues and forget about you.

2. Most vet boards are comprised of 5-8 members. Most of those members are practicing veterinarians, with one or two being consumer advocates who actually shill for the vets, so it's like having all vets on the board, while they feign concern about you and your case. I saw that firsthand during Joey's hearing. As veterinary practitioners, these veterinarians presumably demonstrate care and compassion for their patients during the day. Perhaps they even bond with some of them. As members of a vet board, they become indifferent, insensitive and callous toward pet parents that come before them and request redress for negligence or malpractice.

About 70-80% of complaints are dismissed. The height of disingenuous behavior, hypocrisy and fraud.

3. There is no intelligent reason that a vet board should have a majority of veterinarians. We know from the vet team from Joey's Legacy that, with rare exceptions, if you ask three vets for their opinions on a case, you will get three consenting opinions. By having a majority of veterinarians in a position to decide the case of an accused colleague, you guarantee that the vote (majority rules) will be a firm bias in favor of the colleague. In my opinion, one veterinarian should be included to provide clinical expertise and the other members should consist of a variety of "plain folk" with varying opinions.

4. The complaint you file is likely to take one year or more to resolve, presuming it is not summarily dismissed. Nobody is in a hurry to do anything relating to complaints against veterinarians.

5. The "disciplinary action" imposed by most vet boards, when imposed, reveals the board's reluctance to punish their colleagues firmly and fairly. Small fines, meaningless periods of probation and other lenient measures ensure that "little Johnny" won't learn his lesson and will likely offend again, perhaps on an habitual basis. Ergo, you might say that vet boards contribute to the ongoing permanent injury and death of our companion animals.

6. Finally, while I encourage everyone to file a complaint with their vet board, please do not have any expectations of success or vindication. Those outcomes are few and far between and, until vet boards are dismantled and restructured with a focus on actual justice for pet parents, we must continue to expose and embarrass these corrupt entities as much as possible to forewarn and forearm the still uninformed. We are confident that John Biffar's documentary will do just that.

***

The Veterinary Boards are not yours or your pet's friend. The vet, good or bad, is the Veterinary Board's friend; and they basically say so in their policies. The Boards do not appear interested in cleaning up their trash and fight to the hilt to protect the bad actors, who seem to get away with malpractice or negligence, over-and-over again.

And the beat goes on.

When Veterinary Boards are comprised almost solely of veterinarians, it proves difficult to get justice. But they have never met Scott Fine.

Joey's Legacy was founded by Scott Fine and wife, Debbie, after their pet, a dachshund name Joey, was killed, a result of a veterinarian who reportedly cut corners via omission of lab tests and then blamed Joey's owner. Joey's Legacy exists to help others who have become victims, would like to do something about it but then run into the Veterinary Board wall.

Joey's Legacy is a 501(c)(3) non-profit organization whose purpose is advocacy for our companion animals. They have assembled some of the brightest minds in the area of veterinary medicine, grief counseling and animal law that can assist those that come to Joey's with claims of veterinary negligence that cause the permanent injury or death of their loved ones.

Joey's Legacy has numerous educational pod casts and zoom casts and has assembled America's first nationwide network of veterinary experts and animal-law attorneys whose mission is to hold practitioners of veterinary medicine accountable for negligence that results in the permanent injuries and deaths of our pet companions.

Most veterinarians are caring and compassionate individuals, well-suited for the profession. There is a minority, however, of veterinarians that place profits before quality care for their patients and are perfectly willing to doctor-the-documents in order to cover up the story.

Joey's Legacy can help you if you are one of the unfortunate owners of a pet who suffered this tragedy. Pets are people too, created by God on the 6th[th] Day. It is interesting that the sea life and birds were created a day before land animals; and land animals were created the same day as mankind began. He had a reason.

Whether it is legal skills, emotional skills or veterinary skills, Joey's has someone who can provide help. Help can be requested through joeyslegacy.org or through Joey's facebook page: facebook.com/groups/JoeysLegacy

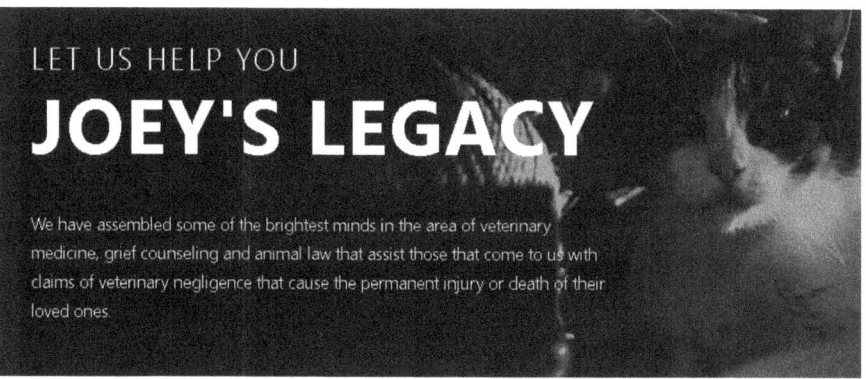

Chapter IV

To sue or not to sue

What do you do if you believe the veterinarian is responsible for your pet's death or injury?
According to the Animal Legal Defense Fund, you have several options that you might check out: aldf.org

-The first and most important, hire an attorney with skills in animal rights.

-Send a written complaint to the state veterinary licensing board. (Good luck on the Board helping or siding with you, but you have to show a paper trail); and it needs to start even before you find an attorney.

-Keep a diary of events.

-Consider Small Claims Court. You can represent yourself, the cost is much less and the case moves quickly. However, the monetary award, the only way to get to the bad guys, is smaller than if you go to regular court.

The monetary award you expect may not be reality in today's courts, though that is changing fast and may simply be the replacement of your pet or the value of replacement.

Currently, courts look at pets as just another piece of personal property, like a lawnmower, dishwasher or bird feeder. With the surge in medical companion pets and special needs pets, things are changing but way too slowly. The Joey's Legacy Documentary, when available, will speed up the education process.

Until a few years ago, the veterinarian would offer you a hundred bucks for your pet, take-it-or-leave-it. Now many awards are in excess of $5,000.
The largest Veterinary Malpractice award in the United States to date is $114,000.00.

In that case, the Los Angeles Superior Court case #119009, Pomerantz v. Schwartz, in 2016, Pomerantz attorney alleged malpractice, violation of California's anti-cruelty laws, fraud, fraudulent non-disclosure and unfair business practices against two West Los Angeles veterinary clinics.

Following are a few tips:

According to Equine Law Blog (equinelawblog.com), winning a veterinary malpractice case requires proof that:

- *The veterinarian had a legally recognized duty to handle a professional matter in a certain way.*
- *The veterinarian breached (departed from) that duty. Almost all veterinary malpractice cases will require expert witness testimony of a qualified veterinarian to prove this component.*
- *The veterinarian's wrongful conduct, and not some other reason, caused the horse's demise or devaluation.*
- *The sum of money lost as a result of the malpractice (damages). Damages in a veterinary malpractice action can include the horse's fair market value or decrease in value, lost profits and others. In the overwhelming majority of states, you will not recover your attorney fees or "pain and suffering," even if you win. A qualified expert, sometimes an equine appraiser, might need to prove the animal's value.*

In addition, or as an alternative, to a malpractice case, a horse owner might be able to file a complaint with the state board that regulates and disciplines veterinarians or has the power to control or suspend their licenses. These proceedings may not compensate you for your loss, but if successful they could result in a taking away the veterinarian's license.

Julie Fershtman

Julie Fershtman is considered one of the nation's leading attorneys in the field of equine law.

For more information, please also visit www.fershtmanlaw.com, www.equinelaw.net and www.equinelaw.info.

There are cases where the veterinarian's actions are particularly egregious. In those cases, it is possible the court will award *punitive damages* for emotional distress and suffering.

Is it worth it to sue, and how much will it cost?

Unlike human medical malpractice, attorneys do not often take the case on a contingency basis (share the wealth) because the awards are so low compared to human cases. So many courts consider your dog or cat to be personal property, like a rocking chair. They do not yet understand Biology 101, or they would understand that rocking chairs have no animal DNA. Nor do lawnmowers.

The price of an attorney specializing in animal rights and the one *expert witness* that is usually needed can be quite expensive, so the average Joe has no recourse. Eventually there might be a state government fund to help the pets of the average citizen, but $5000 in legal expenses is not unusual.

How prevalent is Veterinary Malpractice?

I knew nothing about this cause in July 2020 when I spoke with Scott Fine and decided to write a book about Joey's Legacy, veterinary negligence and the coverups often involved.

I thought at the time I would be fortunate to get 15 stories and 150 pages, but within 3 months I had 60 stories and nearly 700 pages. That is why there is a *Joey's Legacy Volume Two*.

In compiling the mostly heart-breaking stories in Volume One, stories written by the victims of this trauma, the prevalence became apparent. This happens way too often.

Joey's Legacy-VetMal Victims is a private group on Facebook and presently has 2,400+ members and is growing weekly. If you have a potential case of veterinary malpractice or negligence, contact joeyslegacy.org for advice.

These cases that are becoming more public every day have been quite secretive in the past. One has to do quite an Internet search to find them, and animal rights attorneys seem to be few-and-far between.

That is where Joey's Legacy can be a great benefit, dedicated to helping the victims and educating the public with advice like this:

SUNSHINE IS THE BEST DISINFECTANT

The most powerful tool we have to seek and obtain justice will be the exposure of the bad actor to the public. This MUST be done in a prudent and legal manner so that the absolute truth you tell, the irrefutable facts you state and the pure opinions that you opine make it difficult, or impossible, for the bad actor to refute. **Lawyers will tell you that truth is an absolute defense to a defamation claim**, and that defamation lawsuits are expensive and often difficult to prove. Our attorneys can review any content that you would like to post in a public forum for potential legal entanglements prior to your posting. Protect yourself!

I understand how emotional this experience is firsthand. It's been four years for me and I'm still on a tear. Once the Florida vet board determined malpractice, I went to one of the local television stations in Fort Myers, Florida and told my story. They ran a story on the vet and what happened. Same with the Fort Myers News Press. They ran a story as well. The vet left town for 2 weeks to allow things to "cool down". Exposure, Exposure, Exposure. However, you must act responsibly so you don't make matters worse.

All bad actors must be exposed to the public so that any companion animal parent will think twice and do their due diligence on the reported actor before allowing their companion animal to engage with the veterinary facility. You must be your own advocate, and allowing Joey's Legacy to assist can be a good resource in your battle for justice. While I encourage everyone to file a complaint with their vet board, you should have no expectation of vindication or justice. I am still waiting for the first success story where a vet board punished firmly and fairly based off a consumer complaint.

***

Many veterinarians face little, if any, discipline from the veterinary boards, maybe a *letter of reprimand*.

Chapter V

Products that can kill your pets

Flea Collars

According to an article in the June 1, 2021, edition of *Resident Community News*, Jacksonville, Florida:

"As of May 2021, the EPA has not formally issued any consumer warnings about, or mandatory product recall of, the *Seresto* Flea and Tick Collars."

Why not?

According to a recent *USA Today* investigative article, March 2021, approximately 1,700 pets died between 2012 when the product was released by Bayer (as in aspirin) and June 2o2o. It is estimated that 25-million flea collars have been sold.

One might think, 1,700 deaths out of 25-million collars is a small percentage; but the figure is inaccurate. Experts in animal welfare claim it is impossible to know the actual death toll because so many cases are unreported or unknown.

The identified 75,000 "adverse health incidents." There have also been "adverse health effects" to pet owners, possibly from exposure to the flea collar which contains more pesticide than most.

As of today, the EPA has failed to inform the public of the apparent dangers of the Seresto Flea Collar, developed by Bayer and sold to Elanco, a 17-Billion-dollar company. Size means everything when it comes to corporate discipline, and the Seresto collar is available almost everywhere that sells flea collars and pet supplies. Amazon is the leading purveyor of the Seresto collar, and most reviews are good. But not all:

1 out of 5 stars Insecticides can cause nerve problems
Reviewed in the United States on June 8, 2018

10 days after placing the Seresto collar on my dog, she suffered a neurological problem diagnosed as meningitis of "unknown origin". She temporarily lost the use of her hind legs and vet bills have already exceeded $5,000. Insecticides in the Seresto collar are nerve toxins which Bayer said cannot enter the animal's blood stream from the collar. However, these toxins have affected the nervous systems of rats in scientific studies. Our dog was scratching and biting herself after the collar was on, and before the toxic episode she was groomed with the collar on. Our cat, on the other hand, is doing well with her Seresto flea collar. If your dog is sensitive to medications, consider not using either this collar or other flea medications that contain insecticides. They are not regulated (yet) by the Federal Drug Administration, and there have been thousands of complaints from pet owners to the Environmental Protection Agency. Some flea collars have been taken off the market due to concerns about insecticides affecting children and entering the water system.

And another:

1 out of 5 stars BUYER BEWARE! Made my Dog VERY SICK!

Reviewed in the United States on April 7, 2021

Bought the small Seresto collar for my 7lb. Yorkie on January 12, 2021. Didn't open the package till March 27th 2021, to have and prepare for the tick and flea season. BUYERS BEWARE! My dog within 10-15 minutes of application went absolutely wild, he was running around in a panic, rubbing the floor, his face, yelping, pacing, laborer breathing, gaging, dry heaving! My husband and I were devastated, wondering what the heck is happening. He said, could it be the flea collar? I immediately took it off, and gave him a bath. He didn't eat that evening and was very lethargic. He drank more water than usual. The next two days or so he was fine. I put the collar on a shelf open, thinking it may have been to strong for him straight out of the sealed packaging and to air out about 2 weeks later, now applied the collar on again. This time we really kept an eye out on him. Approximately 2 hrs. After wearing the collar, it started again, in addition, he was vomiting this time around. I was done! I looked up on line, and in addition the reviews. To my surprise, I see several articles on Seresto collar on pets severe reactions, deaths, and even humans getting severe reactions to Seresto's product. We are consulting with our vet next week for alternatives and going to have our dog checked, and put the veteran aware of our situation. Not only is this product dangerous im.my opinion, but USA today, did an article, interview with a representative of AMAZON, and the EPA to ask Seresto to recall it's product this week. I will ask AMAZON for a full refund, even though my window for my purchase was closed in February. I am also, going to contact, Customer service of AMAZON, SERESTO, AND THE EPA to file a complaint. funding a fellowship at the center for expanded coverage of agribusiness and its impact on communities.

Dog Food that Kills Pets

Aflatoxins, produced by fungi found on many crops, ie. Peanuts and corn, are poisonous carcinogens caused by Aspergillus flavus and Aspergillus parasiticus, mold that grows in rotting vegetation and grains. Enter Midwestern Pet Foods.

Midwestern Pet Foods is a major manufacturer/provider of pet and domestic animal foods.

The Food and Drug Administration has warned pet parents and the world in general that some of the pet foods have "fatal levels of aflatoxin" that has led to nearly 100 dog deaths. The company has experienced several recalls.

The symptoms of aflatoxin poisoning include sluggishness, loss of appetite, vomiting, jaundice and diarrhea. Aflatoxin poisoning can be fatal and may cause liver damage.

Hill's, the manufacturer of the heavily-pushed Science Diet, had a January 2020 recall of 25 brands of wet and dry food because of high levels of Vitamin D. In June 2014 they recalled several brands for possible salmonella contamination.

According to PetHealthNetsork.com:

When ingested in poisonous amounts, vitamin D can result in

life-threatening elevations in calcium and phosphorous, leading to acute kidney failure and death.

The following chapters are actual stories of Pet Parents who have suffered negligence and loss at the hands of poor veterinary care.

Chapter One

Sierra's Story ("Sissy")

J. Tindell

Our beautiful, 9 year old AKC Purebred Golden Retriever, Dual Certified Service Dog and Registered Therapy Dog for our 6 year old daughter suffered horribly and unnecessarily from an incomplete and unapproved "Economic Euthanasia"…

Sierra was more than just an amazing dog; she was my little girl's service dog – from birth.

Originally trained for my bedridden father, a USAF Korean War Veteran who suffered with PTSD and seizures, Sierra was naturally adept at detecting oncoming silent seizures and providing him with much needed support. When my mother, who had severe, deteriorating COPD, developed hypoxic-induced Alzheimer's disease, Sierra transitioned effortlessly to provide daily assistance in my mother's care, preventing her from wandering and performing "seek/recover" of her when necessary.

When my parents passed away, our little family had no idea the great value we would inherit with Sierra. Not only did Sierra provide me with daily support, she was the first to discover and alert us to our newborn daughter's infantile seizures. Holding our child still to prevent injury, Sierra would lay her head and paw gently across her. Sleeping next to her baby bed, Sierra watched our little girl throughout the night, just as she had done for my father before her. As our daughter grew, so did her need of Sierra.

By the tender age of 5 years old, our little girl and Sierra had become inseparable. Sierra had not only become her constant companion, but also her guardian angel. Sierra became a constant in our lives, too, an invaluable asset, enabling us to enjoy life outside of our home and bringing us a sense of security and peace within it. There was a great comfort in having Sierra, or "Sissy" as she was lovingly called by our daughter. With Sierra by her side, we knew our little girl was safe. Sissy became her lifeline. And ours.

All that was stolen from us when a veterinarian at a Specialty Clinic took Sierra's life away, because he deemed we could not afford treatment "IF" treatment was necessary or even an option. And now we are without her...

On September 12, 2019, we decided to take Sierra to our trusted veterinarian of more than 30 years to evaluate a small growth that had become an enlarged, hardened cyst on her side. Up until this fateful day, Sissy showed no signs of discomfort or pain. Because we loved her so, we wanted to be sure it wasn't something more serious, such as cancer. And if it was, we would spare no expense to provide her treatment, even mortgaging our home, if that's what it would take to help her.

Unfortunately, our own wonderful veterinarian was away at a veterinarian conference, along with all the other vets at his practice. In fact, all the veterinarians in our Central Florida area were gone to this conference. A relief veterinarian from Miami was filling in at our vet's office for emergencies. We decided to meet with him for an evaluation instead of waiting for our vet to return the following week.

The relief vet seemed very knowledgeable and showed concern for Sierra. Worried that the cyst on her side could have grown through her chest wall, attaching itself to her ribs, and rendering it inoperable, he ordered x-rays. He gave her something to help her lie still for the x-rays and physical exam, even though she was not exhibiting any kind of pain. In fact, earlier that morning, just before the exam, Sierra had been playing ball in the yard with my daughter - running, jumping, and fetching enthusiastically as usual.

Moments later, he returned with Sierra and her x-rays. He stated he could not tell from the preliminary x-rays whether or not the cyst had attached itself to her ribs, but unfortunately, it had grown in a very bad place. What he thought he did see, however, was the possibility of cancer beginning to form in her liver. He stated he couldn't be sure of either of these diagnoses without further evaluation. He recommended further diagnostics to include more x-rays, an ultrasound and bloodwork. However, he was unable to provide these services as there were no ultrasound technicians that day and he was only the emergency relief vet. He recommended for us to schedule a followup appointment when our vet and technicians returned to the office. Or, in the interim, we could take her to a veterinary Specialty Clinic to be evaluated by multiple specialists, including an oncologist if treatments were needed, and was hopeful they may be able to shrink the cyst or aspirate it. Although convenient, he indicated that this "one stop shop" of specialists and therapies would be expensive.

He did not recommend euthanasia at this time as her gums were pink, her eyes were bright and she was still active: eating, playing and not in any apparent distress. He did recommend to monitor her for changes in those signs and, should they appear, to contact a Veterinary Hospice, such as Lap of Love, to have her passing done at home ... to honor her and give her dignity and a pain free passing, as she so deserved. He indicated he did not know the time frame of when this would take place, stating it could be several months, or even a few years, depending on the growth of the cyst. He stated we did not need to "rush to euthanize" her right away. He advised us to trust Sierra; she would let us know when it was time.

With this information, we left the room to make a payment for the visit, feeling concerned and wanting to help our beloved friend, but with limited means to do so at that very moment. The receptionist, whom I've known since my childhood, recommended Care Credit, a credit card to help pay for veterinarian expenses so we could have options, knowing that if her care required even further funds we would tap into our resources, such as our home. My husband applied for the credit card and was approved, using it that day at our vet's office before heading off to work.

Once home, I called the Specialty Clinic to make an appointment for Sierra. Because no appointments were available until November 16th, they advised me of a "work around" if I wanted her to be seen sooner. For a $500 fee, I could bring her through their Emergency Room Department to be evaluated immediately. The ER vet, along with any specialists, including a veterinary oncologist if cancer was a concern, could evaluate Sierra on the same day, and they would perform all the necessary diagnostics for a full work-up to include x-rays, ultrasound and bloodwork, just as the relief vet had recommended. I would need to bring her records and have her recent x-rays sent over electronically. This additional $500 charge to do it this way had to be pre-paid over the phone. Any additional treatment plans would be extra. I called my vet's office and had them send her records and digital x-rays to the Specialty Clinic in case we decided to take her.

I took Sierra outside to play in the yard with my daughter and then brought her back inside for a drink of water, a well-deserved treat and a lie on the cool tile floor, as our Florida heat in September is almost unbearable.

As she lay there, relaxed and happy with her head on my foot, gazing at my daughter next to her, I called my husband at work and said, "We love her so much, and she's given so much to us, we should take her to the best vet money can buy. Our vet won't be back until next week. Let's see if there's a way to shrink this cyst. Let's be sure she doesn't have cancer." He agreed, so I called the Specialty Clinic back and paid the $500 fee with the Care Credit Card over the phone. I told Sierra to "load up" because we were "going for a ride!" She dropped her ball and jumped into the car. Making the long drive on the interstate, I drove our beloved Sierra to the veterinarian specialists for a thorough evaluation, with my little girl in her carseat, riding alongside her best friend in the whole world!

It was a fateful decision that has left our small family inconsolable.

Upon our arrival, Sierra jumped out of the car and we took her to potty in the grass before entering the Specialty Clinic. Unlike our vet's office, which has separate animal entrances with spacious, designated dog and cat waiting areas, this Specialty Clinic had only one entrance in the middle of the building and a long, narrow front waiting room with all of the animals together. It was crowded that day with many animals and two particularly aggressive, rambunctious large dogs. Not wanting our gentle Sierra to get hurt when passing these two dogs while she was escorted to the Emergency Room, I requested attention to my concern. A Vet Assistant came out from behind the counter, took Sierra by her leash and walked her through a shortcut behind the front desk to bring her to the ER Department in the back.

The receptionist handed me paperwork to fill out, which included a consent to evaluate and treat. I also signed a separate DO NOT AUTHORIZE for any procedures without my prior approval. She then informed me she could not verify our newly opened Care Credit Card. She asked for the password to our account in order to verify our credit limit online or else they couldn't evaluate Sierra. I gave her the password and we waited…And waited.

3 hours

Slowly the overcrowded, long and narrow lobby dwindled down to only a few remaining clients. Finally, only one other client, and ourselves, remained. We were called back to a patient room to speak with the Emergency Room Vet. But where was Sierra?

The ER Vet informed me that Sierra had a growth on her side that may or may not have attached itself to her chest wall, unfortunately rendering it inoperable. He stated he did not perform any diagnostics at all, but had gathered the information from reading the report my vet's office sent over to the Specialty Clinic…and he recommended immediate euthanasia! He stated I could not be with Sierra for this procedure, and since it was closing time, I would have to come back another day to pick up her body.

I was shocked!!! After waiting now nearly 5 hours, this ER Veterinarian had only read the report??? And he wanted to put our dog down immediately??? Without any diagnostics whatsoever???

"Is it because of the cancer?" I asked tearfully, to which he replied that he "didn't know anything about any cancer." They had not done ANY diagnostics. No x-rays, no ultrasounds, no bloodwork. NOTHING. When I asked why not, he informed me because "the outcome would be the same – she needed to be euthanized." I expressed to him our concern about Sierra having cancer as the relief vet at our office had said Sierra's x-rays showed the possibility of cancer developing in her liver and had also indicated that there may be a way to shrink the cyst, which is why he recommended the Specialty Clinic – to evaluate the nature of the cyst on her side and so she could be seen by an oncologist, if needed. I also expressed our desire to go through a Veterinary Hospice should we need to euthanize her in the future. But we came to seek options, not euthanasia.

The ER Vet then stated there was no way the relief vet could tell if there was cancer or not from an x-ray and claimed the relief vet had "lied." Only an ultrasound and bloodwork could show cancer. I requested the ultrasound, which I was told would be done in the ER at arrival, but he declined to perform one because he deemed it was "unnecessary." And now, by this time, the ultrasound "tech" had left for the day. When I requested bloodwork, he stated again it wasn't necessary and the oncologist was not there today, anyways. He stated they had not done any tests or drawn any fluid. He continued to insist "It doesn't matter, the outcome is the same. She needs to be euthanized immediately." He went on to explain that even if it was cancer, he knew we would not be able to afford the treatments. He had seen our Care Credit Limit was only $2500, with only $1100 remaining available. So, there was no need to do any diagnostic testing on my dog.

I couldn't believe what I was hearing! My little girl started to demand, "Where's my Sissy dog? I want my Sissy back! Bring her back to me now!"

The ER Vet asked me to have my little girl wait – by herself – in the empty lobby. My little girl who is never separated from her service dog, or me. I took her to stand just outside of the door to the lobby hallway where I could see her from the room. While briefly outside of the room with her, I called my husband at work so I could introduce him to the ER VET over the phone to help make sense of everything when we returned to the conversation.

When I re-entered the room, it was suddenly dark inside, with the only light coming in through the open doorway from the lobby. The ER Vet had turned off the light and stepped into a darkened corner of the room just behind the door. He was agitated and in a hushed voice asked, "What is it going to take to get it through your head that she needs to be euthanized? The outcome will not change." To which I responded, "The diagnostics that I brought her here for. I want an ultrasound. I want bloodwork. I want to be sure it is not cancer."

He resisted, telling me, "Regardless, the outcome will not change." I demanded my dog back, as I had never, ever been separated from any of my pets at a vet's office like this in over 30 years. "I want to see her –now." He then offered for me to leave her there and come back tomorrow to have all the testing done, and he would not charge me the emergency room fee. Why would I leave her and come back tomorrow? I was already there now. I had been waiting over 5 hours. He relented and stated there was a "tech that could do a quick ultrasound of her liver, but it wouldn't be anything "legal;" it would not be part of her medical record," to help me come to terms with the need to euthanize our Sierra. He stated I was to not trust the relief vet at our office, but to trust him. He stated "to help decide," he wouldn't charge me for the ultrasound. I agreed to have the "quick scan" done.

He left the room, and I quickly pulled my daughter from the doorway where I had been watching her, back into the dark patient room with me. While I was speaking to my husband on the phone, my little girl insisted, "Don't trust him, Mommy! He's going to do something bad. They are going to give Sissy something she shouldn't have! I just know it! Don't do it, Mommy! They are just tricking you! They are tricky people here!"

My husband responded by advising us to bring our service dog home and take her back to our vet on Monday. He remained on the line, while another Specialty Vet came in the room and turned the light on. Sitting on a stool, she informed us the ER Vet asked her to "talk sense to me." She continued to say it was necessary to euthanize Sierra immediately. She told me I would need to leave Sierra at the hospital morgue, frozen, until we were ready to dispose of her body, they would not charge me a fee for the euthanasia nor for the "morgue hold," and to "call ahead to make sure the dog had thawed." She stated they could take care of her remains for us without charge, also.

I repeated to her we did not want to euthanize Sierra today, we were returning to our vet on Monday to have her re-evaluated, and should our vet recommend euthanasia, we would do so with a Veterinary Hospice at home. When she questioned how we would deal with the cost of our dog's remains, my husband told her we had it covered financially and we lived on sufficient property to legally bury our animals.

She then explained that the needle biopsy was "Nasty!" The ER Vet had drawn out brown fluid from the cyst when Sierra was first admitted to the ER. She stated she didn't know what that indicated, but "it wasn't good." She said Sierra was in a lot of pain, with labored breathing, but we could not see her nor could we be with her when she was euthanized.

Wait! What?? What biopsy??

I questioned her because the ER Vet had told me he didn't perform ANY diagnostics or procedures at all, including a needle biopsy. The Specialty Vet quickly covered her mouth unaware and then said, "You'll have to ask the ER Vet about it."

None of this made sense. My head was spinning as I felt highly pressured to euthanize my dog sight unseen, without me. Why could we not see her? Where was this sudden, severe pain with labored breathing coming from? Only this morning we were playing fetch in the yard…

She responded with silence and left the room.

When the ER Vet returned, he remained in the ER hallway instead of entering the patient room and was undeniably agitated. He said he had no idea what the fluid from the needle biopsy meant. He said he threw it away. He said it wasn't diagnostic. He said he didn't test it because it wouldn't change the outcome. He then stated the quick ultrasound showed that the liver looked like it might be slightly, abnormally shaped, possibly indicating cancer. And that even if it was cancer, he didn't see me driving to Gainesville for chemotherapy, as they didn't offer chemo at their Specialty Clinic, which I later discovered was a lie. And since nothing would change the outcome, he said Sierra should be euthanized immediately. And since they were closed now, I would have to come back for her tomorrow.

I said, adamantly, "Give me my dog."

I was then told to check out at the front desk and once I paid, Sierra would be brought to us in the front lobby. Again, we waited. By this time, not only were there no other clients, nearly the entire staff was gone and all of the lights in the building were turned off. As we waited in the darkened lobby, my little girl said she was afraid. When I asked her why she was afraid, she shared, "I am afraid that they did something to Sissy and she's going to die in the car. She's going to die in the car on the way home, Mommy. I'm scared they did something bad to her."

I assured her they didn't. That they couldn't because I signed a paper that said they couldn't. But still she fretted anxiously, wringing her shirt hem in her hands…

FINALLY, Sierra was brought out to us – but not on a leash like how we brought her in. She was on a stainless steel gurney cart!!! She was laying on top of pee pads, reeking of a rubbing alcohol-like smell. Her forearm had been shaved extensively and was wrapped tightly in a bright pink stretchy, guaze bandage. Although her eyes were bright and twinkling, and she was holding her head up looking at us with relief and anticipation, she was drowsy and did not attempt to move off the cart.

I asked the technician who brought Sierra out to us what had happened to our dog's leg, but before she could respond, the receptionist said it was protocol, a preparation done upon arrival "just in case" they needed to do any procedures. It all seemed odd, but the technician and her assistant ushered us out the door quickly. It took all three of us to load and slide Sierra with a blanket and pee pads into the backseat of my car, next to my daughter in her carseat. The rubbing alcohol-like smell was so strong it burned our eyes in the car. My daughter rolled her window down to breathe easier. Sissy rested her head on my daughter's lap.

As we started to leave the parking lot, my little girl's voice began to tremble, "Mommy! Something's wrong with Sissy...she can't hear me. When I say her name, to 'watch me,' she doesn't move..." When I looked to the backseat, Sierra's eyes were heavy and starry, with a glassy, glazed look in them. Her mouth wasn't held right. Her eyebrows weren't right. Nothing about her facial expressions was right. I called her name, but she did not respond; her gaze remaining fixated forward, in a far-off dazed stare.

I immediately pulled over before leaving the veterinarian Specialty Clinic's entrance way. The few remaining cars of the staff went speeding past me. No one stopped to assist me as I tried to flag them down. The parking lot was deserted. I stood outside of the car, trying to get Sierra to respond. But it was like she couldn't see or hear me. She moved her head slightly to be more comfortable on my daughter's lap. Worried, my heart dropped and I called my husband.

I was going to try to drive to Gainesville for the highly regarded University of Florida Small Animal Hospital, but couldn't do it. The drive was too far and I knew something was dreadfully wrong. My husband advised me that he had just left work and would meet me halfway to help get Sierra home.

As I drove up the on ramp of the interstate, the traffic was in a gridlock. It was rush hour. To complicate matters, there was a large scale construction project in progress. I couldn't turn around! I couldn't get to an exit to get off the highway! I was stuck in bumper to bumper traffic on the interstate.

Suddenly, Sierra let out a horrific cry and began wrenching and writhing in pain, thrashing her body about in the backseat, slamming into my daughter repeatedly, gasping for air.

"Mommy! Mommy! Sissy is dying! I told you Mommy, I told you! I told you this was going to happen, Mommy! Help her! PLEASE!!!"

Trapped. On the interstate. With our dog suffering horribly, inconceivably without comfort. With my 6 year old terrified and screaming. It was horrific, the scene that unfolded in my rear view mirror. All because I wanted to give her the best of care, a second opinion, another look by a "specialist"...

Finally, I was able to pull off the highway to a side street in a now dark and unfamiliar area to meet my husband. We switched vehicles on the side of the road so he could drive Sierra home alone. Our little girl, grief-stricken and emotionally overwhelmed, immediately fell asleep in the quiet sanctuary of the backseat of the car. My husband drove ahead of us without any contact or conversation, later sharing with me that it was a devastating ride, one that he would never want to do again. Sierra was actively dying and she suffered greatly. It was too late to reverse the process...and now there was nowhere to go for help.

As we pulled into the driveway of our home, our little girl immediately awoke and ran beside her daddy while he carried her Sissy Dog inside. He laid Sierra down on the cool tile floor. She was struggling to breathe, gasping for every ragged breath. We placed a soft fan to blow gently on her face and stroked her beautiful, soft golden fur and held her, and with heavy hearts and tears, we said our goodbyes. I covered our exhausted child with a blanket and a promise to wake her when her dog had passed. She fell asleep in her Sissy dog's bed nearby.

Then, slowly, Sierra's breathing became less labored and I laid down beside her, to comfort her. That's when I noticed it. Sierra's back was misshapen... her spine grossly misaligned. But it didn't matter anymore. She would soon be free of this undeserved, terrifying pain that broke my heart. She took four deep, slow breaths and then, with a sigh, she was gone. Her face twisted in agony, blood stains from her mouth on the floor. It was more than awful. It was horrendous. It was gut-wrenching. And it was unnecessary. This was not our first dog death. We have been through several, both natural and euthanized. But nothing, no never, nothing ever like this.

The following day, our long time, trusted vet called about Sierra's passing. Saddened by the news, he recommended we speak with a Veterinary Hospice for Bereavement. In speaking to the counselor on the phone, she explained to me that in pet euthanasia there is a 2-step process, and once the first injection, called Twilight, is administered, clients must continue with the second injection for euthanasia. Once the first shot is administered, there is no going back, otherwise their beloved pet will most likely die an excruciatingly, painful death, as different organs shut down, especially if the pet is septic. In fact, this particular Veterinarian Hospice makes the pet owner sign an agreement that there is "no turning back."

I was also informed that "brown fluid" in a needle biopsy indicates a severe infection, and that if drawn inappropriately, can leak into the blood stream and cause rapid sepsis throughout the body…and in turn, pain and labored breathing as vital organs shut down.

Then I was told there is such a thing as "Economic Euthanasia."

Economic Euthanasia is when veterinary care is bypassed based on the inability to pay for the cost of care. A choice when the progression of the disease will result in euthanasia eventually…(Humane Society Veterinary Medical Association, 2018) This decision was made by him, not us.

"You cannot afford the treatments. I saw your Care Card credit limit…The outcome will not change."

This ER Specialty Vet decided, based on his assumption of our supposed inability to pay and the likelihood she would be euthanized eventually anyways, that Sierra, our service dog, our friend, our Sissy, should be euthanized – immediately.

When my husband went to speak with the ER Specialty Vet about what had happened, the vet did not deny or admit to anything, and in being evasive, kept repeating to my husband that, in his opinion, the outcome would have been the same. He sat silent when questioned about the shaving of Sierra's forearm, the smell of rubbing alcohol, her sudden distraught state while here and, the fact she was evaluated earlier that day and was in no apparent distress when we brought her here, yet suddenly died, only hours after being seen by them, a painful, horrible death. That she was walked in on a leash for a second opinion and came out on a gurney and died the same day.

Then there were the medical records. Just a few scantily written lines that basically repeated what the relief vet had stated. We asked for a copy of the quick ultrasound, but there was none. I was informed by a staff member that there was no record of it because the doctor, not a tech, who performs and reads the ultrasounds, was not there that day – at all. My husband pressed the ER Vet about the results of the fluid biopsy he had extracted from the cyst. The vet stated he had thrown the sample away without ever, even testing it…that it wasn't necessary because we could not have afforded treatment, whether it had been cancer or not. "The outcome would be the same."

What happened? And why? Why wasn't Sierra given the diagnostics? We brought her to be evaluated, not to have a second opinion of our vet's notes. Why did she suddenly die? Did she become septic from the unauthorized needle biopsy gone wrong? Was she given medication to start unauthorized euthanasia, but since I wouldn't give permission, they couldn't proceed with the second injection? Did she fall off the rolling table as she was not strapped in? Were we prematurely judged that we could not afford her care? How does he know what we can and can't afford?? As my husband pointed out to the ER Vet, we were left with more questions than answers.

The problem is – it was NOT his choice to make. He TOOK our choice away when HE DECIDED that we could not afford her treatment. HE TOOK OUR CHOICE AWAY WHEN HE TOOK OUR DOG AWAY! What right did he have to do this? Our world has changed dramatically with our loss of Sierra and we are heartbroken. Our dog suffered a horrible death. Our child suffered a horrible heartache. Our family suffered such a great loss.

We came to them seeking interventions to bring quality to her life…we left without her life having any quality remaining.

This is Sierra's Story, but she was so much more…

Sierra wasn't just a dog. Sierra was OUR dog…Our highly trained and specialized Service Dog. Most importantly, she was a part of our family. She made us whole. She spent half her life taking care of my parents and the other half caring for my daughter and me. I brought Sierra to this veterinarian Specialty Clinic to help her, to help prevent future suffering for her. I left with her experiencing the exact opposite of what I wanted for her. For me. For my little girl. Sierra suffered so much and died.

And now, I just want to know… WHY?

Maybe the outcome would have been the same, but we could have prevented her suffering. We would have had time to prepare our daughter for the loss, our hearts for the grief and our home for a new life to be our daughter's four-legged angel on earth while we came to terms with the sorrow of our angel dog in Heaven.

But all of that was STOLEN by a decision that a judgmental and careless vet, whom we trusted with all our hearts and Sissy's life, made that day based on his assumption that we did not have the financial resources to provide for her care. He ROBBED us of even the basic right of an animal owner, the decision to give her a peaceful passing.

"Nothing is more difficult, and therefore more precious, than to be able to decide..." Napoleon Bonaparte

Now our lives will never, ever be the same without her. We will miss her forever.

She is gone, but not forgotten.

Every night our little girl curls up in her Sissy's dog bed and cries for her. Every excursion outside the home without Sissy is a dreaded risk and full of emotional upheaval. The turmoil we experience daily on so many levels because of this vet's indifference...With every step my child takes without her, we are reminded of Sierra's absence, and her tragic and senseless death.

As Thucydides, the ancient Greek philospher once said:
"The secret to happiness is freedom...and the secret to freedom is courage."

Sierra gave us all the courage to enjoy life, and to enjoy it freely! That freedom to step courageously out of your own door and into your destiny... Sissy was our courage and our confidence. She had been trained so well to provide so much. And so much more was stolen away from us when our dog was made to suffer and die, needlessly in my child's arms.

My little girl summed it up best when we buried her Sissy dog with my daughter's favorite toy and she said, "A mistake is one thing, Mommy. You can forgive a mistake...But when you lie about it, that's a whole 'nother thing...It's wrong."

Sierra – our beautiful, beautiful golden girl. Our friend, our companion, our helper, our Guardian Angel, our family, our Sissy.

Working. Alerting. Recovering. Dual certified as a Medical Alert Service Dog and Registered Therapy Dog, she was the most intelligent and dedicated dog we've ever known. She was a game changer for our family. She gave us a freedom we would not have ever known without her. And for that, I am truly thankful.

Current Training Value of $50,000. Life Value – immeasurable.

Trained extensively through the following organizations:
Pawsitive Action Foundation / New Horizons Assistance Dogs
Sunshine State Service Dogs / Topaz Assistance Dogs
Wallace K-9 Training Center / Genesis Assistance Dogs
King Valley Collies for Mobility & Support – Distance Training

ADI (Assistance Dogs International) – Professional Evaluators
Pet Partners (formerly the Delta Society) – Therapy Evaluators
Demonstrated Skills:
Seizure Alert, PTSD, Anxiety, Alzheimer's Seek/Recovery Response, Vestibular Balance Assistance, Retrieval Skills

Community Involvement / Grand Openings:
1st Therapy Dog Team – Nemours Children's Hospital Lake Nona, Florida
1st Therapy Dog Team – University of Central Florida's School of Medicine

I want others to know that they are not alone in their anger when they discover that our pets have no value according to the current law that does nothing to protect them. Our pets can easily fall prey as innocent victims to the actions of a medical community that is not held accountable for negligent or malicious acts on our animals for whom they are entrusted to provide care. The animals we love are devalued by the law, less than personal property, and this is a travesty that breaks my heart every day.

There has been nowhere to turn – until now. Thank you Joey's Legacy for standing up and shouting from the rooftops for the voices of the silent innocents whom we have been given such profound charge over. The good you do not only honors Joey, but works diligently to protect others.

God bless all of you who join this tremendous force to create justice and a safer medical community for the lives of our beloved pets, the hearts of their owners, and the veterinarians who are honorable in their chosen profession. Thank you for your collective vision and for making this book of collected experiences possible and available for the world to see.

Thank you, Scott Fine, for being such a steadfast support and for allowing me a place to share our grief. We miss her so much. We love you Sissy <3

By **Your Side"** - A Service Dog Anthem for Sierra and RangerMusic

and Lyrics by J. Tindell@ 2012 copyright

By your side is where I long to be
By your side is where I'll stay.
When you call, I will come to you.
When you fall, I'll keep you safe
By your side.

By your side, I will walk with you
By your side, faithful and true.
When you're lost, I will be your guide
When you're found, you will find me too
By your side

With every step I take and every move you make
When you sleep and when you wake
My eyes are watching you
I give my life to you...

By your side, I will wait for you
By your side, beckoning
You're not alone, don t be afraid
Reach for me - I'll always be
By your side.

By your side, by your side.
I'll always be - By your side, by your side...

Always Together

Chapter Two

Barney's Story
Honoring my boy Barney
Natural Wellness for our Pets!
By Sherri Willingham

My passion for animals and natural healing came together in a big way when I was able to connect the two for my love, Barney the senior rescue GSD. I met my boy Barney in 2011, while working at a community animal shelter as a kennel attendant. He was a mangy, emaciated, flea-ridden GSD, with ears eaten away by fly strikes. As sick as he was, he was sweet and affectionate, and I connected with him immediately! He was 'estimated' to be 7 years old, but honestly it's difficult to read a dog's age when they have been so badly neglected. None of his issues mattered, as I promised him I would never let him suffer another moment in our life together

I have a background in computer systems, and worked in the aerospace industry for 20 years. After I left this career, I enjoyed learning yoga, and spending time with my jr. high and high school aged children. I have no medical background, no formal education in health, just a lifelong interest in being healthy with food and exercise.

Roll back to 2009, I had been very sick, with MRSA, for two years. During that time, I was prescribed a dozen different rounds of antibiotics, and I either had an allergic reaction, or the MRSA abscesses came back within a couple weeks.

I took control of my health and began a quest to find a holistic solution. I found a group online that had gotten rid of MRSA using diet and special essential oils, and not antibiotics! What I also learned is that most times when we have an infection or virus, it's because our immune systems are not strong.

Did you know that it takes our bodies up to 9 months to recover immune system strength from one course of antibiotics?

Using these special 'medicinal' grade essential oils (not the ones I had previously bought from the health food store for their pretty smell.), I began to help my body heal. I have not had a MRSA outbreak since, and I keep these oils in my medicine cabinet for any indication of any type of illness.

Back to Barney's journey, his first couple years were fraught with chronic ear infections, intestinal parasites and infections, skin infections, and lameness in his hind legs. I did everything the veterinarians told me to do; antibiotics, GI medications, flea products, medicated baths, and steroids. He would get better for a while, then one of more illness would come back with a vengeance.

I should have realized that his condition was similar to mine; a weak immune system being continuously assaulted with toxins and medications depleting his good gut bacteria.

I was already feeding him the 'best' grain free kibble, and I had started using natural products for his health conditions, but he continued to have issues, mostly ear infections and hot spots. I knew that I needed to keep digging.

In 2015, I stumbled across a documentary called "Pet Fooled", where I was educated on what is in that hard dried 'food' we have been told we need to give our pets. It always leads back to the money. The pet food industry is a $60+Billion business, that seems to only be feeding its board members and stockholders, instead of nourishing our animals. These corporations are connected with all aspects of our pet's care, from sponsoring colleges and classes at Veterinary schools, providing 'free' food and other products to the students for their own animals, and teaching the nutrition classes at the schools. These companies are completely invested in and dependent on these new practitioners buying into this ridiculous notion, that we feed our animals nothing but processed nuggets with high levels of chemical preservatives, and low level of nutrition.

Once I ditched the kibble crap, and started feeding Barney whole unprocessed food, like any animal in the wild eats, his health took an immediate and dramatic turn. Imagine years of daily medications, special baths, laser therapy, chiropractic, accupuncture, Chinese herbs, and then changing that bowl of food to real human grade food fixing EVERYTHING! And not one practitioner, not even the 'holistic' ones, suggested feeding a whole food species appropriate diet. Not one.

At this point I began a mission, to tell every pet lover what I have learned. **Real food matters!** I was able to reach a large group of animal parents through my essential oils business and customers.

We all want the very best for our animals, but we don't know what we don't know!

The more pet parents I talked to about using natural products for many of the things we would traditionally go to the vet for, the more I saw heartbreaking stories of animals becoming ill or dying from other commonly used protocols.

Flea and tick products that are prescribed for monthly use, even for animals with chronic health conditions, or living in areas that are low risk for infestation, causing sometimes irreversible damage. Besides assaulting the immune system, these neurotoxins have been linked to seizures, as noted in an FDA warning letter published in 2018. There are natural non-toxic ways to prevent critters, starting with the diet, and including natural sprays.

Then the topic of vaccinations and the horrible effects from over-vaccination were coming up. Since Barney was a sickly senior, I already knew intuitively not to vaccinate him, but I was shocked by what I ended up learning. Our pets are being sickened by an aggressive schedule of over-vaccination, that has been arbitrarily imposed by the pharmaceutical companies for no reason other than profit. From starting out at 8 weeks with a slew of toxins, our animal's health is jeopardized with every set of shots. We trust that our vets would never give our furbabies something that posed more of a risk than a benefit, but they do. Mostly I believe because they don't have time to do their own research, and because they are educated on the 'safety' of vaccinations by the pharmaceutical reps. Like the fox watching the hen house.

No vaccination should EVER be given to an unwell patient, as stated clearly in the package insert. Based on my research, I also recommend spacing out any shots that you decide to be given, instead of all at once, thus reducing the toxic load.

Because most vaccinations provide the needed immunity for 7-15 years, almost every one is not necessary. Using a blood test called a titer test, the level of immunity in the blood is measured, and shows that a specific vaccination is not necessary. In many states, this is now accepted for the rabies vaccine!

This titer service is available at a minimal cost through Dr. Robb at Protectthepets.com.

The last thing I address with my pet parent friends is reducing the toxic load in the home. Based on my research, Air fresheners are a chemical wasteland of toxins for our pets and ourselves. These 'fragrances' are comprised of a list of ingredients that studies show have been linked to respiratory illness and cancer. The same goes for cleaning products, that our pets can walk on and absorb through the paw pads, or breath in and circulate through their bloodstream. I learned one of the most toxic products we can use are laundry dryer sheets! They seemingly coat our laundry with these chemicals and follow us and our pets around wherever we go! There are natural products that are safe, effective, and inexpensive that can be used in place of all of the above.

My Barney gained his wings in 2018, after 7 wonderful years of companionship, and teaching each other about love and life. I strive to help others realize we can support our pet's health in ways that are not taught in traditional settings.

I am so passionate about letting people know there are options for our health care. For me, the doctor, vet and pharmacy are not my first line of defense. I have most everything I need at home, that I can use. There are some things we don't have control over, but truly many things we do!

You can reach me at essentiallysherrilynn@gmail.com
or join our Facebook group:
https://www.facebook.com/groups/essentiallyoiledpetz
or go to my website:
my.doterra.com/protectyourpetz

Barney

Chapter Three

Bim. Bimka. Bimushka. My boy.

(June 18, 2013 adoption day - October 12, 2017)

Written by Olga.

Please note, ALL information is factual, and can be confirmed by legal documents. I did not sign any confidential agreement, so I want to use my right to freedom of speech without worry for a defamation of character lawsuit. This is not libel, or bashing. This is just my story.

This story about my chihuahua boy Bim and his tragic painful for many hours slow death in incompetent hands of ignorant and careless veterinarian and her team. The story about the Vet Board and system protecting bad vets.

The story is quite detailed and long, but explaining details and time frames in this particular case is critically important. Thank you for reading.

Just imagine.... What can be worse when you run to a vet you know and trust, trying to save your loved one, knowing it can be life threatening issue and every minute is important... to the vet, who is supposed to help your four legged child, and then have your furbaby die because this vet and assistants did not even try hard to save him? Even more - they made your baby die more painful, because they did not do the most important procedure, but instead gave him prohibited medications, inadequate treatment seeing him dying bleeding all over? And then brought the dead body of your loved one with a smile on their face? Blamed YOU, accusing YOU trying to protect themselves?

This is what happened to me and my baby boy on that day. October 12, 2017.

The day I will never forget.

Defendants (names abbreviated)

CVet. Dr.BS, owner of CVet, DVM, who was not present at the clinic on the day of the incident, but supported the treatment of my dog.

Dr.HH, DVM, CVet veterinarian taking care of my dog on the day of the incident. No longer works there.

I adopted my boy on June 18, 2013 from Solano Animal control (aka high kill shelter) during my vacation in CA. I was told he was 5 years old. He was very happy and excited leaving that hell shelter. He jumped in our van like he knew us for a long time. Bimka started a new life with us spending fantastic time at the most beautiful West Coast beaches and parks while driving home. In a few days we came to our home in WA. I took Bim to a local Pet Clinic for an exam. He seemed healthy.

We had never been separated since. Bim had been by my side for 4 years. He had always been there for me for a snuggle or giving me kisses when I needed them. Bimka was the sweetest boy. He completely stole my heart. He was very intelligent by nature, not yappy at all. Bimka loved children, people, companies, dogs. He was very sensitive, emotional, very outgoing and full of life..... He wanted to please me every second and followed me everywhere. I have never seen that loyal dog. His tail was ALWAYS wiggling, with no stop, so we always made some jokes that one day it will be broken because it never rest-). Bimka loved to smile. He made ME smile or laugh every single day because it was just much pleasure to see how happy and funny he was. How he smiled, the way he played, howling when wanted my attention, how he was step dancing when he was excited.... Because of his positive attitude, I called him "my depression pill". I did not have any depression, but Bimka was still my non official emotional support dog. He helped me a lot to stay positive after a car accident when I was not able to do my favorite yoga. Some people in a park called him "mummy's boy". Because I was protecting him like a hawk, and he was just too attached to me too. He knew we loved him and worried about him. My boy was an ideal dog to have around. However, I still was nearly neurotic about him. I always was afraid that because of his hyper temperament and adventurous nature he might get in trouble because he had some episodes of escaping at the beginning. Bim was so special to me. He was my word, and we both had some sort of separation anxiety from each other.

All my family deeply loved Bim, not just me. My mom, an elderly lady, had been visiting me every year staying with us for many months, and was extremely attached to Bim. Before Bimka's tragic death she spent a lot of time with him walking, they often slept together.... We all traveled together, hiking, staying in dog friendly hotels, and visiting many tourist places together all the way on the West Coast from South CA to Canada.

Bim health.

I do not know how Bim was fed before I adopted him. All I know he was very food oriented and a beggar. Bim was on a healthy homemade food diet, but, unfortunately, he was addicted to dog treats. In 2015 he had one episode with a stomach upset after eating some cookies he begged for. He was taken immediately the same day to the CVet clinic. That day Bim was seen by Dr.BS, defendant. Dr.BS made a blood test immediately, and it was good. Dr.BS didn't answer my questions clearly enough what could be wrong with him, so the only answer to myself was - he had a reaction to cookies. Bim was in normal shape just in a few hours running and playing that day. To avoid another episode like that, Bim never was given the same cookies again. If Dr.BS was concerned that Bimka might have some serious possible issue, he should have discussed it with me. In my opinion, failure to communicate and describe potential risk with a pet owner is not right. *Later, DrBS repeatedly stated under oath that my dog died because of a chronic issue mentioned in an autopsy report. Same time, DrBS stated that he did NOT offer diagnosis the same day, but we both agreed that if Bimka has the same symptoms again, we will do XRay and ultrasounds. However, before we filed a lawsuit he was pretty defensive saying "radiology and further diagnostics were declined" by me. Also, his paperwork from that day had some incorrect information about chicken strips, Bim was never given.*

Bim was a healthy boy with no signs of serious illness that needed an urgent vet visit. *Later, Dr.HH and Dr.BS told under oath that my dog had a deadly process that cannot be fixable by the time I brought him to the vet and what caused his death. They explained that "dogs cannot speak", and sometimes owners only recognise their own dog being sick when it is already too late and the dog cannot be saved. While I agree with their statement about other owners, it had nothing to do with me.* Being with Bim 24/7 and very sensitive about him being well I am confident that he was in good physical shape. While he was a bit down the hill for a couple weeks before he died, he still did not behave as a sick dog, was playful and happy until his last day. Night before he was in perfect shape! He never had any diarrhea, mucus stool, his appetite was always great. While Bimka did have some chronic gastro issues and the necropsy report also mentioned it, it was not deadly if treatable and it could be managed with the right diet.

Bimka's tragic death

Sometime before October 12, 2017 Bimka somehow had an accidental access to a beef bone. I was very against feeding bones to my small dogs, but our big German Shepherd rarely was given some beef bones from a pet store by my husband. It was always under supervision. When Shepherd ate meat off the bone, it went to a garbage. It is still a mystery how Bim got access to the bone, but a tragic accident happened. Neither me, or any family member gave any bones to Bim directly. *Later, the defendant lawyer tried to represent me as a neglected owner feeding bones to Bim, or/and not keeping an eye on him, trying to find some excuses for unforgivable vet unprofessionalism.*

I remember, the night before, Bim ran from downstairs and asked for treats from my husband. I still remember his happy eyes, and he was very playful, came to me to show up like "mom, look what I have", and soooo happy running back. That night he slept with my mom, and, according to her, he was sleeping uncomfortable.

The following morning, on October 12, 2017, I awoke at about 6:30 a.m, went downstairs to take Bimka out. Mom had already woken up and said that Bimka was outside, but something was wrong with him. Then I noticed he was acting strange, vomited white foam, his body clenched, and it was visible he was in pain. I never saw him like that. Because we had an appt we were waiting for a few weeks, mom asked if we should leave him home for a couple hours, but after I noticed a vomiting pink stain (meaning blood) on the rug next to tiny, but sharp bones, I knew **immediately** that I must take him to the vet ASAP.

For a minute I had a hard decision who I should call - CVet, the vet I already knew, or emergency. I decided to give a call to my vet first, and it was the biggest regretful decision I will never forgive myself for. I called them, and asked if they can accept me or I should go to an emergency. I did mention over the phone about bones and pink stains. Whoever spoke to me over the phone said I can come, so I did. If they said - take him to an emergency, I would with no problem. Wish they did !! *Later the vets and the defendant lawyer blamed me that I did not bring my dog to an emergency.*

Now I learned that regular vets do not know many important basic things. Then, I was naive thinking ANY veterinarian must know bones obstruction treatment, and I was thinking it can be done in ANY clinic. Dogs eat bones, ribbon hairs, plastic hangers, cable ties, socks.. you name it. It is a common issue, dogs are dogs, like toddlers, they have a tendency to chew anything they can get into their mouths. I do believe that taking care of dogs with blockage of foreign objects is a BASIC knowledge for ANY vet. According to public info, Nationwide pet insurance reports foreign body ingestion as one of its most common claims, demonstrating the severity of this pet safety issue. In 2018, policyholders filed more than $11.5 million in claims for foreign body ingestion for dogs and cats combined. Secondly, I already knew CVet. Unlike unknown doctors at some local emergency clinics and horrible "stay away" reviews about most of them. So, I did trust CVet by the moment I brough Bimka in. This is why I made that choice.

While still at home, for a bit I was thinking if I should give Bim some oil as first aid that acts as a lubricant and laxative and may help bowel movement, but decided the vet will know better what to do. Meanwhile, Bimka went from 1str floor to upstairs, came to my closet and he was digging, making his bedding on top of my clothes I left on the floor, and making him comfortable. When I came to check him out and grabbed him, this was the first time I noticed a strange breathing sound and bad smell. Even though he was walking, he clearly wanted to be left alone. He clearly was in pain. So... I carefully put him in a blanket and ran to the clinic, I was speeding and speaking to him "Bimushka, we will help you, you will be alright, my boy". *Later, Dr.HH blamed me that I brought Bim too late, already him having diarrhea and being lethargic, which was a false statement.* My mom was holding Bim in a blanket. This is why we knew he did not have diarrhea, because his blanket was clean and dry. My mom was very confident about him not being lethargic. This made me seriously upset when Dr.HH said "you brought him too late" after Bim died. I am 100% sure I brought my boy ON TIME, when he had chances to survive, when he started showing first symptoms and acting wrong. I am not that type of pet owner who will wait days or even hours to see if something changes for the better. I especially understood that bloody vomiting and sharp bones are seriously dangerous.

While driving in a car for appx. 15 minutes, he vomited 3 times white foam, and clearly <u>felt better</u> after it. He even stopped shaking for a bit after vomiting. This made me think that vomiting might be a good thing to help him, but it must be done by a professional.

We came to the vet clinic at appx.7.45 a.m., just before opening. AT, CVet assistant, was the one who we saw first. I immediately mentioned that Bimka most likely ate bones, he MIGHT need surgery, I am worried about the bad smell from his mouth. She said - yes, he smells stinky. Then Dr.HH showed up, I mentioned to her immediately that I suspect he ate bones, since I found sharp tiny bones with pink stains. I repeated that he might need surgery because of blood in vomits. She answered calmly, words to the effect that there was absolutely no need to do it right away, mentioning fluids most likely help. *Later, she told under oath that she had many cases when fluids helped with obstructions.* I did require an XRay myself, as step number one to confirm bone obstruction. We also agreed about a blood test and fluids at the same time. *Later the defendant lawyer accused me that I was offered expensive treatment and I declined it. She did not explain what expensive treatment it was, but clearly tried hard to find many excuses for unforgivable mistakes.*

My mom asked me if she can stay with Bimka. I answered: "Let's don't interrupt them doing their job". *Later the defendant lawyer asked me why I did not stay with Bim during the exam if I had separation anxiety from him. I believed it was not a typical exam. It was an emergency visit and I was expecting the vet to do some important procedure immediately to save my dog's life.* Even in emergency owners are not allowed.

Later, Dr.HH said that Bimka bit her during the exam. When a dog is lethargic, as Dr.HH claimed him being at the moment of arrival, he will not fight for his life and bite! and run on the stairs. Bim was NOT EVEN CLOSE to be lethargic when I brought him to the clinic. 100%. He was in pain, but he was alert.

We left the clinic at appx 8.15 a.m. On our way to an appt, we were discussing how <u>lucky</u> we were for not leaving Bimka at home alone and he was at VET hospital with specialists being SAFE. Wish I knew.... I feel extremely guilty and still blaming myself for leaving my boy with them without my attendance and controlling every step. I paid my price for trusting that vet. He was not safe there. Not at all. They just left him behind, as I believe to be true.

Later, because of the investigation and both defendants' answers at depositions, I found out that two veterinarians and a few assistants were working that day. It was not a busy day at all, no other emergencies. Small enough room with ability to monitor closely a critical patient using important equipment the clinic had, but none of it was used. Respiratory rates, heart rate, blood pressure, temperature.... nothing was checked. NOTHING was monitoring. Extreme case of carelessness and negligence, in my personal opinion. What I found out because of the brilliant work my lawyer did, was way worse that I was thinking when we filed a lawsuit. We opened a can of worms. Thus, CVet had at least a few other cases when dogs died because of bone obstruction (it was confirmed by Dr.BS at deposition). Dr.HH was working without a renewal licence, and had other negligence complaints. None of the assistants were licensed. Another vet, who was working that day, Dr.Sweeney, also had some incident when the dog died because of her mistake (med. overdose). Dr.S was not Bim' doctor that day, but she saw Bim's condition. Both vets and technicians did nothing, not contacted me, not warned me, not recommended to take him to emergency. They knew he was dying because of the necrotic smell. Or they were THAT ignorant for not understanding it???!!! The rotten smell was way too strong and everywhere... As I see it, they just decided FOR me that MY dog will die. They did not give any chance to even try to save him. I personally think they are ALL responsible for Bimka's death.

I still cannot explain why I trusted CVet so much. Sometimes I think if I brought him to an emergency, I would be more careful. I have had different experiences with local vets, from unacceptably horrible ones to a very positive. My yorkie had an excellent and adequate vet for over 10 years, but he retired. I had experience with a canine neurologist who was very caring, and volunteered his time trying to help my other fatally ill dog. Btw, he was the one, who once told me: "You are from only those 2% of owners who fight for a dog's life. Most owners just put down their dogs after a known diagnosis". *Later, the defense attorney asked me if I sued that vet because that dog died too. "What for?", I responded, "That vet was trying to save my dog's life!".* But some vets, I dealt with, were just ridiculous with their treatment plans. *Later, the defense attorney blamed me for refusing their "expensive" treatment as an excuse trying to represent me as a frugal owner.* So after dealing with some incompetent and unadequate vets before, I was quite untrusting of many of them. After trying a few local vet clinics, I decided that CVet is better. I considered Dr.BS as a very experienced good vet. I was so mistaken. Now I will never blindly trust any vet. I lost hope after this tragic experience.

Back to that day. At 8.53 a.m. I called Dr.HH. She told me that XRay at 8.44 am showed Bim's body full of bones, and asked my permission to put him on fluids, and do blood test. I agreed, of course. But at the same time I remember that I became upset and complained to my mom because Dr.HH was asking my permission to do it now, when we already agreed about it before I left the clinic at 8.15 a.m. and by 9 a.m. I was thinking they were already saving his life for at least 30 minutes!!! Doing enema, make him vomit, or whatever needs to be done in emergency situations to take care of bone obstruction. I missed that red flag. Later I found out that my boy was just left without any treatment for even longer when I was thinking he had already been treated. The dog in critical condition that was brought in the clinic at 8 a.m!!

At the moment I brought him to a hospital, I was expecting that my boy might need surgery ASAP. Because of bloody vomiting and found sharp tiny bones. However, I also knew that sometimes in obstruction cases the vet can help the dog by making the dog vomit, doing enema or endoscopy that often helps. Surgery is the worst case scenario. This is what I knew by that time. But I am not a vet, and did not know the difference of treatment depends on bone location. So when Dr.HH said (before I left the clinic) she wanted to give him IV fluids because they often help, she made me relaxed thinking maybe his case was not that bad and it would be good for him to avoid surgery. <u>The surgery was never recommended to me in the morning.</u> when I asked if he might need it at 8 a.m. Even when I called at 8.53 a.m. <u>my very first phrase was: "does he need surgery?".</u> Dr.HH said calmly already knowing he is "full of bones": "I do not want to do surgery for now, I WANT to AVOID it, his bones are not big, GOOD for him (exactly what she said), they might move." I felt just relaxed. This is what I was hoping for. I WAS ready to do a surgery IMMEDIATELY in the morning if she mentioned the importance of it. She just did NOT consider the surgery at all in the morning. She wanted to do fluids. Period. Her decision. Not mine. She did NOT mention any sharp bones, but did only talk about small ones. *Later the defendant lawyer blamed me at arbitration that I did not request the surgery. Like I suppose to teach a licenced vet (Dr.HH finished UC Davis School, considered as the top one) what must be done. According to her, it was MY fault for not doing it. Just a poor excuse for negligence and ignorance.*

The most disgusting and unforgivable thing is that later, Dr.HH along with Dr.BS accused me that I DECLINED the surgery MYSELF. This false info they both provided to a necropsy company and to the Vet Board. Even though Dr. BS was not present that day, and only trusted Dr.HH words. I never signed any declining form, and none of the paperwork confirmed I declined it. At arbitration, she told that according to her experience many owners cannot afford veterinary bills and she experienced this all the time. I agree - many cannot, and from my personal experience, being an animal advocate, I know it too, but what it has to do with me if many cannot?! The truth is - I never told her that I <u>cannot</u> afford the surgery, and I will NEVER accept her statement accusing me of declining surgery. Wrongly accusing me was one of the reasons I took a legal step. Also, at deposition, Dr.HH told that I WAS GIVEN OPTIONS for FB REMOVAL VS IVF, and I WANTED to elect IVF. I NEVER EVER REFUSED TO DO A SURGERY as later she told under oath. **It was a VET decision, NOT mine, to put Bim on IVF.** Plus, I am not frugal when something really important must be done. The life of my loved one depends on it. Who would care about money knowing their dog can die ?!?

Later, when Dr.HH responded to the Vet Board that the surgery in the morning would be a best option for Bim. Same time in arbitration and deposition she repeatedly told she wanted to keep Bim on fluids. *Her controversial responses to the Vet Board, at deposition and arbitration only confirmed she was not honest.*

I still believe it to be true that avoiding to do a surgery in the morning was Dr.HH' biggest mistake and what cost my dog's life. Because of that smell already started in the morning, Bim needed surgery immediately operating his dead tissues, but he was just "left to die". Dr.HH never recognized the necrotic smell thinking it was a dental smell. The vet, who finished top vet school!

These two images made at 8.44 a.m. showed **where the obstruction is in the small intestine**. Later I received a couple veterinarian consultations about the importance of doing surgery immediately: "If it is known to be a sharp bone, surgery should be done immediately to prevent any perforation of the intestines. Endoscope only works if the object is still in the stomach. You cannot scope objects out from the intestines". Another vet response was: "I will not wait so long. As if case stable now who knows what will happen after. Surgical interference best option". I also did my own homework at legitimate sources. . According to a reputable veterinary article, if the object has made it into the intestine, surgery is imminent. Time is critical since an intestinal or stomach obstruction often compromises or cuts off the blood supply to these vital tissues. If the blood supply is interrupted for more than a few hours, these tissues may become necrotic or die, and irreparable damage or shock may result. Another veterinary article states: if intestinal obstruction happens, food, fluids, gastric acids, and gas build up behind the site of the blockage. If enough pressure builds up, your intestine can rupture, leaking harmful intestinal contents and bacteria into your abdominal cavity. This is a life-threatening complication.

This is what happened to my boy. However, Dr.HH was so unprofessional that even during arbitration she still told "Bim died UNEXPECTEDLY". According to CVet assistant Shawnae B. "it was traumatic for her because Bim was vomiting blood and had blood coming out of his rectum. He was spraying blood from his rear end. The smell was horrendous". How ignorant can a so-called vet be for not understanding a necrotic smell? The rotten odor was everywhere. UNEXPECTEDLY???!!! My boy had all his organs falling apart for HOURS. This is why the room had a necrotic smell. UNEXPECTEDLY???!!! Bim came to the clinic having consumed bones at 8 a.m. Radiographs that morning at 8.44 a.m. confirmed their presence. He died at almost 4 p.m. After 8 !!! long hours being in horrible pain and bleeding all over? UNEXPECTEDLY !!! ??? What a vet she is if she didn't know what it can be???!!!!! And did NOTHING about it?

Is this how US Davis teaches their students?

But let's back to what happened hourly that day..... At appx. 11.40 a.m., I returned to the clinic and was shocked that my boy was still under fluids. I was sure that by that time Bim was already "ready to go home". On our way to the clinic, me and mom were speaking that Bimka is probably already relaxing after important cleaning procedures and waiting for us. I had absolutely no bad intuition at that moment. However, when I saw Dr.HH, it made me seriously worry. First of all, Dr.HH looked nervous. She said: "Poor boy, he is in pain, I gave him pain medication". This was a HUGE red flag. He shouldn't be in pain if he had bones removed either by vomiting or enema or fluids, as I believed. I asked her: "Did you make him vomit? She said 'he puked twice a bit". You see, even being on Cerenia (She administered him *CERENIA* which is ANTI vomiting med, and contraindicated in dogs and cats suspected of having a gastrointestinal obstruction), my boy did fight for life, he wanted to vomit and "clean" his body from bones.

This time I was not as trustful and nice like I was in the morning. My tone also changed, I became more demanding... Why so long? This was the first time I thought I had to take Bimka to another clinic/emergency, but Dr.HH promised that she would do another XRay in 40 min, and hopefully bones will move. Additionally, she stated clearly that Bim' blood test was good, I still remember her satisfied face when she told me that like "nothing serious", when actually it was very bad, as it was confirmed the next day by Dr.BS, and later by an expert during the investigation. I remember, I counted time if I took him immediately to an emergency. Simple logic and math was that it was more safe for him to be under treatment already, that wasting at least 2 extra critically important hours and risk waiting with no help if I took him to an emergency. But she didn't even mention the emergency. She promised to treat him for another 40 min. Because it was "only 40 min" I agreed. I asked her if I should stay, but she said there was no need.

A second set of radiographs (without barium contrast) were taken at 12:45 p.m. Instead of going home we stayed near the clinic waiting for her call. Dr.HH called me at 1.06 p.m. and said that, unfortunately, some bones were still there stuck, he needed a surgery, but NOW she was worried because he started to have a bloody diarrhea. According to an expert who evaluated my case "diarrhea is not a contraindication for surgery". I asked Dr.HH: "Are you sure you did everything right?" and she answered with a very confident voice : "We did our best, all we could". So I agreed on surgery. I told her: "I don't want my boy to die". *Not because I decided to finally do it as later Dr.HH repeatedly was saying at deposition and at arbitration.* Because SHE WANTED TO KEEP HIM ON FLUIDS THAT LONG. It was also stated in her written notes. She ignored professional advice from radiologists suggesting surgery much earlier. XRay from 8.44 a.m. already showed bone obstruction that must be surgically removed. What Dr.HH was waiting for???!!!! When he started internal bleeding and died in pain from multiple organs failure? Her written notice after appx 2 hours being at the clinic showed that he started to be lethargic. Cerenia also gives side effects like lethargy and bleeding diarrhea, what I learned later. Well.. I still shake my head how everything was done wrong. Her explanations were too controversial... She did not remember anything, even who was responsible for doing some procedures to Bim. It was just a mess and hard to even listen to her answers and false statements during deposition and arbitration. It will be never understandable, forgotten, and forgivable. The most ridiculous sounding phrase in the end was "I take my work very seriously".

Back to that day....At 1.06 p.m. call Dr.HH mentioned she was going to do surgery next hour. Her voice didn't sound confident enough this time. She did not say a single word about him smelling bad, dying, etc. I wanted to be in the clinic, but because she said there was no need, I came home thinking my boy was doing surgery at this moment. *Later I found out that by that time he was spraying blood from everywhere.* I was by the door ready driving back to the clinic when at 2.09 p.m. I received a call from her and she told me that she was continuing to keep him on fluids, she was nervous to do surgery because he was very weak. Again, not even a single word about the danger of death, so even understanding he was not doing well, I couldn't even think he was dying. According to an expert who evaluated my case "This is an inexplicable poor clinical judgement, as clearly the doctor's prescribed course of action failed".

Dr.HH also mentioned the calming voice that most likely Bim would need to relocate to emergency service at 5 p.m. and we agreed to meet by that time at the clinic. *Later she stated that I "expressed financial concerns and did not want to transfer him to the 24 hr facility due to the cost".* The truth is - we even discussed what emergency was better and I even asked the last name of the vet she would recommend. We agreed about the Redmond emergency. However, after we spoke, I already knew that something seriously wrong was going on. I remember, my mom was panicking what they did wrong if that took so long. I called them soon after. Ali Trudgeon picked up the phone. She transferred to Dr.HH, who started to talk fast that Bim became lethargic, they increased dose (didn't know what was it), and new medication (I didn't know which one), and he immediately died after. My boy died just before 3.40 p.m. According to written notices, Bim became alert when they checked him last time... then he was FOUND dead in his ward.

I was ready for anything that morning.... Surgery, recovery from surgery, extra care, high vet bills, but ... not his death. I couldn't believe what I heard. " WHAT?! did you say Bim died?" She said: " Yes, he passed". All I remember, I threw my phone away and broke the screen. I believe I screamed, but I already was not myself to clearly understand. I started running from wall to wall without understanding what I was doing. My poor mom had a different shock reaction. She was sitting like a zombie staring at one place and didn't say a word. My mom was trying to stop me going back to the clinic, because of my condition at that moment, but nothing stopped me. I sped up again, and when I came there, the first person I saw was Ali Trudgeon coming from a back room holding my Bimka in a different blanket and she was smiling. Yes, I was not mistaken. SHE WAS SMILING. I remember her smile. This is why I was thinking for a second, maybe my boy was alive, they did something to bring him back to life, I still was thinking maybe they were mistaken saying he was dead. "Is he dead", I was asking, she said "yes". Then Dr.HH came, and I started yelling at her " You killed him, I told you he needed surgery". Her first response was "you brought him too late". I hardly remember details of our conversation except some of her phrases like "Even my dog(s) died from bones". *Later, at deposition she refused saying this phrase. What vet she is even if her own dog(s) died from it, and she still does not know what must be done?* I was crying putting my face to Bimka's dead body, I was kissing him. Bim was still warm, but became cold while we were there. My mom was still in shock saying nothing, just petting his dead body. Then my son came trying to figure out what caused Bimka's death. Bimka was in someone's blanket, not the blanket I brought him in. And because I saw blood around his rectum, I knew the blanket was dirty with blood, so they hid it.

Next morning I came back to a clinic to pick up frozen Bim's body and drove to another side of the city to do a necropsy. I still did not believe that Bimka could not be saved. I was offered to do a necropsy at Crossroads, but, of course, I refused it. I needed an independent party. Same time, I spoke with Ali Trudgeon about Bim cremation and double checked if I was able to receive a claw paw print (standard cremation package). I was told - YES. Later all I received was an urn with ashes. This time Ali Trudgeon said the opposite thing pretending she didn't know what I was talking about. I had never received any claw paws from my boy. Just a tiny print on his medical record. It was another example of them being sloppy, careless and cynical. Then, I found some info on their web about how they respect their clients, with a pic in frame with some dog printed paw. After they lied to me that I would receive a claw paw, it was kind of painful to see it.

Same day I spoke to Dr.BS, owner of CVet. Firstly, he confirmed that a blood test was not good, and said that "the treatment was questionable". I told him that I believe Dr.HH responsible for Bim' death and his death was completely preventable because the surgery was not done on time when I brought him when he was stable. I did say that Dr.HH wasted important hours. Dr.BS said that Bim was too weak to do surgery. His exact phrase was "What is the point of doing surgery if he could die anyway". *Later, during the deposition and arbitration he refused that he told this phrase.* I responded: "At 1p.m. - maybe, but not at a time I brought him in the morning". He said that fluids are the right thing to do. I responded: "Yes, but for how long?" But that time I did not know that even fluid therapy was done terribly deadly wrong with inadequate low doses. He was not saying a word when I mentioned the time missing. He also said that he needed to go over everything to give me a better answer. Next time when I stopped he was pretty cold saying "Her treatment was right, I would do the same". *Later, Dr.BS mentioned multiple times that Bim was an unfortunate candidate for a surgery, because it was impossible to cut a certain amount of dead tissue. But they did not even try. How they knew how much "dead tissues" were there?* Ironically, after the case was closed, I found an online 1 star review about a local emergency. It was also an intestinal obstruction case review. Despite the horrible unprofessional service there, and very complicated surgery because of wasting two days untreating, a significant amount of intestinal was removed. Still. DOG WAS SAVED because of a professional surgeon. The owner complained about very bad careless assistants, and because of it, dog lost much of his organ, but HIS DOG WAS SAVED!!!!!

After I requested all health records for Bim, I had a shock.

1. Bim was administered CERENIA, anti-vomiting medication that was contraindicated in his case. While Cerenia did not cause his death, I still believe that this medication did cause additional problems (leathady and bleeding diarrhea known as side effects). Later I received a few answers from other veterinarians saying that giving this medication without going to surgery or monitoring the potential obstruction is not a good idea, and even though It is a fantastic medication to prevent vomiting. It should NEVER be given in cases of possible obstruction, as this can mask the signs of an obstruction and delay appropriate treatment. Additionally, the fact that this drug is controversial in patients with suspected gastrointestinal obstructions was confirmed by a top expert who evaluated my case. *Later, during the investigation our expert confirmed that this is not only medication that was prohibited in his case, but yet, still given to him.*

2. Dr.HH clearly told me that Bim' blood work was good, and it was bad. According to an expert, Dr.HH greatly underestimated his level of dehydration and physical compromise.

3. Bim received a total of 200 mls over seven (7) hours of intravenous fluid bolus. Meaning he received nothing that could help him even a little. According to an expert, a prudent calculation for a small patient that was significantly dehydrated, hypotensive, and experiencing continued fluid losses (vomiting/diarrhea) would have been 90-100 mls/kg (324- 360 mls) over the first 1-2 hours, then followed by patient reassessment. That is a minimum of 160-180 mls/hr. over the first two (2) hours.

4. Additionally, Dr.HH compounded this error by the administration of HETASTARCH, which is <u>contraindicated</u> in Bimka's case. <u>It has a greater risk of poor clinical outcomes compared to other intravenous solutions, and may increase the risk of death.</u>

5. The blood test was done only after 3 hours of Bim being in a clinic knowing he was in critical condition. According to an expert, it was an inexcusable delay.

6. Bim was given Buprenex, a strong pain medicine. If you see the first XRay and last XRay Bimka's body shape changed a lot. He was dying very painful.

7. I signed up for Barium treatment at estimate, but they never used Barium that must be checked every 30 minutes, not 4 ! hours between XRays. The four-hour delay between the first and second set of radiographs significantly compromised Bimka's chance of survival. *Later Dr.BS responded that they do not even use Barium.*

8. According to Dr.HH written notes, Bim was <u>found dead in crate</u> after 15 minutes… Think for a second… My boy WAS FOUND DEAD. *Later both vets tried hard to pretend how they closely monitored him. Two !!! Vets in a small room, and MANY assistants. Yet, he still WAS FOUND DEAD. Later Dr.BS answered*: "He was never left unattended; our ward has constant presence In our treatment area". **Bim WAS <u>FOUND</u> DEAD.**

When I received an autopsy report, it was another traumatic experience. I picked up the report at CVet and decided to read it right away, of course. The autopsy report stated in detail that Bimka died because he had multiple bone foreign bodies. It was stated very clearly that **"certainly at an early point in this process, removal of the bones from his stomach could have saved his life".** However, first I read in the report that the "owner declined the surgery". I had a shock and started crying …. where it came from? Just a few days ago, I had a conversation with people from a necropsy company complaining about CVet for not doing the surgery. That was clear enough to understand that CVet provided them false information. Crying and upsetting I walked back in a clinic asking WHY… I saw Shawnae B, a technician, who looked respectful and understandable to me. She immediately asked how she can help me. The only one. I saw a group of people sitting behind the counter and all giggled...while I was crying in front of the counter showing them the report and asking WHY they provided false info. I left. It was too stressful for me. They had a good fun time. Later I found out that the group are the same people working the day Bimka died. In my personal opinion, they ALL did not act as caring people respecting other life, nor having any compassion.

Then I had to face another painful episode. Yes, AGAIN. Being heartbroken, devastated I wrote a Yelp review about CVet. It was saying shortly "If you love your pet, stay away. My dog died at this clinic because of unforgivable ignorance and lack of compassion" . You will not believe what happened next. My review was marked AS FUNNY by Shawnae B (her name pop-up) and 3 other people, clearly all from CVet. I deleted my review. I could not stand it anymore. I had enough. IT WAS FUNNY FOR THEM….. WHO ARE THOSE PEOPLE!?

For "dessert" to already listed experiences with the CVet team, already felt I was trumped in the mud, I received a warning letter from CVet signed by Dr.BS that I must pay the bill for THAT visit, otherwise he will report me to a collection agency. I wrote a check with the sign "under protest". I already started a legal process against this clinic. I had enough.

PS: **According to a top expert with 35 years of major experience, who evaluated my case, cause of death was complications from severe dehydration, hypotension, multiorgan failure and endotoxic shock as a result of inadequate patient assessment, care, and monitoring rendered by Dr.HH and CVet. Dr.HH and CVet fell well below the standard of care in their treatment of Bim. Dr.HH had not conducted herself as a reasonable, prudent, and skilled veterinarian. In her expert opinion, lack of appropriate, aggressive supportive care, surgical intervention, and/or referral were the proximate causes of "Bam's" death.**

The expert also mentioned that Dr.HH' acts were unforgivable and "Better to have a negative exploratory than a positive autopsy," "which unfortunately denotes "Bim's" fatal outcome".

Investigation and lawsuit.

I knew from the very beginning I would not let it go. I was lucky to start working with a top attorney who took my case, and I will be forever grateful for all the hard work that was done helping in my case.

Firstly, we filed a complaint to a Vet Board. Unfortunately, It took nearly a year, and I was extremely not satisfied how poorly and unprofessionally the Vet Board took care of my case. They blindly believed the defendants, none of them called me or asked any questions. Their report was very poorly made and it was clear enough that they did not even read or care about my point of view. Plus, they lost all my files, and it took them additional months to find it. In the end, they closed my case - nothing wrong was found. *Later, the defendant attorney used their decision against me*. The following people who took care of my case are: Sue A. Moriyasu, D. V. M., Reviewing Board Member, Deonna Chartrey, Case Manager, Scott Bramhail, Investigator, Staff/Panel present: Elizabeth Davles, Michelle Zachry, Aja Senestraro.

In positive note, Dr.HH was subjected to discipline by the Washington State Department of Health for failing to provide proof that she completed continuing veterinary medical education for a period between January 30,

2015 and January 29, 2018. I was about to file a complaint about them, but was told this will be a waste of time. So we proceeded further and filed a lawsuit. Then we had to deal with a defense attorney, who made the whole process more miserable trying to protect bad vets. I am naive, I guess, but I truly believe, this is just so wrong and unethical to accuse and blame an already devastated, heartbroken pet parent who provided excellent care to her furbaby, who would do anything to save him. It cost nothing to be a decent person. On deposition and arbitration I was accused that I had chosen holistic because I tried to save money (ridiculous, because holistic vets, actually, way more expensive), I was accused of being a frugal owner who brought a very sick for a long time helpless dog too late. Bad frugal owner will not spend over $8k on a fatally ill dog as I did to my other rescue. Bad owners will not bring a sick dog to an emergency immediately next hour after showing first symptoms. Frugal owners will not start a legal process trying to bring justice for a dead dog. We had to deal with insurance who claimed Bim was ONLY $100 and we want "too much" . After ALL I already went through, being slandered, to consider my boy, who was everything to me, who was PART of me, who was my FAMILY member, my word, like something not valuable. Well.... Even if the law says a dog is a piece of property, "it" WAS VALUABLE piece of property to me.

The top expert did prove veterinary malpractice, unforgivable ignorance, and far below veterinary standard care. Both Dr. BS, the owner of CVet and especially Dr.HH REPEATEDLY LIED under oath. Insurance attorney still did not care. Her hypocritical phony 'I am sorry for losing Bimka" cost nothing, when I was accused and ignored when we tried to reasonably settle.

After 3 years dealing with it…(It wouldn't take that long, but after the Vet Board closed my case I was not well. I felt helpless. It took me at least 6 months to get back to understanding I was strong enough mentally and emotionally to continue…):

I am the prevailing party in my lawsuit against Dr.HH and Dr BS. Judgment is entered against Defendant BS DVM, HH, DVM in favor of me.

But sadly, it is a bittersweet victory... While veterinary malpractice was confirmed, and I was awarded veterinary bills and some legal cost, as well as sanctions for discovery abuse by defense counsel in favor of me, I was not awarded even a dollar for emotional support or instrustic value of my boy. As a result, I am in significant financial loss. No apologies from defendants, either. Despite excellent and hard work by my lawyer, I closed the case and even though we had many chances for a better outcome at supreme court, it was still a risk because of the cost of litigation. Plus, it would take another year and would ruin my health more. My head is half white due to stress already. I stutter every single time I speak about that day and think about Bimka's suffering. First time in 50 years of my life. I am very worn out physically and emotionally. My whole family is affected. I already know enough and I do not need to prove anything else. I always knew I was right. And thanks to my fantastic lawyer who proved a vet malpractice even though the Vet Board found nothing wrong. On a positive note, I do not have a confidential agreement but right to freedom of speech. Now my story is public. Maybe my story will help other pet owners to stay away from bad vets or maybe details mentioned in my story will save another dog's life...

However, as for today, both defendants do not have any disciplinary notice, so a new complaint to a Vet Board must be filed again. Hopefully, they might take action this time. There are multiple bad reviews about Dr.HH and CVet from many unhappy pet owners who had negative experiences with any of them, including the death of the pets, many are public. Everyone can find them. As I believe to be true, the level of ignorance and lack of compassion is unacceptable for Dr.HH to continue working with animals. I lost my dog, but do not want other pet parents to experience what I did. No other innocent animal should suffer in incompetent hands of the vet who does not respect their life and feeling. I have been working on the page "Justice for Bimka".

Epilogue

It's been a few years since I lost my boy due to an extreme case of veterinary negligence. It still hurts to think about how much he suffered at CVet' hands.

I am an adequate person with dignity, and always have been a great owner for ALL my dogs. I do not deserve to put myself, my whole family in this position, ruining my life because of it. I would not waste anyone's time, a significant amount for legal fees, if I declined the surgery as Dr.HH and Dr.BS claimed to protect themselves, or I was not caring enough about my Bimka, or brought him too late. Otherwise the only person I would blame is myself. But I not only lost my four legged child, I also had to deal with the accusing, disrespect, slander, cynical attitude that made me feel like I was trumped in the mud. It is just unacceptable and unforgivable. Additionally, I was extremely disappointed with the Vet Board and dealing with insurance. Vets are protected. I experienced absolutely nightmares with all those people.

I do know, I will live the rest of my life with this pain and never forgive myself for trusting CVet. This was a horrific experience. I went through absolute hell that day. But this is not just about me. This is about my innocent Bimka. I try to be strong. Life is going on. What is killing me just to think how my poor boy suffered for 8 long hours bleeding all over and I was not next to him. He died very painful, and the vet did her "best" to make him die harder by not doing the right things causing undue and exquisite suffering, without giving me an opportunity to provide Bimka with emergent veterinary care. I still have extreme anger and extreme grief. I miss my boy terribly.

I do know I won't forgive her careless, heartless, incompetence and complete lack of peacefulness at the end of my dog's life. One day I will forget about them treating me as garbage, laugh at my reviews, and be cynical, dishonest. But I do know that the way they treated my innocent boy who died left alone in pain spraying blood… will be NEVER forgivable and NEVER forgotten.

I also want to say something else. None of us is perfect. We all can make mistakes. Some mistakes can be forgivable, or, at least, we can find some explanations, or excuses. But what cannot be forgivable is extreme indifference to life in professions when this is a MUST have. Veterinarians are not car mechanics fixing a broken car. They are dealing with suffering LIVE animals and owners who love their pets dearly. I do believe, negligence and cruelty is unacceptable in a profession that requires compassion, respect, and honesty when caring for animals in need.

PS: The last day, when I finished writing this story about Bimka, I took my 17 y.o. yorkie for a walk. It was a nice sunny day, but a little rain started. Then I saw a Rainbow in the sky. I smiled and started to cry at the same time. I had an interesting feeling that maybe it was some sign and my Bimka was running there happy…. My little sun beam Who was loved beyond definition. Who will be Forever Be My ALWAYS.

My experiences with vets. Written by Olga.

Being a huge animal lover, advocate and owner of a few rescued dogs and cat, I have had a lot of experience with many vets in WA since 2004. Below are a few examples of what I had to deal with during all these years. I am writing this not because I want to bash anyone. I do it for the sake of other animals, and hope that details in my stories will help other pet owners to avoid what I went through. Our pets depend on us, please be a protective and educated owner.

Kitty Story. 2005. Torture euthanasia.

Kitty belonged to a close family member. He was a bit older, but still had many years to live. He was an outdoor, a bit wild, Himalayan cat, and did not let touch him much. So one day he let me do it, and I knew and saw something wrong with him. I ran to an emergency with him. I was given the list of all possible diagnostic tests, but we started with XRay, as I told the most important thing to start. XRay showed that his body was full of fluids. With a very confident voice, sounding like a good professional who explained many details about all potential risks and Kitty's future, the vet recommended putting Kitty down as the most humane way. Pretty much he was pushing to do it. By that time I was trustful to vets, did not have much experience with them, but the doctor was very confident about him being right, so we agreed, only because we did not want Kitty suffering. I do remember, I was asking if Kitty might have any pain during the procedure. Again, with a very confident voice me and my son were told that there was nothing to worry about. No painful procedure. So we agreed. Then the horror started. Without using any sedation, the assistant made a death injection directly to a vein. This unprofessionally done procedure caused him undue and exquisite suffering for a LONG time. It was a torture. I had never experienced euthanasia procedure before, I think it took maybe 20 minutes at least....He was bleeding from his month while dying and gasping for air. Then the same doctor came and told the assistant with an extremely indifferent voice "yeah, not enough, add more". They acted like they changed oil in a car. No compassion at all. ZERO. Assistant added a dose, and Kitty finally stopped breathing. Not immediately still. It was absolutely a sadistically done euthanasia with no compassion to a poor innocent animal. Later I found out that this doctor was known for recommending putting animals down when they would have been saved. Probably, Kitty would have been saved. At least, he did not deserve suffering that way in his last moments. This doctor is passed now, but the clinic (Aerowood) still has many horrible reviews.

Lesson from this experience: never blindly trust any vet. Get a second opinion. Ask many questions about details how eutanasia must be done, what medication they use (there are some prohibited medications to certain breeds due genetic), and never euthanize your pet without sedation first.

Polina's story. 2010. "What do you want?"

Polina was my puppy mill rescue. In 2010, after nearly a year of her rehabilitation, she became ill. To make a long story short, after MRI at a specialty clinic she was diagnosed with a fatal brain illness/autoimmune disorder. Her regular vet recommended putting her down immediately, but I found Dr.S, neurologist, at SVS, WA, known as best in the state. He was very caring and adequate. He also volunteered his time contacting a specialty vet from Boston, who specialized at Polina' illness, trying to figure out the best treatment for my dog. Dr.S is retired and no longer practicing. However, before we started work with him, Polina was misdiagnosed with a liver shunt (liver shunt might have neurological symptoms), and was under treatment with an internist at the same clinic (vet no longer works there). With that vet I had a bad interaction. When her treatment did not help, I called her, saying that Polina was dying. Her irritated response was "WHAT DO YOU WANT?". I started yelling at her: "WHAT DO I ???!! want???!!! My dog is DYING, we need a neurologist appt ASAP!!!" SVS is an EMERGENCY hospital. Just saying. By that time I already knew that if the treatment was not helping, it was a bad sign, and my dog would need steroids. Only after yelling at the vet, she prescribed prednisolone the same day, and SVS scheduled an appt. with a neurologist the next few days, while at the beginning I was told I had to wait a few weeks to see him. After Polina started the treatment the same day, she became immediately better. She lived for another 9 months. PS: still a question if the rabies shot that was given Polinka a few months earlier caused her autoimmune disorder.

Lesson from this experience: Don't be afraid to be aggressive to save your pet. Sadly, sometimes to save your dog you HAVE TO BE aggressive enough, otherwise they do NOT care.

After sadistic euthanasia experience at Aerowood, when I brought my poor Polina to put down to SVS, I had to be the same aggressive. I WAS afraid that my already suffering girl would go to the same hell as Kitty went. I was very clear asking her to do work right. Luckily, it was an absolutely opposite experience. Except for two young technicians with zero compassion, who were chatting, indifferent to my dying dog, and were not able to put a catheter. But euthanasia was done highly professionally. The vet put her to sleep first, then left me for certain time to say "goodbye" to my dog while she was sleeping, but alive, and only then came with "blue" final injection. Polina was calmly sleeping. I told my girl how much I loved her and she was my best girl. She was relaxed, even her tongue was out.

She did this only when she was happy, relaxed, and free of pain. And that sign made me sure she was not suffering that moment. She was not even shaked. I did not believe she was dead. Wish I knew the name of that doctor. I couldn't find her name in documents. She was sitting on the floor and cried with me. She was reading the Polina file before the procedure. That doctor WAS CARING.

Bim experience. 2016. Inadequate money oriented advice.

My tiny 7 pound dog was bit by a bigger chihuahua we knew. At the beginning it was not even noticeable. Absolutely no blood, nothing visible. But being a loving mom, I paid attention to any small signs of anything wrong. Next day I noticed my boy didn't want me to touch his neck. I found a tiny (size of my small nail) wound under his fur, and it was just a bit infected. Still enough for me to be in the clinic the same day. I was very confused about the procedure I was recommended. Actually, it took me some time to even understand exactly what they wanted to do with my poor dog, because I couldn't even imagine that a vet might recommend 4!!! stitches under anesthesia for a few hours. SERIOUSLY?! I could not believe the doctor was that inadequate to recommend that, I would call, sadistic procedure at THIS PARTICULAR case. I ended up buying antibiotics from them, just in case, and did a holistic treatment using some creams from pus/infection, and applications, including aloe, myself. Good for me I knew how to treat it and had anti infection medication purchased at the local pharmacy. If someone does not? Poor dogs! The vet did not offer anything re. local treatment, but thank him, still gave good advice to keep the wound open to heal better. In a week my dog even did not have a scar left. In my personal opinion, if the vet does not know a holistic treatment like medicated cream for such small issues, and wants to put the tiny dog in hell under anesthesia, something seriously wrong going on. Looked like it was more money oriented advice, definitely, not the best interest for a pet. I am not frugal, and IF needed, will pay whatever it needs to be done, but I was very proud of myself being smart enough to save my dog from unnecessarily suffering and risks (that cost, btw, over $800 or so, not my concern, but clearly their interest), and having great outcome treated him myself for less that $100. Also, I seriously dislike the assistant that day. She did not look like a person who really loves animals. Anyway, It was my last visit to that clinic.

Later I was reading a sad review written by a person, who lost her loved one due to wrong anestesia (it was a dental procedure) at the same clinic. They reported this incident to a Vet Board, and the vet had a disciplinary notice, according to their public review.

Aspen experience. 2020-2021. Did all the shots cause her illness?

Aspen was an older rescued white Shepherd dog. We needed a new vet and decided to try VCA Bellevue. It was a big regret. A few very serious enough cons to avoid VCA forever. Personally, I wouldn't take our dog at first place after the VCA vet refused to accept her (attention!) being SICK and BLEEDING, if they do not make a RABIES VACCINE FIRST. However, my husband followed the vet advice, and regretted it later. As I believe it to be true, absolutely NO CARING VET WILL PUSH ON SERIOUS VACCINE TO AN OLD SICK BLEEDING DOG. PERIOD. Yes, it is required by law, but there are always exceptions if the dog is sick and old, and I have seen some local vets who are way more caring. (copy): *The American veterinary medical association says the vaccination isn't a requirement or necessary for every dog. Most recently, the research indicates that dogs over 10 or 12 years of age should not be vaccinated because their immune system can be compromised, and also, by the time they are that age, they have received adequate protection. Research has demonstrated that over vaccination can cause harmful adverse effects in dogs. Immunologically, the rabies vaccine is the most potent of the veterinary vaccines and associated with significant adverse reactions such as polyneuropathy resulting in muscular atrophy, inhibition or interruption of neuronal control of tissue and organ function, incoordination, and weakness, auto-immune hemolytic anemia, autoimmune diseases affecting the thyroid, joints, blood, eyes, skin, kidney, liver, bowel and central nervous system; anaphylactic shock; aggression; seizures; epilepsy; and fibrosarcomas at injection sites are all linked to the rabies vaccine. senior dogs are more likely to suffer adverse effects from rabies vaccinations. It is medically unsound for this vaccine to be given more often than is necessary to maintain immunity, yet scientific research strongly indicates that the 3 year booster interval required by state laws may be unnecessary.*

PS: After a few months, Aspen suddenly became sick. She was diagnosed with DM (Degenerative Myelopathy), became paralyzed in a week and went to Rainbow Bridge soon after. While DM is caused by gene mutation and typical for particularly white Shepherds, DM is also known as a side effect of Rabies. So it will always be a question of what caused the DM in our dog.

Additionally, VCA FAILED the urine test. They found NOTHING. When I took Aspen to another vet immediately after, they DID find a serious bacteria.

VCA sells ROYAL food from their office. ENOUGH to avoid. Anyone who knows the shocking truth about the commercial dog food industry and watched Pet food exposed documentaries, checked consumeraffairs.com site, will leave those offices immediately. I did not see it the first day due to closed windows (Covid).

That day, beside Rabies vaccine, Aspen was prescribed expensive medication that did NOT help her, and later I found out that she was resistant to it. "Sensitivity test might be recommended in the future" was mentioned in her record. Why didn't the vet do it right away?! Clearly, it is not their interest to find the right solution from the start. Experiences with expensive drugs that might not help, extra useless appointments... Their philosophy about over vaccination, the way they operate... clearly, the clinic is money oriented. The estimates I received for some procedures were twice higher than different clinics nearby. After not being satisfied with their service, knowing we have to find another vet, I required records, and found some false information about details re. Aspen visits. Same time, the tone of the vet, while she was speaking to me, was very defensive, if not aggressive. VCA, Thanks for nothing and wasting my time and money. Most important - our dog's health ("thank you" for Rabies shot again - you might be responsible for Aspen sudden disorder and death). Never again.

Lesson from this experience: Avoid any clinic selling/recommending commercial dog food. Never let an uncaring vet do ANY shots without a TITER test, especially if your dog is sick, OLD. Require TITER test. We have a titer bill in Arizona! SB1353 ANTI-RABIES VACCINATION. Learn about The Rabies Challenge Fund.

So. I took poor Aspen to another local private clinic. Cannot say I was too happy taking her there, but I needed XRay ASAP, and some clinics were not available for a sooner appt.. I knew this vet, he was an old school type vet and had been in business forever. He was nice to my other dog before, but she was misdiagnosed there, also. My other dog case was a bit complicated, and he was understandable enough and even took back some medication he prescribed. So I decided to give him another chance. However, experience with Aspen made me decide that I will never go back to the same clinic. There were some Pros: Aspen had a sensitive test, and was under right treatment this time. They made the right urine test to find bacteria. However, Aspen, being calm, and not an aggressive dog, was given absolutely unnecessarily sedation called ACE (Acepromazine) for simple XRay procedure. This drug has been documented to cause problems in dogs with the MDR1 mutation (according to the Washington state University webpage, the MDR1 mutation has been found in German Shepherds). Poor Aspen was completely out of shape for at least 3 days. She was not able to walk after injection, and 3 people tried to put her back in a car after the XRay simple procedure. She was not able to jump from the car when I brought her home and 100 pound body just fell down on the concrete driveway. Her hind legs were paralyzed. She was nearly dying. Like under heavy drugs. It was painful to watch her. When I called the vet he was quite irritated saying "She will be fine" like I am overreacting. The vet also was not familiar with what a BRAF test is. Luck of education? Again, I started to look for another vet because we still needed to do an ultrasound to make sure our girl did not have any bladder tumor. Unfortunately, nothing around was available for next month, and it was quite urgent, so I had to deal with the same vet. But this time I had to make sure NO MORE ACE. I already figured out that this old school vet was not up to day to recent studies. He overdosed her with a med that is prohibited for her breed. Ok, he failed, but it could be a lesson. But what happened next was just unacceptable. I told him clearly - I do NOT want ANY sedation. However he told me AGAIN that they MIGHT use sedation to do ultrasound. I asked him: "What is the name of sedation?" I was sure that knowing Aspen's reaction for it, he would have mentioned another one. Nope. He told me agan - Acepromazine. Hello???!!! So, already being experienced, I HAD to write that I do NOT give my permission and decline using ACE on my dog. Guess what happened next? They got irritated at least. Like I was making problems for them. Excuse me, this is MY dog, and I have to fight for her being safe if you don't care or have too short a memory. This time I was simply afraid to leave Aspen in his office and brought her only after their call informing the mobile vet came. Ridiculously, he charged me $50 for "surgery room use" the same day. Beside nearly 500 ultrasound cost. Aspen was not in his clinic all day, and no surgery was done. It was absolutely a rip-off, and clearly not appropriate in this situation, but I "let it go". You ask why I had to deal with them? Only because we needed this test soon. I will never come to the same clinic again. It was the very last visit there.

Lesson from this experience: Do DNA is that possible. Do not trust unethical breeders because often they sell mixed breeds lying about breed. If any rescued a mixed dog, please, DNA is important, because there is a list of prohibited drugs for certain breeds. For instance, Australian Shepherd, Border Collie, English Shepherd, Longhaired Whippet, McNab Shepherd, Old English Sheepdog, Shetland Sheepdog, Silken Windhound, Rough Collie, Smooth Collie, German Shepherd, American White Shepherd, English Shepherd have MDR1 gene, and ACE (Acepromazine), Aspen had a bad reaction for, is only one of them. ACE can be fatal for boxers. This sedation might be used by your vet for a simple procedure, or surgery. And you will never know. Know your rights! ASK what sedation your vet is using. It might save your dog, even from death. You can find more information from reputable sources like WA state University website.

Lesson number 2. Do sensitivity tests before starting antibiotics treatment. It will save your time, money, and most important - yourpet health.

In the end, just before our girl went to Rainbow Bridge because sudden MD disorder took her too fast, I had 2 more experiences with a local "euthanasia" aka "home vet" companies I put in my own black list. It was only related to compassion issues. Some really did not care about our poor paralyzed dog suffering at home when I asked for an emergency visit, even those who represent themselves as "compassionate and caring". Luckily, there are still compassionate people that really do care and those who helped our poor girl Aspen crossed to Rainbow Bridge peacefully immediately after my call...

There is hope we have good compassionate and educated vets.

But bad vets must be known. For the sake of the animals who depend on us.

Bim

Chapter Four

Buffy's Story
Sandy Gosselin

Buffy was a young and healthy dog UNTIL she went to Jaffe Animal Hospital in Palm Beach Gardens. What that vet inflicted on poor Buffy was horrifying.

After she died I learned this vet has over a decade of priors including a previous suspension. Why are repeat offenders allowed to remain open for more business?

I stupidly trusted and took my dogs to that vet for about 15 years. The boards failure to protect the unsuspecting public and their innocent pets cost precious Buffy her life and forever impacted mine.

At the 1st hearing they permanently revoked his license BUT 3 months later they changed their permanent revocation to a 50 year suspension and then all within months they gave him his license back. Why?

What he did to poor Buffy was dead wrong. Time doesn't fix everything, She's gone.

Invite others to help protect others, inviting EVERYONE to sign the petitions found on Justice for Buffy page on Facebook.

Hope to find Justice for Buffy and protect others. Hope to find a legal way to change what's NOT acceptable.

Buffy should still be here. Veterinarians should help the sick feel better, the old live longer and not kill the young and healthy.

State Board Eases Restrictions on Veterinarian Who Botched Spay

BY CARMEL CAFIERO, DANIEL COHEN
MARCH 22, 2016

WSVN — It's been years since a South Florida veterinarian botched a routine surgery ending with the death of a beloved dog. For years, the owner has been on a mission to convince authorities to take away his license. Investigative reporter Carmel Cafiero is on the case.

Buffy was a champion show dog. She was also Sandy Gosselin's pride and joy.

Sandy Gosselin: "She was the love of my life. She was my little sunshine. I'll spend the rest of my life missing her."

Sandy took Buffy to the Palm Beach Gardens office of Dr. Richard Jaffe to be spayed. She says the procedure took hours and that Buffy was sent home in pain. She says she sent text messages to the vet all night– but he did not responded until the next morning when he sent this text indicating that he thought Buffy would "b alright."

Sandy Gosselin: "I called him immediately. I knew he was awake so I called him twice in a row and I left a message like, 'She's not all right and she's in pain and what do I do?' And he just ignored me."

Sandy rushed Buffy to another vet… but it was too late. The dog died from internal bleeding.

Sandy Gosselin: "And all of a sudden, I was like, 'She's not breathing.'"

Sandy made it her mission to make sure no other pet would suffer like her Buffy did. She attended meetings of the Florida

Board of Veterinary Medicine, the people who would be responsible for disciplining Dr. Jaffe for Buffy's death.

Sandy Gosselin: "I'll never forgive myself for spaying her, and I'll never forgive myself for trusting him."

A transcript of the first hearing about Buffy in 2014 reveals the former board chair accused Dr. Jaffe of "incompetence" and called his behavior "inexcusable." And since he had been in trouble several times before, and the board considered him a "danger to the public," the board revoked his license.

Dr. Jaffe filed an appeal in court which allowed him to practice while it was pending. The board ended up reinstating his license with restrictions last summer. Among those restrictions was the requirement to have another vet monitor his work.

Dr. Richard Jaffe: "I do."

But at a hearing this month, Dr. Jaffe wanted that changed.

Edwin Bayo: "We believe that Dr. Jaffe can safely practice without on-site monitoring."

He and his attorney argued, paying another vet to monitor his practice was expensive.

Dr. Richard Jaffe: "Giving me some relief with on-site supervision would allow me to– free me up financially, allow me to put money back into things were I normally would put, alimony, the practice, etcetera's."

The board agreed, but said Dr. Jaffe would still have to be monitored when doing surgery.

Board chair: "The motion carries."

Dr. Richard Jaffe: "Thank you board members."

Sandy was disappointed.

Sandy Gosselin: "And you know, they seem to protect the vet instead of the pets."

Dr. Jaffe ignored our questions.

Daniel Cohen: "Could you just respond to that?"

Sandy meanwhile is not giving up.

Sandy Gosselin: "I want justice. I can't bring Buffy back, but I feel like others should be protected."

Carmel Cafiero, 7News.

Buffy

Check your Vet

My young and healthy dog died from a routine spay by a veterinarian who has over a decade of complaints on public record, including previous suspensions. There are veterinarians who have many years of multiple wrongdoings, including more than one suspension and even revocations of their licenses, still allowed to be open for business. It is often difficult to easily access this information online. If these records were required to be posted in their waiting room, it would warn the unsuspecting public and their innocent animals before it's too late.

Veterinarians should make the sick f❀ better, the old live longer, not kill the young and healthy. Please help us change what is NOT acceptable. IF we do nothing, Nothing will change. Invite you to help support Justice for Bufty _please help protect others from the horror a veteonarian inflicted on my young and healthy dog
We are still TRYING to find Justice for Buffy

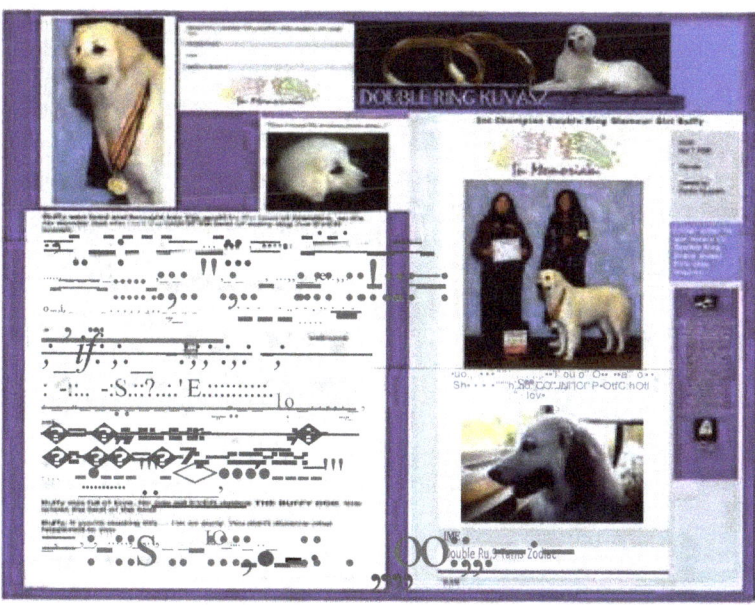

Chapter Five
Otis "Oatmeal"

1/24/10- 2/1/2020
He existed- He has a soul- He is loved- He is our family

Otis was a once in a lifetime dog. He was not just any ordinary pug, he was a super pug! He was so in love with life, he was the best little man ever. He loved his mommy, daddy, two younger brothers –Rajer and Max- his nana and her dog, Sabrina. But at the end of the day he was a mommy's boy, we were two peas in a pod. We did everything together. I brought him to work with me. He went on all vacations with us. Otis traveled to more places than many people have! Otis was the best man at our wedding and he took his role very seriously!!! He was our "King of the castle" and he had just the right amount of mischievousness in him that was absolutely loveable and gave him quite the personality. You could never be mad at him! He was like a little old man! Otis brought smiles to everyone he encountered. We used to take him to pug parties in Chicago, and let's just say, Otis was the one who got the party started! He was so full of life and made everything better. He loved his long walks, loved to cool down in the lake or river. He loved adventures, loved to smell, and smell some more. We would walk and always have to back track 10 feet so he could sniff a particular tree and mark it. I remember one time Otis and I went for a long walk in a large forest preserve. We got completely lost and water was in short supply. I looked at Otis and said "find the way out" and he would sniff at cross points and give me the look of "follow me" and sure enough he got us out! At bedtime he always was under the covers snuggled into me and I would fall asleep to his extremely loud and passionate snoring. I am so lucky to be his mommy. He is the best thing that ever happened to me. He is the love of my life.

For Otis, more than one vet failed him, so I refer to it as the "system" failed him. It was our primary veterinarian of 4 years and then a 24/7 Specialty Hospital- known as the "Mayo Clinic" of all of the Chicagoland area. In February 2019, I brought Otis to our 'former' primary vet of 4 years, (IPAH), for an ear infection. During the exam we decided Otis needed to have his teeth cleaned. Since he was 9 he had to have routine blood work. I got a call from IPAH vet, Dr. C, stating that Otis's liver enzymes were elevated. Something told me to have an ultrasound performed. After the ultrasound we got a call from Dr. C stating that Otis had a form of cancer called Hemangiosarcoma and expressed his condolences. He made that diagnosis based on the ultrasound results. He stated Otis had a mass on his spleen and nodules on his liver. The next day we brought Otis in for a chest x-ray to see if the cancer had spread to his heart and lungs. It did not. Dr. C did not offer us any options, such as going to a specialist. He authoritatively stated that Otis needed his spleen removed, and that it was the clear course of action. That Monday Otis went in for an emergency splenectomy. A biopsy was taken of the mass and the nodules on his liver and after what felt like a year, we finally got the call from Dr. C. Everything came back benign! My husband and I cried tears of joy. Dr. C, however, failed to find out what caused the mass on his spleen and nodules on his liver. Dr. C also did not discuss with us any potential/future consequences, etc. No follow up or guidance post-operative. Sadly we blindly trusted him to act in Otis's best interest.

In September 2019, Otis was diagnosed with anemia and diabetes after I brought him in to IPAH for bloodwork. The night prior he strangely collapsed and had a hard time for a few minutes gaining his composure. We saw a Dr. B at IPAH (our first time with this vet as Dr. C was off that day), and he put Otis on 20 mg dosage of Prednisone and Vetsulin. Otis did not do well on the Prednisone. Almost immediately we were alarmed by Otis's behavior and voiced our concerns about prednisone. I called several times to Dr. B and Dr. C regarding our observations, but I was dismissed. I was met with no collaboration or any other options. A few weeks after receiving his first dose of prednisone, I rushed Otis back noticing pale gums. Dr. B said we needed to immediately take him down to U of I Champaign. My husband and I raced down there where Otis spent a week undergoing tests and essentially was a guinea pig. U of I came back with an intestinal bleed. Once he was discharged, I made a follow up appointment at IPAH, as U of I instructed us the next step was to have blood work tests in 4 -6 days. Apparently word got back to IPAH that I told U of I that I was very unhappy with how the Prednisone was being handled. Our follow up appointment in mid-October was with Dr. C. He did not even look at Otis when he entered the exam room. He told me we didn't see "eye to eye" over this medication and that meant "I did not trust him." I asked him if he was terminating us and he said yes, then got up and said, "No further communication" and walked out of the room. I proceeded to have a full blown panic attack and became hysterical. Dr. C was our vet for 4 years! Had Otis not been terminated in this regard, we most likely never would have gone to BGVSC. After IPAH did the unthinkable, we had to find Otis a new primary vet quickly as the blood test was needed. IPAH did not give us any referrals and refused to treat Otis until we were set with a new veterinarian. We hustled to find another primary vet by the beginning of the following week. Our new veterinarian initiated testing and monitoring his blood CBC every few days and after that first week, the vet personally contacted me urgently to inform us that "we needed to rush Otis to [BGVSC] for an emergency blood transfusion." I was later told had Otis not been taken, he would have collapsed and died. This ties into how IPHA violated ethics/oaths/principles. You CANNOT terminate a very ill dog. Furthermore, IPAH did not give a referral, nor did they treat him until we could get him into a new vet. The new vets were outraged that IPAH removed Otis's spleen. They told me IPAH should have first done a fine needle aspiration for biopsy. This is how [BGVSC] came into the picture. I still cannot believe what he had done! I have filed a complaint against IPAH for violation of oaths & principles they swore upon to become veterinarians. My last update was my complaint was moved to prosecutions.

FIRST VISIT at BGVSC:

Otis was hospitalized at BGVSC for a blood transfusion on October 22nd, 2019. What caught us completely off guard was a doctor came in for barely 5 minutes to give a clinical impression. Immediately after hearing our boy was going to be hospitalized and the doctor left, two women walked in. The one woman was evaluating our finance plan for the day, ushering us to apply for financial assistance via Care Credit. I was strongly encouraged to "request the highest amount, you never know." The other person was present to give us a written estimate. I realized that they expected us right at that moment to have $2,865.00 for the deposit. We were told if we could not pay, they would bring Otis back out to us (to leave and die). My husband and I knew we were being told we would have to drive an hour home to get our checkbook. They would not even begin treatment until confirmation of payment was received. We frantically drove an hour back home to get finances in order and then called in payment so Otis could begin his blood transfusion. This is One of TEN blood transfusions throughout the experience with BGVSC.

We raised our concern with BGVSC that Otis' prior Splenectomy may have contributed to his current anemia. This became an ongoing curiosity and we questioned repeatedly about this. Was the removal of his spleen the eventual cause of his anemia? Red blood cells are stored by spleen. Internal medicine refused to answer these questions and disregarded it. This was the first question of many that went dismissed and unanswered by BGVSC. My point is we came to BGVSC to get answers since they are a specialty hospital. I do not see why they never questioned or mentioned the splenectomy ONCE. Perhaps if they did further investigation, I may have had some sort of answer. But BGVSC does not provide answers nor collaborate with patient families. This was our first taste of being left in the dark.

We were referred by our former primary vet because Otis's RBC blood count dropped dangerously low. We were sent to BGVSC for a blood transfusion. We were sent there because they were close in proximity and were known as "the best" and a "level 1 trauma facility". Otis had 10 "partial" blood transfusions at BGVSC during his time with them. We were greeted by Dr. R (internal medicine) during our first or second visit. He informed my husband and I that if Otis needed more than a couple blood transfusions than he would need a FULL blood transfusion (a very risky procedure essentially draining ALL blood out and putting in completely new blood) which is a $12k procedure. We only heard about that ONE time. So why did he have to have TEN "partial" blood transfusions? We never got an answer.

Otis tested positive for the Coombs Test down at U of I Champaign Vet Hospital in early October. His symptoms resembled an auto-immune disorder. Once Dr. R took Otis off his medications for said disorder, Otis's RBC kept dropping at a faster rate. I brought this up at least THREE times to Dr. R. Are we sure this is not IMHA because he tested positive for Coombs, can we retest for Coombs? All questions dismissed immediately. Dr. R had his agenda set on how he was going to treat Otis, and nothing was going to sway him, not even with Otis's life on the line. There is further testing that could have been done to absolutely rule out IMHA but that was never done. During one of our first visits the only thing I thought was "great" was Dr. R sending our Otis's blood to Cornell University to see where his iron levels were at. Otis had an extremely low iron count at 9. Dr. R gave the full impression to my husband and I that this was the answer. He had an iron deficiency that caused his anemia. Dr. R started to give Otis monthly long-lasting iron injections. However, it did not take too long to find out this was not the cause and it was not helping with his RBC. First occurrence of "false hope."

Due to the high dose of Prednisone and the fact Otis had to be slowly weaned off it, Otis went completely blind in mere hours on December 13th[h], as the Prednisone had accelerated his diabetes. Blindness came on suddenly and as a complete shock. No veterinarian ever mentioned this possibility, even though it is a common side effect of diabetes/anemia cases. We were instructed to consult an eye specialist to treat Otis. Furthermore, to monitor blood, BGVSC finally applied the FreeStyle Libre technology to Otis after we had already been there for multiple hospitalizations. They applied it for us to better monitor his glucose without having to prick him for blood. Meaning they were running out of places to extract blood, since they were doing this over an extended period of time. This should have been discussed at the very beginning. However, this is just a classic example on how the doctors improvised as time went on. There was never a clear treatment plan. All we heard was "Otis is a complex case."

BGVSC suggested "add on" treatments that they swore by. They have this apparent state of the art "oxygen chamber." Otis had about five 1 hour-long treatments in it, when suddenly one day, a nurse tech, not a doctor, told us that they received a "memo" stating the Freestyle Libre could potentially "blow up in the oxygen chamber." So, they had to keep taking it off and re-applying it. We saw no difference in Otis from these "oxygen sessions." I was extremely traumatized that my boy could have blown up.

None of the specialists spent any quality time with us. They talked so fast and were in the room and out before you even blinked. Again, the longest a doctor there spoke with us lasted no longer than 5 minutes. All of our questions, or thoughts were immediately dismissed. We were left completely helpless. BGVSC at no time offered any guidance, support, or counsel. I had to consult with a third- party vet (out of state) to help me interpret test results and explain it so I could understand. I cannot understand a veterinarian at BGVSC who talks like they are on "speed" and then exits the room before you even realize the one-sided conversation has ended. The third-party vet we worked with to consult and get guidance felt it was a definite case of IMHA and the findings of scope were mere "coincidental." Hence why I kept asking about the IMHA and Coombs testing. I felt I was talking to the wall. It was beyond frustrating and I cannot explain how helpless my husband and I felt. I had reached out to some alternative specialty hospitals', however we are very limited geographically, especially when Otis RBC dropped to fatal levels. In addition, if we went somewhere else they would have had to repeat all the testing. I could not put Otis through it again and we could not afford to pay for repeat testing.

In January 2020 Otis had the upper GI scope with BGVSC. The results of the upper scope stated Otis had an "ulcerated mass" in his upper intestines. Dr. R said it was a "risky" surgery as the mass was located right by his pancreas. Dr. R never got into detail about the risks involved or how any complications could be fatal. We were under impression it was "risky" due to the fact Otis was age 9 and already had multiple procedures. Enter Dr. M. Dr. M (co-owner of BGVSC) removed the mass that was found during the scope. It was Dr. R's impression this was causing the internal bleeding, even though the report of the GI indicated no fluids around the mass. Mind you, my husband and I never actually met Dr. M at any time in person. He telephoned us only at surgery time. I asked why this mass did not show up on ultrasounds, x-rays, CT scans, etc. I never got an answer. Dr. M merely called me to say, "We got it all out." It was a two-minute one-way conversation. I was never able to get the full clinical summary or any details on this "duodenal resection" surgery. What I do know is Otis developed a severe case of pancreatitis. Honestly, at this point, we are completely skeptical as to what has unfolded. Congruently, I diligently worked with my third party outside vet (not our primary vet) to try to put together exactly what happened to Otis. We were seeking alternative professional opinions.

We had one last procedure performed. Again, Dr. R failed to be upfront that this procedure carried a lot of controversy (a common theme) as I later learned from my own research. He placed tubes in Otis's stomach region to bypass the pancreas, essentially shutting it down to recover. Prior to the procedure, Dr. R stated a "resident" suggested "draining Otis's gallbladder to help offer relief." I would expect that to come from Dr. R and not a resident. Another "resident" recommended to Dr. R to get a kangaroo pump feeding tube. This way Otis could receive his food nutrients as fluids for a 12-hour continuous block while he slept. Otherwise, I would have been trying to administer his nutrition all day as he wouldn't eat on his own. All Dr. R said to us about the gallbladder was that "a lot of fluid came out." Also, I need to emphasize that after the procedure was complete, Dr. R told us he would have "a fresh start," regarding Otis's condition. Here we are again, another example of "false hope." There were so many times my husband and I embraced and cried in joy after hearing "promising news," that led to countless times of "false hope" to only having reality crash down on us.
It was that night when we came to visit Otis a nurse tech that we had never met nor seen before, came out and sat across from us in the lobby area. She stated she was there during the procedure and they got an "enormous amount of black sludge." This was so very concerning to us and caused great panic. Dr. R merely stated "fluids." Finding an "enormous amount of black sludge" is far different than "fluids." Why am I hearing this from a nurse tech and not Dr. R? This nurse tech also said that "Otis has a probable GI bleed." Let us just say that the room started to spin for us. I told her that the WHOLE reason for the removal of mass and Dr. M's surgery was to "STOP the internal bleeding in GI tract" as we were told over and over. How could Otis have a GI bleed now when we were told by Dr. M and Dr. R they got the source of the bleed removed? I felt almost like I was in the Twilight Zone and experienced major Déjà vu. We had done a 360 degree turn and were right back where we started.

When Otis was discharged, they gave us Peptamen, a fluid like Ensure for humans, for his nutrition via tube feeding. After two days I noticed he was leaking the fluid (not digested) through his anus. I called immediately and was told "this is normal, and they actually call it the 'Peptamen poopies.'" They made a joke of something VERY serious. They failed to care that Otis was losing (WHICH I SENT PICTURES OF TO THEM) a great deal of essential nutrition that he desperately needed to keep his strength AND to live. We should have been instructed to give subcutaneous fluids along with the tube feedings. They never gave me an answer about how much water to put in the feeding tube to keep Otis hydrated. I had to wait SIX hours for Dr.

A to finally call me back regarding WATER. He stated Otis had been receiving subcutaneous fluids via IV but that he did not think it was necessary to give him more. Further indicating that the Peptamen should keep him hydrated (which it did NOT) and if I wanted to, to administer 10ML of water four times a day. I asked Dr. A in person if we could try an appetite stimulant with him to encourage him to eat. I even stated, "Can we try something like Entyce?" He dismissed that one too merely muttering "we could." But he never did. Here I am and I feel like I am the ONLY ONE fighting for my boy's life. Not one time did they ever make any attempt to collaborate or to even be on the same page with other doctors at the hospital. All of their responses/answers contradicted one another.

I put in at least four phone calls (and e-mails to the internal medicine department) while Dr. R was out of town. He left the day after Otis's tube placement. Dr. A took on the role as Otis's "vet" there. It was clear as day Dr. A and Dr. R had not consulted each other on Otis's case at all. Otis was leaking a clear fluid with a small amount of brown fluid. I was told by Dr. A that "this is normal and unless it smells foul it is not an infection." Two days after this conversation with him, I asked him to look at the pictures of Otis, and commented to him, does this look normal and not infectious to you? As I stated before, Dr. R was gone for the next week. Apparently prior to leaving, he got the results from the "sludge" culture from Otis's gallbladder. Honestly, it was a fluke the results of culture were even communicated to me, but I happened to be meeting with Dr. A that day. A meeting I insisted on. He brought Dr. J in with him which I found odd. She remained mute and an orderly fixture in the corner, as he did not want to be alone in the room with just myself, clearly. I wonder why not? Dr. A stated Otis still had cancer. I told him Dr. R stated that Otis was "cancer free" that prior Thursday. There was absolutely no explanation or concern on these two strikingly different answers. He proceeded to state that "the fluid in Otis's gallbladder tested high in bacteria," but I was not provided any more information other than about an antibiotic they wanted to put him on. According to Mark's Drug Store (who works alongside this vet hospital) told my husband this antibiotic "would either kill our dog or help him." We never received this type of warning from Dr. A. In addition, the dosage amount the vet hospital put on clinical summary was way off from what the pharmacy label stated. I called and spoke to a nurse tech who stated to follow the pharmacy label. I feel this was their way of making us go away permanently, prescribing our Otis this very powerful, very dangerous antibiotic. They were aware we were running out of money. As I had since day one, begged and pleaded for a payment plan to be told "they do not offer payment plans." Not until one of our final appointments, when I made a couple of strongly worded comments (not threatening by any means) did they approve a payment plan of sorts. What about the other thousands and thousands of dollars we ran around in a frenzy to collect? When striking up conversations with other clients in the lobby area, we learned about payment plans. We discovered that BGVSC offered payment plans the ENTIRE time, they just offered them selectively.

Otis was dying and three days later I had a vet come to our home to give Otis a shot so he could go to Heaven as I held him in my arms. He was such a fighter through all of this. A rare truth, BGVSC told my husband and I, that Otis was "a very strong little boy." He wanted to LIVE. He was the glue to our family. He knew how loved he was/is and all the plans we had for him and his little Sheltie brother, Maxwell. This veterinarian service that came to our home was referred by BGVSC and it was absolutely awful. The veterinarian rushed us. I wanted to hold my baby boy longer but he was whisked away from me and put in the trunk of her SUV. My husband and I stood on the driveway and watched our beloved boy being driven off. Otis died. And to be quite honest I died with him that day. I was in complete shock by all this and I will never get over the guilt of not being able to hold my boy longer.

We never got an answer as to what took our sweet boys' life. Not one doctor could provide a definitive answer or diagnosis: cancer, infection, autoimmune disease. We were always told "Otis is a complex case." I would think that would motivate the doctor to work harder, sadly no. The doctors were not interested in discovering more about the complexity of his condition. Otis was just another number to them. We did not receive ANY condolences. BGVSC knew we were going to be putting Otis to sleep, yet they had some employee call us to "confirm Otis's appointment with Dr. R that Monday." I was shaking, talk about horrible. My husband got on the phone and demanded to know if they "actually read any of the files at all," but the tongue-tied woman on the other line, per usual, could not answer the question!

To this day, I continue to research my sweet Otis's case trying to determine exactly what happened to my boy. He was ill but stable when we first brought him to BGVSC, but as time progressed, his condition went downhill under the care of BGVSC.

Pets admitted to hospitals are going to have serious ailments that can be easily diagnosed. Some pets arrive with complex cases that are more subjective. If humans can have multiple health ailments and be treated with transparency, why are pets any different? They are not immune from multiple issues happening at once. These "veterinarians" do not want to be bothered with additional work and accountability. Then when you lose your beloved pet they can rely on their "we told you it was a complex case." It is 2020, how are vets not trained appropriately in complex cases? And what exactly defines a complex case? It appears to us Otis's case was complex because they did not know how to handle it and did not want to be bothered. Therefore, we should have been referred to someone who could handle it. Veterinarians need to do what is in the pets' best interest. Dr. R, 100% could have referred Otis to another specialist. He made it clear he had his agenda set on how to treat Otis. We never had a chance. Looking back, we wish we would have taken him to my husband's alma mater UW-Madison. We are tormented on what we could/should have done. But the simple fact is we trusted, that as veterinarians, they would be able to help our boy and that they care about the animals they worked with. We falsely believed they became veterinarians because they truly "cared." Sadly, the veterinary world (as odd as it sounds) has become increasingly corrupt and veterinarian hospitals are financially motivated and morally lackluster. Corporatization is hitting the veterinary industry. My husband and I saw upfront in full display the toxic lack of emotional intelligence. BGVSC is guilty of being only interested in hospitalizing your pet for profit. Specialty centers have high level specialists and superior tech tools granting them the ability to stabilize your pet. There are large financial windfalls in hospice…hospitalization, as pharmaceuticals can be administered adlib while under practitioner care. Please be vigilant about questioning all procedures and tests the doctors recommend. Yet keep in mind, they do not like these types of pet owners. To them, it is a waste of their time. As their mind and agenda has been set in a manner that does not always correlate with that of pet owners. Not their problem.

Our beautiful little family is now brutally broken. I cannot handle nice days. They are Otis days and I am SO angry that he is not here to enjoy, he SHOULD be. Otis was robbed of his right to enjoy and live out his senior years. His little brother, Maxwell, is very depressed too. He spends most of his time snuggling into Otis's special pillows. When I can get Maxwell to play, he chooses Otis's favorite toys. The house has become so quiet and lonely. I will never see my boy again in this life. He is gone forever until we meet again in the afterlife. I cannot wait for the day of our joyous reunion.

However, I am determined to get justice for my boy. I started a Facebook advocacy group and a website (www.justiceforotis.org). I was blown away by how many families came forward to share their story of how BGVSC harmed their pet. It was quite shocking. I soon realized that this is a national epidemic, revealing unethical and immoral veterinary practices. Misleading, price gouging, incompetence, and flat out blatant lies have corrupted the veterinary industry. It is my mission and goal to expose the dark side of the veterinary industry. I am not saying all vets are bad. What I am saying is there are too many "bad actors" and their fellow colleagues should be holding them accountable. The Veterinary Board, state licensing board, etc. needs to hold these vets accountable. What I want pet parents to take away from this is to never blindly trust your vet. Vets are not entitled to respect, they need to earn it. Stand your ground, ask questions, and be assertive. Allow yourself to have the option of a second opinion. Do not let the broken system do to you what it did to us. They manipulated us in our hours of darkness, at our most vulnerable.

I know Otis is watching down and proud of me for raising awareness. I know I am not walking down the street alone- I know he is with me everywhere I go. Love never dies. A soul never dies .I know we will be reunited again, one sweet day. We love you Otis. Our sweet beautiful baby boy. Mommy loves you Otis.

Chapter Six

BOSTON'S STORY
Katrina Hughes Heiser

I was looking for somewhere to donate this year in honor of my BOSTON who was taken from me. I had asked for recommendations on Schnauzers Well Loved where I could donate. There were a lot of wonderful recommendations but there was one that hit my heart. JOEY'S LEGACY. When I read about what ya'll do I knew this is where my BOSTON would want me to honor him.

My Miniature Schnauzer (BOSTON) was born September 8, 2014. And passed away on July 17, 2020, while at Sienna at Six Veterinary Hospital Missouri City, Texas 77459 in the care of Dr. Manny Sanchez. I have been taking my four Schnauzers to Sienna Six Veterinary Hospital on or around April 2018. The girls behind the counter and the techs have always been very helpful, kind and sympathetic to my 4 Schnauzers and myself.

BOSTON has always been taken in for anything I was requested to bring him in for, also a few other things like ear problems or allergies. He did get Cytopoint injections about every 3 months for allergies. He would just scratch a lot and the shot always helped. I'm one of those dog owners that makes sure my dogs are taken care of. I've never been told that BOSTON had any life-Threatening issues or that he had any problems other than his ears and allergies. I was always told BOSTON was a healthy dog. I've always been told all of my dogs were perfectly healthy.

I had taken BOSTON in July 13, 2020 because I had noticed for a few days that he had started drinking a large amount of water and that his stomach was larger than normal. But everything else seemed normal. He was eating, defecating and urinating normally. He played with his siblings and was his perky self. He had lost a few lbs. But I had been told that he needed to lose a few lbs. anyway. I made an appointment for July 13, 2020 and Dr. Manny Sanchez saw BOSTON. Blood work was done during this visit. I'm dumb when it comes to medical terms or looking at things about how high or low things need to be. Dr. Manny Sanchez called me on July 14, 2020 and said he thought BOSTONS pancreas might be a little inflamed and his glucose was a little higher then he would like it to be. Dr. Sanchez said for me to bring him in the next morning July 15, 2020 and he wanted to keep BOSTON over night to give him IV fluids and antibiotics and that should do the trick.

Dr. Sanchez called me that evening and said BOSTON was resting comfortably, but that he wanted to keep checking BOSTONS levels because his glucose was a little high and he wanted BOSTON to stay one more day/night to watch his glucose levels. Dr. Sanchez called me the night of July 16, 2020. and said that BOSTONS glucose was still a little higher then he wanted and that BOSTON was diabetic. Dr. Sanchez said that he recommended BOSTON be given insulin twice a day. Dr. Sanchez said that I could pick BOSTON up the next morning July 17, 2020 and they would so me how to administer the shots. I was up and ready to leave the morning of July 17, 2020 to go pick up my BOSTON. My phone rang and it was Dr. Sanchez and he said, " Boston didn't make it" I screamed WHAT? Then Dr. Sanchez said "Boston has passed away "I was in total shock. I think I hung up my phone and just ran out the door to get to the hospital to see my BOSTON. When I ran in the door there was a girl (wish a mask on) I have no idea who she was at that moment I only knew she was a girl and said she would take me to BOSTON. I walked into an exam room that BOSTON had been in many times and my BOSTON was laying there. He wasn't happy to see me like he always was or respond in anyway. My BOSTON had really passed away. I knelt down on my knees to get close to BOSTON on the floor in a dog bed to kiss him, hug him and talk to him. I asked the girl to please let me talk to Dr. Sanchez. She told me he was not there. I knelt there holding on to my BOSTON crying and kept asking WHH?! The girl told me she had tried doing CPR on him, but she just couldn't get him back. My husband left work to come up there. We both just could not believe BOSTON was gone. When I took BOSTON in on July 15, 2020. I hugged and kissed BOSTON and told him everything would be okay and that I would be there in the morning to pick him up. I was told my BOSTON would be there only one night which turned into two nights and then was told I could pick BOSTON up on July 17, 2020 but my BOSTON was dead. After spending a long time with my BOSTON and asking several times if Dr. Sanchez was there yet? When I got home without my BOSTON I called Sienna Six for the next 3 days several times a day asking to talk to Dr. Sanchez. They would tell me they gave him my messages every time I called. On the end of the third day of calling I asked if I could make an appointment to come and talk to Dr. Sanchez. I was given an appointment for July 20, 2020.

When I arrived one of the girls who worked there come up to me right away and just took me into an exam room. I sat there waiting alone in a room I had brought BOSTON into many times over the years. I just sat there in tears waiting on Dr. Sanchez. When he does come in he said, " I'm sorry I haven't called you back, that's my fault" He sits down on a stool and just looks at me. I said," What happened to my BOSTON?? After scratching his head he says, " I really don't know" He told me that at least four times every time I asked " What happened to my BOSTON?" and " What did they do to my BOSTON?! Every time he said " I don't know. To this day I still do not know what happened to my BOSTON. On July I brought my BOSTON home in a wooden box. This was NOT how it was supposed to be.

On July 30, 2020 I had already made an appointment for another one of my Schnauzers FENWAY to have blood work to have his phenobarbital levels to be checked because he is on it twice a day for seizures. Fenway also had a knot that had come up on his back that I had been in there for many other times to have it checked and was always just told it was nothing. I had also had them look at it this time because the skin on the know had changed colors. This time they made my appointment with Dr. Solis. I haven't seen her but maybe 3 times since I had started bringing my 4 Schnauzers there. The tech that was in there came in and said he needed to take Fenway for his blood work. and check the knot. I had never had then take one of my dogs out of the room for blood work or anything, they always did it right in the exam room while I was in there. I told the tech that I would rather they do that in the exam room with me in there. The tech left the exam room and Dr. Solis came back in the room and said, " I need to take Fenway for his blood work " and picked Fenway up and left the room. I guess I was just sitting there in shock. The tech brought Fenway back in the exam room a little time later. He said, " Man when she poked Fenway's' knot it started just gushing blood, but they put some kind of glue stuff on him to stop the bleeding." I looked at Fenway's knot to see what she had done. It was still bleeding a little, but soon stopped. The tech told me that Dr. Solis would call me with the results. She didn't even come back in to discuss anything. Dr. Solis did call me back about the blood results. She said Fenway's phenobarbital levels were good, but wasn't sure what the knot was. She told me I needed to make another appointment to bring Fenway back in to do a biopsy on the knot. I was still just like I am today so upset about my BOSTON but that was where I took my babies to be taken care of. With Covid I couldn't get in to see any vets. Dr. Sanchez had lifted the drop off order. I was scared to find another vet because I didn't want Fenway going in without me. They set me up with Dr. Solis again this time. When she came in she said, " Let's wait a little longer and see if the knot goes down, make an appointment for 4 weeks to see how the knot looked. then" She then asks me how Fenway was doing on his thyroid medication? I'm sure she saw my puzzled look on my face. I said, "Fenway is not on any thyroid medication. She looks at the computer screen and says, " Hummmm, I guess he's not" Then she tells me that some of Fenway's blood work was not back yet, but she would call me when it did. I called for two days several times a day to see if the other blood work for Fenway had come back in. I was told late afternoon of the second day of calling by the girl that answered the phone, that she had given the doctor all my messages and that one of them would for sure be calling me back that evening. I never got a call from Dr. Sanchez or Dr. Solis. I felt that I was treated very differently after the death of my BOSTON. And it seems to me that they were no longer concerned about Fenway's knot or telling me about his blood work. I feel that Dr. Sanchez did something to cause my BOSTONS death and that are not going to tell me what they did wrong to my BOSTON.

I wrote a detailed letter about what happed with my BOSTON and how I was treated when I took Fenway in after the death of my BOSTON. I had gotten BOSTONS records and X-rays that were taken the morning of my BOSTONS death to the Texas State Board of Veterinary Medical Examiners to ask them could they help me with this and find out who was responsible for BOSTONS death and WHY did BOSTON die? All I received was a call from someone who said his name was Michael Campos and that he was an investigator and had received my envelope concerning BOSTON. He said he was not a Veterinary but he wasn't really sure what I wanted. And told me he was going to call Dr. Sanchez and have him call me and tell me why BOSTON died. And I haven't heard from anyone else and my BOSTON will be gone 5 months on Thursday Dec.17, 2020.

There has not been one day in almost 5 months that I have not cried or completely broke down. I love my other 3 Schnauzers with all my heart, but my BOSTON and me had a bond like I've never had with another. We would stare and look into each other's eyes and then BOSTON would smile at me or come prancing over to me to get in my lap to give and get love. BOSTON was my protector. I've never had anything like this with another animal. I am totally lost and I so want my BOSTON back with me.

Chapter Seven

Edouard's Story
Agnes Meunier

Losing my best friend...

17 years ago, I was in France for Bastille Day. One of those days in the South of France that has nothing to learn from California in terms of scorching heat. I ran early morning to a big store nearby to grab something to eat as I was planning a picnic on the beach later on and as I was walking out, the security guard at the door told me that a kitten was dropped in a bush by his mother and had been crying for an hour and that the mother scared by the traffic and the people in the parking lot would not come back to get him. Afraid that he would die from dehydration and heatstroke, and after hearing him cry for a while, he had decided to take him in. Why did this guard talk to ME out of the thousands of people going in and out of this mall? I will never know. He opened a shoebox. I looked at the kitten, found him a little ugly but endearing at the same time, he had the umbilical cord still attached and his eyes were still closed. I said "okay we will take him and we will find him a good home once he is on solid food". From this point on, this little life so tiny that he could sleep on the palm of my hand changed my entire life for the best. I took him to the vet immediately who told me "He is too young, he will never survive, the best would be to euthanize him" "Nope" I responded, "We will give him a fighting chance". Okay says the vet: I have warned you: He is too young, he is never going to make it: What is his name? I was caught off guard by the request as the vet was giving me no hope: "I need a name to put on his file" growled the vet. I thought about the place he was coming from and I decided he would be named after the founder of the grocery store at least for now. That's how the name Edouard (Edward in French) came about. Countless sleepless nights followed because a kitten is like a baby, they need their bottle every 2 hours. But this little fellow who was sleeping in a tiny basket next to my head rapidly understood that if he was climbing out of the basket and trying to suckle on my nose, I would wake up and feed him. I stopped setting the alarm as he was taking care of waking me up for food. I still remember clearly this little creature latching on the bottle, holding it between his minuscule

pink paw pads and those tiny ears going back and forth as he was avidly suckling... He was so beautiful, I could not take my eyes off of him! Since I had to bottle feed him often I started taking him everywhere versus going back home every 2-4 hours. To this effect, I purchased a large tote so his little basket and his bottles could fit in. Among the things he understood as a baby was also that he would have to stay put and quiet in my purse if we were in a grocery store (because pets are prohibited in stores in France) until I could go to the bathroom to feed him secretly but if we were in a pet/garden store, it was just fine to stick his head out of the tote. How was he able to tell from the bottom of the tote whether we were in a grocery store or at "Botanic"? I never figured it out; but to this date, this big male cat will remain in my purse if I tell him to sit in it. Edouard grew up to be a beautiful and very athletic cat who also loves to ride in a car and to go to a drive-through just to have fun watching people's faces when they realize that he is a cat and he is totally unfazed by being all windows down at a drive-through, waiting for food. I knew I loved this kitten from the beginning, I did not know that he would become my best friend, an extraordinary cat with a wicked sense of humor and a taste for travel, plane trips, road trips, vacations, and hotel rooms. He is the type of cat that will be on a leash in an airport's overcrowded boarding area and remain seated and as calm and chill as a businessman having fun watching people walk by and then look twice when they realize he is a cat. But what took me by surprise is how much love he would give me and how much love I would have for him. I know it sounds cliché but he truly is MY family, the love I have for this cat goes way beyond what I ever thought possible and I would give ANYTHING for the latest part of this story to be inaccurate. Edouard has followed me everywhere, from France to the US through thick and thin, rich or poor, here or there, he has been with me for 17 years and was always by my side. This cat knows everything about me and we read each other so well that it is scary.

Shortly after our move from EU, few day after a vaccine, I noticed a lentil-shaped tiny bump under his armpit. I took him to the vet who removed the mass and sent it to the pathologist and to a different lab (I already lost a cat to malpractice, I am now double-checking everything), The report came back as "Low-grade lymphoma"; working in cancer research myself I was very suspicious of the diagnosis because he had no other signs (no abnormalities in his blood test) yet the oncologist immediately started insisting on starting the chemo immediately... In spite of me pointing at his blood test and telling her that if it truly was lymphoma, his blood test would show something, the oncologist kept on insisting even going as far as telling me that I was a bad pet guardian because I was jeopardizing his prognostic! I trusted my gut and refused the chemo, asking her to wait for the second lab which came back as "vaccine material and reaction to the excipient", the first lab recanted their report and confirmed they made a mistake... Disgusted after having lost a first cat overdosed by a vet, having been lied to by the vet board who refused to take my complaint while I had the acknowledgment in writing of the overdose, and now having been confronted to yet another of those malpractice stories, I decided that I had enough of California and decided to go live in my dream city: Boston. I lived there for a few months, came back to pick Edouard up in CA after I found a house and I was ready to live my dream with my husband and my fur baby!

Shortly thereafter, in March 2020 Edouard started sneezing profusely then getting a nosebleed... I took him to my regular vet, she drew some blood and wrote in his file what would unleash hell: "Kidney disease". Looking at his blood test and working in cancer research for decades, seeing that only his BUN was elevated, I knew immediately that something was really wrong. I started thinking of cancer right then and there. Next nosebleed I took him to the famous Angell Medical Center ER (they are on the show Animal ER on Animal Planet) I started asking for a CT scan, and I remember this vet as if it was yesterday, she would NOT get out of the loop: "It is kidney disease". I remember discussing Edouard's epistaxis, unilateral epiphora, and snoring and she went on to say: "Oh that's a sign of cancer" and... Yet she refused to do the CT scan (it is written on his file) while she gave me something to manage the nosebleed!. At this point I started searching frantically for a vet that would order the CT and I kept on banging my head against vets that would stubbornly stick to their initial diagnosis "he is 16, his elevated BUN is kidney disease, no CT"... My experience in cancer was telling me that something else was wrong and really wrong (elevated BUN and normal creatinine and specific gravity mark a slow internal bleed which most of the time is cancer) and I needed to get to the bottom of this but I was hitting a brick wall. Édouard had been misdiagnosed in the past: a vet "diagnosed" a lymphoma he never had (it was a vaccine reaction) so my gut was telling me to press ahead. One vet, two vets, three vets, four vets, at Angell, all refusing to do the exam -a simple CT scan- I was begging for, I took him to the ER in the hope that they would do a CT. At this point, I changed clinic went to VCA South Shore saw ER DVMs and Internal Medicine DVMs, all refusing to do a CT, they insisted on doing an ultrasound of his kidneys: "This is the GOLD STANDARD they said, It will show the extent of his kidney disease", and I thought "Okay the only thing they want to do is cash an abdominal ultrasound, let's let them have the money and be done with it, we will do the CT next!" But when the ultrasound came back with " kidneys in perfect condition, kidneys medullary structure in perfect condition, abdomen unremarkable" the very vet that was telling me that an abdominal ultrasound was "the gold standard" and would show us how his kidneys were, started making all kind of excuses "there are microscopic things happening in his kidneys that we don't see on the ultrasound (I thought it was the gold standard?) this is kidney disease". At one point one of their urgentists (who ordered the ultrasound) sedated Edouard to look at his mouth and   Did not look at his nose and wrote kidney disease in his file while he had just said that Edouard did not look as if he had kidney issues AT ALL. I asked their internal medicine specialist: Are you 100% sure that only kidney disease can cause all this? "I am definitely positive you have to accept the diagnosis" she responded.   I took him to Tufts, they tried again to lodge an ultrasound, the Vet in charge lectured me and tried also to get me to sign a $4000 estimate with an immediate $3000 deposit "to run some tests" but still refused to do a CT scan, I took him out right away. 4 days later Edouard started to bleed again and I took him to another ER (Ethos) I almost grabbed the eighth vet (a UK trained vet) by the neck, poor thing, she is the only one among the famous Tufts University, Angel Medical Center, VCA, etc to finally look outside of the "he is 16, it can only be the kidneys" and she came out of the exam room, with tears in her voice and said " you know what? I think you were right all along I think he has a mass in his nose: the vets at large, have really dropped the ball on Edouard" you could see how embarassed she was for her colleagues and how sorry she was for the ordeal I went through: she ordered a CT for the next day. The internal Medicine DVM that did the CT and a rhinoscopy told me (It is also written on his report) "BUN elevated caused by internal bleed and cancer? I see that every day! It is likely a tumor or a fungus but regardless it is extremely serious and life-threatening"

I called the Medical Director at Angell to let her know about the repeat misdiagnosis expecting that she would at least try to right the wrongs done by her team knowing that they are the only ones in the area to have a linear accelerator capable of delivering Stereotactic radiations which is the ONLY treatment that works on this type of tumors   She first said that she would help but as I was anxiously waiting for the CT and rhinoscopy/biopsy to be over, the clinic director at Angell called me to tell me that they were refusing to treat Edouard as "this type of cancer rarely have a good outcome, and in addition, you called to tell us that we misdiagnosed him and this generated a breakdown in our communication, don't ever come to Angell again, you can go out of state for treatment" I was dumbfounded... Those incompetent vets had missed an aggressive nasal adenocarcinoma delaying his care by a full half-year and making the prognostic even worse, but in addition to that, they were directly trying to hurt his chances of remission by refusing to treat!

In the middle of the pandemic, I packed two suitcases in minutes and flew with Edouard back to CA by the next available flight so that he would receive proper care: radiations and chemo because on top of being wrong in the diagnosis, those people also refused to right their wrongs. Almost $50 000 and a year later, Edouard is still there but nasal adenocarcinoma is merciless and the months that went by while he was receiving no treatment took their toll. Edouard, this beautiful and pure heart with such an angel face, who happens to be the main part of my own heart, the love of my life, the very best thing that ever happened to me is, I believe, losing his battle against cancer as I write those lines because of sheer incompetence (still right now I am very disappointed in the Medical Oncologists he is seeing). He is next to me but not the same and even though I am sure he knows his days are numbered, he is cheering me up. I feel like such a measly miserable human being compared to this braveheart... I know that the moment is coming, where I will have to make a decision that, cowardly, I don't want to make. He is my light, my life, my joy, this little soul gave me more than I have ever dreamt I would receive and I am losing him because of bad luck and incompetence. What if I had gone to the eighth vet right away? What if? What if? What did I do wrong that this beautiful soul whose only sin has been to love me and be loved by me has to go in such a terrible way? I just wanted to share his story with you and the love I have for this cat as the road is coming to an end, I also wanted to share a picture of him because this picture, taken less than a year ago, captures this softness I see in his eyes every day for 17 years. This is really who Edouard is: this extraordinarily smart cat with a heart as big as the universe born in France, well-traveled and so exceptional that he has left his pawprint forever on whoever met him over 2 continents. I just wanted to tell the world how exceptional he is and how much I love him.

This is Edouard, he was already sick but we did not know (see the epiphora). This is the 16-year-old cat that they wrote off, so heathy that the vet who anesthetized him to look at his teeth requested records to verify his age as he would not believe that he was 16 ! This is the cat they messed up completely...

Edouard

Chapter Eight

Fancy's Story
March 22 2009 – July 21 2020
Anthony and Pamela Jo Sirilo

Fancy came to me in December 2014 at the age of 5 ½ years when her owner passed away who was a distant family member. Since I had her litter mate, Lacey, they called me to see if I wanted her. Of course, I said yes. Previous owner was a smoker so Fancy had a cough when I got her. I took her to the vet and she was given a steroid shot. Unbeknownst to me steroid shots can cause diabetes. I was not made aware of that possibility prior to her getting the shot. When she started peeing on the carpet, she went back to the vet with what I suspected was a urinary tract infection. That was confirmed but she also had sugar spilling out into her urine which means diabetes.

After several months we finally got her blood sugar under control with 2 shots of insulin a day and a special diet.

My quadriplegic son moved back home in March 2015 and the two of them bonded right away. He said it was because she knew he was sick so they had that in common. She would ride around on his lap or on top of his feet in the wheelchair and cuddle with him at night. Out of all the cats I've had over the years, he had never had a relationship like this with any of them. She loved me too but not like she loved him.

On July 7, 2020, I noticed she had peed on a towel on the bathroom floor which wasn't like her. I called my vet the next day and took her in. They ran tests and determined that her blood sugar was low but she had sugar in her urine which wasn't right and she had a urinary tract infection. They gave her a shot of antibiotics for the infection and sent her home. She had also become finicky about eating and that wasn't like her. Fancy would scream at me if I wasn't getting her food fast enough so I knew something was wrong. I called my vet and made another appointment to bring her back in for a glucose curve the following Wednesday. That morning, she only ate half of what she normally eats and I gave her a half dose of insulin and took her for her glucose curve. The Vet advised he thought she might not be diabetic anymore so I was to continue to feed her special diet and monitor her blood sugar.

That night I couldn't get her to eat and when she did, she only licked at her food then threw up. At that point I was concerned that she might have pancreatitis because her symptoms were the same as a previous cat, I had that had had that disease back in 2011. She couldn't be saved after several days up at the original Emergency Vet Hospital in North Oklahoma City and had to be put to sleep.

I panicked because I didn't want that to happen to Fancy and I knew that supportive treatment needed to be started as soon as possible if this is what she had. I was also concerned about her not eating because cats that go 24-48 hours without food can get fatty liver syndrome (hepatic lipidosis) and that can be life threatening as well.

At 3:00 am Thursday morning 7/16/2020, I drove her up to the new Emergency Vet Hospital in Oklahoma City now owned by a large corporation about 16 miles from my house. This new hospital is huge compared to the old one. Because of Covid 19, I am unable to go in with her so I handed her over to a girl at the door and explained to her my suspicions of her having pancreatitis. All she said to me was "do you want an abdominal ultrasound?" I declined at the time not knowing why she needed one. They diagnosed my previous cat using a fPLI blood test while I waited in the waiting room.

I went and sat in the car waiting for the E.R. doctor to call me. It was hot and humid and I was very tired given the time of day. When he called, I advised him of her last two visits to our vet and that she had had blood work done and I was told it was fine. He advised they would do additional blood work and I assumed it would include the fPLI for pancreatitis. He also advised they would admit her, hook her up to an IV and keep her for the night so the critical care doctors could look at her in the morning. I agreed and went home after prepaying them a large sum of money.

That morning, I got a call from one of the critical care doctors who told me Fancy's blood work looked fine but she still wasn't really eating. I assumed that included the fPL1 test for pancreatitis so she didn't have it after all. They ran another urine test to see if the infection she previously had was gone and it would be a day or two before the results were back. They kept her Thursday night.

Friday morning, 7/17/2020, they called and said she had eaten just a little bit of food and they were sending her home. I paid them additional funds and went to pick her up. She came home with a bottle of Clavamox Drops which is an antibiotic, Entyce which is an appetite stimulant and Maropitant tablets for nausea.

I got her home and could tell she still didn't feel good. I gave her medication and she ate a little bit. The next morning, she wouldn't eat at all. I called my vet and they suggested baby food meat so I went to the store and got some as well as some other cat foods I thought she might eat. Nothing worked. She ate a small amount of honey roasted turkey breast from the deli, something she would normally have gone crazy over but not today. That afternoon, I called the emergency vet hospital and advised Fancy still wasn't eating and I was still concerned about her getting hepatic lipidosis, fatty liver syndrome.

I was advised I could bring her back now or wait till in the morning because the critical care staff wouldn't be there until then. I felt like she needed to be back on fluids so I opted to take her back at that time. I dropped her back off and came home after paying them another large sum of money, the E.R. doctor on duty called and advised she needed an abdominal ultrasound to check for pancreatitis. It was at that time that I learned they never ran the fPLI blood test. According to him, they don't use those anymore because they aren't very accurate. Upon my own research online, I discovered that isn't true. They don't do them because they only cost $50.00 verses the ultrasound which costs $400.00.

This is my cat. I don't care about the cost, I just wanted her to get treatment and get well. Something I trusted them to do but was learning that my trust was misplaced. I agreed to the ultrasound which now couldn't be done till the next day because they didn't have a doctor there that could do it. Keep in mind this is an emergency/critical care hospital but these staff members are not on duty 24/7 like I think they should be. They hooked her back up to the IV fluids and I started praying because I knew at this point this was going bad. Everything that I had done to try to get her the treatment she needed as soon as possible stopped once she entered that building.

Late Sunday morning I got a call from one of the critical care doctors who said they would get to her ultrasound as soon as they could because they had another patient to attend to. There was no urgency to treat her at all. At this time, I paid them another large sum of money. The ultrasound was done and to my surprise, they discovered she had pancreatitis! I told them that 3 ½ days ago. They then decided she needed a feeding tube and it has now been around 108 hours since she has eaten anything appreciable. Her blood work is now coming back abnormal so they had to correct that and get her electrolytes corrected before they could give her anesthetic for the procedure.

She made it through the surgery but I was advised they had to wait until 9:00 pm that night to start feeding her so she wouldn't get nauseated. Per her medical records that wasn't true as they feed her right after the procedure. There is also a note stating they were going to increase the amount of food they were giving her but per other notes that didn't happen.

Cats can get a condition called refeeding syndrome if they are fed too much after not having eaten for a while.

Monday morning, I was advised there was no change in her condition. She was depressed and just lying in the cage. I'm still praying for a miracle at this point and holding onto any hope I have that she will make it through this.

Tuesday morning, 7/21/2020, a glimmer of hope! The critical care doctor said she looked better and had raised her head up. However later that afternoon, Fancy took a turn for the worst. By this time, she was having liver problems, something I was concerned about from the beginning but they weren't and now she was having trouble breathing so she was placed in an oxygen cage. The critical care doctor advised she had run some tests but had no idea what was going on. Breathing difficulty is a symptom of Pancreatitis. Why didn't she know that? She said she also had something going on with her eyes darting back and forth and said they could do an MRI on her brain if I wanted but she thought at this time we might want to consider putting her to sleep as she was a very sick little girl and might not make it through the night. I asked if she had been getting anything for pain and she said no. She said she didn't think she was in pain. A cat that's in pain won't eat or drink and will present as depressed.

At this point I am losing it. I thought I had this under control taking her to the hospital at 3 in the morning so treatment could be started. They didn't listen to any of my concerns. They had no urgency in treating her. They don't have the ability to communicate and they just plain don't care about the animals they are treating. Since this large candy company bought them out, all they care about is the money.

My son and I got in the van and drove to the hospital Tuesday night crying all the way. They brought Fancy out to us, feeding tube still in her neck. She was gasping for breath as they placed her in my son's lap and proceeded to stop her heart. I can't tell you how heartbroken we were and still are over this. Fancy trusted me and I feel like I let her down. This large emergency vet hospital and all of the doctors there let all of us down. They charged me thousands of dollars to kill my cat.

I obtained her medical records from the emergency vet hospital several days later and was shocked to read them. Her discharge paperwork on 7/17/2020 shows they had diagnosed her with Sepsis which is a blood infection and can be fatal. They advised me they couldn't feed her until 9 pm the night of the feeding tube insertion but the records show she was fed right after the procedure. She was put in an oxygen cage because of her breathing difficulty but none of that is in her records. We have no idea what her oxygen saturation was. Now we are wondering if she really had to be put to sleep.

They denied her treatment. I believe because I declined the ultrasound the night, I took her up there, they didn't test her at all. Nor did anyone explain to me why the ultrasound needed to be done. They should have done the blood test and if it was inconclusive then we could have done the ultrasound and I would have agreed to that. They just did the minimum and charged me the maximum. She didn't get the treatment she needed in time to beat this. Per their own website under how to treat a cat with pancreatitis it says under Diagnosis that the fPLItest is a highly accurate test in diagnosing pancreatitis but they advised me otherwise.

Under Treatment it says it's truly supportive in nature, and its aggressiveness depends on the severity of the pancreatitis. In severe cases, hospitalization is required for restoration and maintenance of hydration, control of pain and vomiting, nutritional support and possibly antibiotic administration.

Unlike dogs and people, nutritional support is vital in cats as they can develop secondary liver disease ("fatty Liver" or hepatic lipidosis) within a few days of inappetence. If the patient is not vomiting and accepts food, it should be offered orally. Otherwise, placement of a feeding tube is essential. An acute severe episode of pancreatitis can quickly lead to shock and death if aggressive treatment is not started promptly.

Fancy got fluids. Maybe if she had been given something for pain she would have eaten on her own. But since she wasn't, a feeding tube probably should have been placed days before it was. She never stood a chance at this large corporate owned emergency vet hospital in north Oklahoma City, Ok.

I have never felt betrayed by a veterinarian before. In this case there were 5 of them. I have always trusted them to know what to do and to do it. This has caused me to not trust anymore. You can't assume they know what to do and that they will do it. You can't trust them. You have to ask questions. You have to do research and know what needs to be done so you can be sure it's being done. Makes me wonder what I'm paying them for if I have to tell them what to do and I'm sure that in itself will have some repercussions. I know one thing. I will never take another one of my pets back to that Hospital.

It's been almost 2 months since Fancy passed and both my son and I are still having a hard time with it. We blame ourselves for not being more involved and for trusting them to treat her correctly and in a timely fashion. I still cry and I can't sleep at night. Do they care? I'm sure not. Do your due diligence and don't let this happen to you and your pet. Rest in peace my sweet baby. We think about you every day and miss you so much!

You will forever be in our hearts. We love you Miss Fancy Pants.

Fancy

 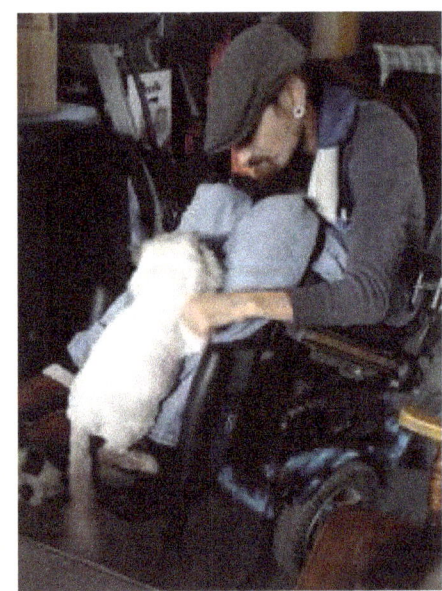

Chapter Nine

Gabriel's Story
Nikki Wharton-Eby

As I have rescued cats and kittens throughout my life, it is not surprising when one or two show up in my yard or on my patio. Last summer a longhaired solid black male kitty appeared on my patio. I named this friendly, affectionate kitty Gabriel. I took him to a vet in a nearby town to be neutered.

My instructions to the veterinarian and office staff were no vaccines other than FVRC and absolutely no Convenia ever to any animal I may bring here! I was so emphatic about the Convenia concern that when I arrived home I called the clinic to stress my instructions! When I picked up Gabriel his invoice was much higher than expected and I learned the vet had shot him up with vaccines ---- AND HAD INJECTED HIM WITH CONVENIA! I LOST IT! A TOTAL MELTDOWN THERE IN HER TINY OFFICE/WAITING ROOM! She tried to usher me into an exam room, but they both had clients in them with their pets. She then told me to leave and "never come back!" We continued with my emotional outcry of my loss in 2019 of my beloved Silver Puff from an injection of Convenia by a veterinary tech at another animal hospital. This antibiotic for specific infection has potential serious, sometimes fatal, side effects, namely anaphylaxis and this is what caused Silver Puff to go into shock later that night with thrashing around and struggling to breathe! A friend/neighbor took us to an emergency animal clinic. I had known the vet who neutered Gabriel for more than 25 years and she deliberately went against my instructions regarding vaccines and the Convenia! I left there with Gabriel praying with all my heart he would not be affected by the vaccines or Convenia.

I had a disturbing suspicion that this vet was using Convenia on every surgical patient "to protect them from possible infection" and without agreement or even knowledge of it by the families! Veterinarians are not informing clients of potential side effects of this or any drug!

I have been advised to share this story from August 2020. I am still deeply shattered by my horrific loss of my precious Siberian, Silver Puff --- whose life I had saved and who I had hand raised and deeply loved since her birth in 2005. She was family. After the heart-wrenching loss of my beloved husband in 2012, Silver Puff and my senior Persian, Nosa, became my emotional support.

The slow-release antibiotic Convenia is often used incorrectly. The possible side effects should be explained in detail to every pet parent whose special furry family member is being treated ---- especially that of anaphylaxis ----
and if this injection is permitted by the pet's family, a signature should be required.

Gabriel is living a happy life in his forever indoor home. I pray his health will never be adversely affected by the Convenia drug nor the overload of vaccinations.

For more information on Convenia, I highly recommend reading Dr. Lisa A. Pierson's article titled Convenia: Worth the Risk? On catinfo.org.

Chapter Ten

Gracie Lynn's Story
By Sandi Flowers

Introduction

"German Shepherds are one of the **smartest dog breeds in the world**. In fact, they are ranked the 3rd smartest breed for obedience and work intelligence, according to canine psychologist Stanley Coren. However, intelligent instincts and their ability [to] adaptively learn is what makes them smarter than most dogs"

My name is Sandi Flowers, and I am married to Doug. In 2015 my husband and I decided to get a puppy. We live on 1.5 acres of land, the perfect place to raise a puppy! We are blessed to own a small business that allows us to work from home. We decided that I would stay home to raise and train our dog and Doug would work either in our in our shop or on-site visiting clients. It was very important to us that our dog not be left alone hours at a time.

I love all dogs, so finding the right dog proved to be challenging. Ultimately, we decided to adopt a beautiful pure-bred German Shepherd which had long been my husband's favorite breed. Her blood line was impeccable, she was beautiful, playful, smart, and fiercely loyal. We named her Gracie Lynn Flowers. At the time I had no idea how much we would love her or how quickly she would love us and integrate herself into our family and all our hearts.

This story unfortunately does not have a happy ending, but despite the pain I feel and will always feel I wanted to write this story in hopes no one will ever have to go through the pain and grief my husband and I went through and more importantly what Gracie would ultimately go through.

The minute I held Gracie for the first time, there was an instant connection and bond between us that cannot be described, much like a new mother who holds her baby for the first time. Gracie was not a dog; she was a baby and part of our family. I had no idea of the love I would have for her and the love she had for me, my husband, our children and our nine beautiful grandchildren. Gracie was so protective of us, especially the grandkids. Because her bloodline was impeccable, we were told the odds of her having health issues were remote. Our breeder was a customer of ours and operates a successful business known as "Bar-Ben Kennels" located in Virginia. On July 24, 2015 we brought Gracie Lynn Flowers home and the fun began!! When Gracie was five months old, we enrolled her in a Puppy training class in which she had a great time, and we all learned a great deal. Upon "graduation" she was a perfectly trained German Shepherd dog! Gracie was always by my side and under my feet playfully nibbling at my fingers and toes. During her first few months in her new home, she only had one accident in the house. After that she went to the door and barked when she wanted to go out. Gracie loved playing ball and we would spend countless hours playing in the yard. Though she had plenty of opportunities, she never left the yard unless she was walking with us or she had to herd my Grandchildren back to the yard. Gracie was very protective of our grandchildren and when one child would cry, she was off and running to save the day. She had the patience of Job, as it was not uncommon to find one of our grandkids perched on Gracie's back, pulling, and tugging on her while she tried to sleep. Gracie had the spirit of child. Back to her favorite pastime; Playing ball. Even though Gracie loved my husband and all our kids and grandkids, she was also determined to spend quality time alone with just me. It did not matter if the weather were rain or shine the two of us could be found playing ball sometimes up to ten times a day, we both had the time of our lives. Gracie loved having the grandchildren (ages one through six) being over at our home. Having the grandkids over meant three things 1) non-stop playing 2) snacking, 3) and best of all, a slumber party! Gracie was healthy, happy, and in good shape.

It was around this time that things began to unravel. I will provide a short story and details of the nightmare both Gracie and I would encounter with these "veterinarians".

I was referred to four veterinarians

1. Elk wood Animal hospital
2. Lee's Hill Pet Hospital
3. Virginia Veterinary Centers (VVC)
4. Friendship Hospital

   One night Gracie began limping around the house. I examined her and did not see anything out of the ordinary. I assumed she may have a pulled a muscle or have a slight sprain that would be cured with rest. I decided I would give it a day or two to see if her condition improved. Looking back now, I should have taken her to the hospital. When there was no improvement, I scheduled an appointment with one of the veterinarians listed above. The vet immediately assumed that because German Shepherds are predisposed to hip dysplasia that must be what Gracie had. This "vet" concluded that we had to put Gracie under general anesthesia in order to take several x-rays. After they took the x-rays, I spent several hours on the floor lying next to Gracie, it was important for her to know how much I loved her and that I would not leave her sight. Whatever obstacles lay ahead, we would face them together. When she was strong enough to move, we left the hospital and got her in the car to go home. Once we arrived my son Austin had to carry her into the house as Gracie was not able to walk up the stairs and into the house. We were told her diagnosis was left hip arthritis and that she would need two shots of Adequan twice a week for six weeks and then once a week for several weeks thereafter. After the third shot I told the vet Gracie had taken a turn for the worst despite minimal activity. I carried her outside so she could go to the bathroom, but Gracie could not play ball or play with the grandkids. To say this broke my heart is an understatement.

By the second week I began searching for a specialist. I had regularly been speaking with Vera who had been Gracie's trainer and who owns Trademark kennels. Vera is the daughter of the breeder I adopted Gracie from and has become a dear friend to me. After I received the x-rays and saw no improvement in Gracie, I decided to get a second opinion and sent the x-rays to Vera in hopes she could recommend an alternative solution or a veterinarian who I would be more comfortable with. After reviewing the x-rays, Vera told me they were the among the worst she had ever seen for a German Shepherd. She assured me she would touch base with her specialist to get their opinion and hopefully put together a detailed plan to get Gracie back to normal. After speaking with the specialist, it was recommended that I bring Gracie in for an examination and x-rays. The diagnosis was a torn ACL. It was so bad that Gracie needed to have it replaced. That same day Vera called to tell me her specialist indicated Gracie had an injury to her *leg* not her hip. The original Veterinarian and I use that term loosely had misdiagnosed Gracie. I spent two months sleeping on the floor nursing Gracie back to health. I spent thousands of dollars on arguably incompetent veterinarians who kept misdiagnosing Gracie's condition. This was frustrating and sad.

I would gladly have paid every cent I had for Gracie to get better. Cost was a non-issue, her health was the priority, not my saving money. I will never go back to or ever recommend Elk wood Animal hospital, Lee's Hill Pet Hospital, or the VVC based on the treatment Gracie received.

Starting in October 2019 Gracie was prescribed Bravecto along with TRI-heart plus and Cytopoint. I did not notice any issues with Gracie except for an occasional loss of appetite and a lot of itching. When Cytopoint proved insufficient, I was told Gracie would need additional allergy testing. The testing revealed that she was allergic to mold spores and dust mites.

The medication Lee's Hill Animal Hospital gave me to help with the allergies, I believe, made Gracie sick and she developed open sours in her mouth. I threw the allergy medicine in garbage.

I tried to coordinate Gracie's sharing records between VVC and Lees Hill veterinarian office. Both veterinarians soon began to communicate with each other in an effort so we would all be on the same page with Gracie's health. Unfortunately, both offices were of no help and were unable to properly diagnose Gracie.

Initial Timelines

- On March 5, 2020 VVC gave Gracie Bravecto (flea andtick medicine) and Revolution T (heartworm medicine.)

- On April 7, 2020 Lees Hill once again proved to me that there was no communication between them and VCC. I received a prescription of Bravecto. (I did not give this to Gracie until July as Bravecto is a three-month pill)

- May 13, 2020 Lees Hill gave me Simpartica. From May until September 2020 Gracie received a double dose of Isoxazoline which is an ingredient found in the medicines that were prescribed to Gracie and would prove to be a factor in her health deteriorating.

- July 2020 Gracie received a double dose of bravecto and simparica and we noticed that she began exhibiting disorientation, stumbling, walking in circles, loss of appetite.

Gracie had free rein to come and go on our property, so I did not check to see if she had vomited or if she had diarrhea while outside in our yard. Gracie was too well trained to vomit or go to the bathroom in the house. However, one morning she threw-up right after eating which was odd. I also began to notice Gracie had not been eating. One night as Doug got into bed, he noticed that it was soaking wet. Gracie had never urinated in the bed before and we thought it was odd since the back door was open all day for her to go out. She stopped eating completely two days before we were to leave on a family beach vacation. I debated going to the vet but thought she just got into something outside. We had left her with a young man that lives in our house that Gracie was very familiar with and loved. Two days after arriving at the beach we face-timed the young man who was watching Gracie and we could see she was acting disoriented. Doug immediately left for home to take her to the VVC. A thousand dollars and another round of x-ray's later the vet still could not determine what was wrong although he said there was a possibility Gracie may have a perquisite. The doctor suggested that Gracie fast for 12-16 hours and then bring her back for more x-rays. Doug told the vet of all the things that were going on with Gracie over the last few weeks and that her ataxia was a problem. With what I learned later I believe she had at least one seizure (When she wet the bed) as time progressed Gracie continued to have a loss of appetite, skin irritation, and Ataxia. We also learned that Isoxanzoline is an ingredient found in bravecto and simparica. These medicines along with the Isoxanoline ingredient can cause seizures, muscle tremors, Ataxia, skin irritation and other neurologic events such as strokes. We were not made aware of this as we (incorrectly) assumed the "vets" knew what they were talking about. Not once did the vets look at her medications and suggest this as the root of the problem. On September 7th, 2020 Gracie came in the house acting funny, stumbling around, and seemed to be disorientated. We left at once and took her to the VCC again. Of course, $500.00 dollars and several x-rays later we left the vets office with no explanation (again) Despite no diagnosis. The "vet" prescribed Gabapentin which we were told was for pain and told to keep an eye on her. Gabapentin as I later learned is an anticonvulsant and analgesic drug that is commonly prescribed by veterinarians to treat seizures, pain, and anxiety in dogs. **No vet mentioned the potential effects of this medicine. Hindsight being 20/20 I believe the vets knew Gracie**

was having seizures but did not tell me because this could have made them liable or at the least incompetent. All they seemed to care about was charging me as much money as possible

In October 2020 I took Gracie to Lees Hill again because she was walking funny. They just could not figure out why, but this did not deter them from continuously charging me for office visits, x rays and antibiotics, even though there was never a correct diagnosis. While at the vet's office I asked them to please reexamine Gracie. That is when they found a swelling in the web between two of her toes. I could not believe that this was not discovered until I asked for a reexamination. Once again, Gracie had another round of x-rays and of course more antibiotics were prescribed without a clear diagnosis. On November 20th, 2020 Gracie began staring at the ceiling and falling on her right side. Gracie could not keep her balance, so I had to carry her to the car and take her to the veterinarians. I frantically called Doug to have him meet me at the vets and when Doug saw Gracie, he knew she was in trouble. The vet said he had never seen anything like this and got on the phone with every neurologist within a hundred miles to look at Gracie ASAP. The vet found one in Washington DC and we left immediately. After a horrifying one-hour drive with Gracie crying and whimpering and her head on my lap we finally arrived at Friendship Hospital where Gracie was rushed into an examination room. Nine hours of sitting in the car because of COVID-19 protocols were devastating to us we could not be with Gracie but we understood the circumstances. The neurologist was not sure what was wrong with her other than offering potential possibilities. One thing the vet did not hesitate to do (of course) was to prescribe more meds and said we needed to get an MRI. We found it odd that they could not correctly diagnose Gracie but had no problem prescribing meds. We left for home at 9:30 PM with a very sick dog and frustrated that none of the veterinarians could correctly diagnose Gracie's condition. This is the beginning of the last forty-seven nights of Gracie Lynns life. What was extremely concerning was the neurologist did not even consider that Gracie may have suffered a stroke. This was a Friday night which meant I would have to wait until Monday to find someone that would give Gracie an MRI. I had my son put a mattress in the family room where I would be sleeping with Gracie. We still had to carry her outside and held her so she could go to the bathroom. She would try to get up but she needed me to be at her side so she would not fall as we walked. She tried so hard to do the things she had done in the past and while her spirit and determination to get better never wavered, we knew she would never be her old self. We have two cats and an English Bull dog who is best friends with Gracie. Gracie was the leader and was the care giver and protector of the other pets. I began searching for a vet with that could perform an MRI. Unfortunately, I had to wait until Tuesday November 24th to schedule and take her to get an MRI.

At this point Gracie was walking gingerly, although she still had to lean against me. Even with her leaning against me she fell every so often. I picked Doug up and off we went to meet with the Neurologist who would perform the MRI. The vets rushed her off and again we had to wait in the car due to COVID-19. Seven hours later the vet called and told us Gracie had several stokes with the latest being on Friday November 20th. We took our baby home to nurse her back to health as best we could. I was not going to give up on my Gracie. Prior to her MRI she was beginning to walk, not very well but she was trying as best she could. It is my thought that she knew I was heartbroken and was trying as hard as she could to get better for the both of us. She did not want to see me so sad. My Gracie Lynn always had my best interest at heart. After the MRI she was unable to walk or move for four days. After the four days she began walking a little, but it was clear she was still not well as of the Tuesday before Thanksgiving. On Thanksgiving Day she could not get up at all, I was able to get some food and water in her, but for the most part she still had to be carried anywhere. Of course, the vets recommend more testing and sonograms. I believed Gracie suffered another stroke while at the neurologist for the MRI. On our way to a follow up visit a couple weeks later at Lee's Hill Gracie began panicking during the ride. I decided to tun the car around as I was not going to subject Gracie to any more stress that could lead to another stoke. I called Lee's hill and explained the situation and they suggested if Gracie were strong enough in a few weeks I could bring her in.

On December 13th it was time for another round of Simpartica. As I prepared to give her the medicine, she clenched her teeth, I thought this must be because of a stroke. Gracie took the gabapentin after I mixed it with a scoop of canned pumpkin. Thinking back, I realized she had clenched her teeth to resist taking this flea and heart-worm medication. I thought she was clenching her teeth due to the stroke she had. I was so tired and worn out by this time and was not thinking clearly. This is not an excuse it is fact. I blame myself every day for not understanding what Gracie was trying to tell me.

On December 23rd I had a plumber come to the house. When he looked at the mattress on the family room floor, I explained what had happened to Gracie. He said "I hope you are not giving Gracie bravecto flea and tick medicine" this scared me to death, so I began doing research on this medicine.   I went crazy absorbing and   learning everything I could about this medication. I could not believe that Gracie showed all the symptoms of this medication back in August and NONE of the veterinarian's thought to check this. None of them reviewed her medication records as a possibility for why she was not getting better.

After I had spoken with the plumber on December 23rd, I called Lee's Hill and requested Gracie's records and a list of all the medicines they prescribed to her. I got a list of the most recent medications that had to do with her strokes. It took three weeks for me to get her complete medical history.

On January 6th at 1:30 in the morning Gracie started crying in pain. I got up and yelled for Doug and Austin to come help me get Gracie into the car. We left as quickly as we could to get to the hospital. I did not know it at the time, but Gracie would never again see her animal pals, play with the grandchildren, or chase the ball with me in the yard. Crying all the way to the hospital I knew in my heart I would not be bringing my baby home. Once we got to the hospital the vet administered an IV to help calm her down. I will forever hear poor Gracie whelping and crying. I kept telling the vet to help her. I could hear Gracie above all the other dogs in there. The doctor came out to talk to us and explained she was having a real bad seizure. He could give her something to help temporally manage the pain and seizures, but she would likely live the rest of her life as a couch potato. Gracie could not live like this any longer. She was meant to frolic outside with our other pets and chase bunny rabbits who wondered into our yard. She was meant to play with and protect us. I am sure now that she was having seizures for months due to the medicines she was prescribed, I just did not know it. I do remember once as I laid down in bed with her and she urinated. I did not know at the time that when dogs have seizures they tend to urinate. By now she had lost her sight in the right eye and she was no longer able to jump up and catch the ball. I would toss the ball a few feet so she could find it easily and bring it back to me.

The evening of January 5th Gracie got one last bolt of energy and wanted to go play ball. It was if she knew this would be the last time she and mommy would ever play together. She wanted to make sure I had one last fun time with her.

We made the painful decision that Gracie would no longer suffer as we lost all hope and confidence these vets could help her. Gracie was to be euthanized as this was the most humane dignified and last act of love we could do for her. The vet brought us into a room where Doug and I cried as we held on to Gracie as tightly as we could one final time. Gracie looked into my eyes and told me for the final time that she loved me. I looked into her beautiful brown eyes and through my tears overflowing I told her how much I loved her, and I was going to send her to live with Jesus. I stayed with her through the procedure and as she took her last breath, I felt my heart leave my chest.

These vets may have taken the love of my life, they may have silenced her but as long as I live, they cannot and will not silence me and my criticizing these veterinarians and Pharmaceutical companies. It is my sincere hope others learn from my experience and make sure to have a doctor that you are comfortable with and trust.

Thank you for taking time to read Gracie's story and I pray it was of some help.

A special Thank you to John Bruton who is a great friend of ours and spent over 20 hours working with me on Gracie Lynn's story. He is the writer I am just a voice.

"Dogs are always good and full of selfless love. They are vessels of joy who never, ever deserve anything bad that happens to them."

Steven Rowley

Gracie Lynn

Chapter Eleven

Greta's Story
Cathy Wilkerson

I've had my share of dogs over the years, but this one…this one was one in a million.

We visited our vet in Stuart, IA on May 26, 2021, with our 6 year old yellow Labrador Retriever, Greta. She had been limping and carrying her left rear leg and would not put any weight on that leg. X-rays determined she had a torn CCL and we discussed options of having surgery performed or letting it try to heal itself as best it could on it's own.

My husband, Tom & I discussed this at home, and elected to have surgery done at Blue Pearl Vet Hospital in Des Moines, so I called and scheduled an appointment for a consultation with them for <u>July 9.</u> Our vet in Stuart, prescribed 100 mg, twice a day of Vetprofen (also known as Carprofen & Rimadyl) which is an NSAID for pain for a torn CCL (like an ACL in humans). A bottle of 60 caplets should get her through until our consultation appointment on the 9th. She was also given over-the-counter glucosamine chews and fish oil capsules for her joints. She tolerated it fine for two weeks. We wrapped her pills in a piece of cheese and she took them willingly. By mid-third week, she began drinking more water than usual & didn't have much of an appetite (which we attributed to our 100 degree + weather). I was having a difficult time getting her to take her meds. She vomited <u>on Thursday morning</u> and became increasingly lethargic. Honestly, I thought it could be a combination of the heat and possibly an upset stomach. I also noticed she was shedding quite a lot, which she normally does when she blows her coat in the spring, so I brushed her and was surprised at how much hair I had collected, but attributed that to the fact that it had been awhile since she had been to the groomer. I even made a grooming appointment that day for early July. I was able to get her to eat a little boiled rice & a bit of hamburger that night, so I felt we were on the right track again.

She vomited twice during that night & again in the morning at which time I called our vet. She was seen that day (Friday) by a different vet at the clinic, who thought she "just had a little upset tummy" from her meds, and was given an injection for nausea "so she doesn't puke in your car on the way home" and was also prescribed Cerenia tablets to help with her vomiting. She also told me to "go down the street to Dollar General" and pick up Famotidine (Pepcid) for an upset stomach, as it's cheaper there "or I can charge you 4 times as much and give it to you here." She was also taken off all her original medication, "until her tummy feels better." I apologized for her being literally covered in dog hair, and she commented that it "just goes along with my job." I brought her back home and she continued to drink, so I was not worried about her being dehydrated, but still would not eat. From that point on, she refused to eat ANYTHING. We tried rice & hamburger again, chicken, scrambled eggs, different dog food, canned food, not even her favorite peanut butter toast. She would not even look at it and would walk away. On Saturday, I put a call in to the weekend vet on-call, (clinic vet #3) and expressed my worries, as I was concerned how long she could go without eating, which we are now on day 4. I was advised to RESUME giving her Vetprofen, as he thought her pain being off meds for a few days was causing her to not be hungry. I only gave her half that evening, (which I had to basically insert into her throat, as she did not want to take it) because I was concerned what a whole pill could do to her on an empty stomach.

Sunday morning (Father's Day), Tom immediately noticed how yellow the whites of her eyes were. Also, her skin & gums appeared yellow and she passed brown urine. I put a frantic call in to the on-call vet again and was told he would call me back after he had contacted the vet we had seen on Friday. He did call back, but was unable to get in touch with Friday's vet. He became quite alarmed when I told him about her yellowness and suggested we take her to Des Moines to Iowa Veterinarian Services, where they "are better equipped to handle this sort of thing." I told him we already have a consultation scheduled for July 9 for her CCL surgery at Blue Pearl Pet Hospital, they already have her records, and could I take her there. He said yes, immediately get her there.

We left her at Blue Pearl mid-afternoon on Sunday. Her doctor called within an hour with her blood work and reported that her liver enzymes, kidney levels and bilirubin levels were extremely high, which was causing her jaundice. She advised us to have her stay overnight, so they could administer fluids and put her on meds to try to clear what they thought was something toxic from her system.

They also scheduled an ultrasound for the next morning. We were absolute wrecks the rest of that day, and I began my search for what might be wrong with her, which revealed horrifying information. Every single symptom Greta had was consistent with Vetprofen toxicity. The jaundice, excessive thirst, vomiting, lack of appetite, lethargy, even excessive shedding...all symptoms of toxicity.

This drug, made by Pfizer, is at the very center of lawsuits, (some of which have been won by pet owners), hundreds of deaths of dogs that are verified by veterinarians and cases too numerous to count of tragic endings for so many pets. Pfizer was also involved in a class-action lawsuit and was forced to pay out monies (pennies, really) to owners ONLY if they would sign a disclosure statement. Very few took the money. A law was also passed in 1999 that requires veterinarians to give a printed out sheet of drug information to owners of dogs that are prescribed this medication. Was I given one? NO. Was I informed of any potential adverse reactions? NO. I did ask if any of the three things she would be given could cause problems, and was told that sometimes the glucosamine can give them an upset stomach, and if so, discontinue for a few days. NOTHING about the Vetprofen and NOTHING on the bottle except for dosage instructions.

The doctor at Blue Pearl was shocked that at the visit on Friday, they saw no red flags and they did not do any blood work, which surely would have shown there was a problem.

I know, through all my research, that this drug does do wonderful things for millions of dogs...until it doesn't.

And our Greta was that one in a million.

Monday morning, Blue Pearl called with the results of the ultrasound. Her liver was shot, she had blood-tinged fluid filling her abdomen, she was bleeding internally. All of her levels had gone off the charts and the writing was on the wall. We could have a liver biopsy done, which would require her to be opened up, but the doctor didn't think she was strong enough and I didn't want to put her through that. I asked if Tom & I could both come that evening to let her go, she didn't think she would make it that long.

I've had to do this before, but this was different. She wasn't old, she had just turned 6! She was healthy in every way, other than her torn CCL and she'd never been sick. And she was my one in a million. My customers who come to my shop, knew she was my mascot, my greeter, always happy to see you, rolling over for a belly rub and relaxing her days away on the shop porch or the deck. This dog had my whole heart. Our Aussie, Reba has always been Tom's dog, but Greta was my girl.

They wheeled her in and I could see that she had lost so much more weight than the 8 pounds that she showed lost at the vets office on Friday, though her belly was distended. She was having trouble breathing. I did get a half of a tail wag when she heard my voice and I buried my face in her neck and sobbed like a baby, telling her over & over how much I love her and apologizing for having to say goodbye. Tom wanted to FaceTime with her and she lifted her head when she heard him say her name. I looked deep into her big brown eyes, because I wanted her to know I was there with her at her end, and to memorize her face. What I saw was that still, unconditional love, even now, but also the furrow between her eyes that pleaded with me to make it stop. I will NEVER forget that look, it will haunt me for the rest of my life. Make no mistake, this dog KNEW she was loved, adored and spoiled rotten to the core. We are having her cremated, instead of being buried in the north yard with the others we've lost. Because she was one in a million and that wasn't good enough.

Why am I telling you all this? Because I feel like I've failed her. I didn't protect her from the one thing that I trusted would make her pain free. I didn't know what this drug can do to dogs that are prescribed it, until I discovered it for myself and it was too late. I wasn't told what to potentially watch for. I wasn't told that she should be having blood draws if she will be on it for an extended period of time, to monitor her liver function, or that she should have had her blood checked prior to being put on Vetprofen. I feel like I basically poisoned my own dog, and I am having a really hard time with that.

I'm begging you all, PLEASE, PLEASE do your due diligence when it comes to your pets and their meds.

Nail down your vet and ask questions, get your answers in writing or record your conversations & above all, do your research! We had complete trust in our vet clinic that they all were competent, and doing the right thing, yet 3 of them failed us horribly. If I had heard one thing about this drug having potentially deadly side effects, I would have researched it and requested something else when I found it to be unsafe for some.

I'm completely devastated that my Greta had to die like this and I truly feel it could have been prevented, or at least discovered, somewhere along the line before it was too late. We DO NOT want anyone else to experience heartbreak like this!

Please give your fur babies a great big hug and lots of extra love. We've still got Reba, who's missing her (big) little sister desperately, but we've always told her we loved her first, so now we'll love her last. Q

PS-to this very day, we have not heard ONE WORD from our vet's office in Stuart. Not one member of the clinic has reached out to us since she was passed off on that Sunday, which speaks volumes to the kind of practice they run.

Chapter Twelve

HAPPY'S STORY
Kim Mortise

"HE'S GONE." Those were the only words that I could find the strength to message to family and friends after the hospice doctor finished injecting the needles. Happy's precious life, and life as his fur brother and I knew it, came abruptly to a devastating end as I held his lifeless body in my arms.

I have worked in the field of education for 30 years. Much of my life has been devoted to educating others as well as myself. I have a strong passion for research and had already spent a great deal of time reading up on canine nutrigenomics to the point that my veterinarian asked me to assist one of her clients. I had worked hard to do all the right things at home for my fur children. I trusted that all the right things were being done at the animal hospital.

It was not until I found the courage to question the hospital after being denied diagnostics for Happy's chronic cough and an enlarged mass that I started to see the shocking red flags. I began researching additional canine health and wellness topics online as well as in books written by leading conventional and holistic veterinarians. I immediately discovered red flags with even the most basic areas of my dogs' health care. One red flag led to another. Based on my findings and a second opinion, my dogs' vet visits appeared to be plagued with mistakes and below standard care. How could this happen? During a conversation soon after my discoveries, I casually mentioned to my veterinarian that I was reading up on additional canine health and wellness topics. Her response was "you're going to read yourself into a black hole." She was right. I did encounter a black hole. That black hole was Happy's grave.

The case is still under review, so I will refrain from mentioning some of the specific details and dramatic, heart breaking events. Trust me. There is much more than what is here. And unfortunately, it is not the first time that Happy experienced questionable care. In 2014, he had major surgery at another hospital that failed to inform me that they did not have overnight care yet thought that it would be acceptable to leave him all alone overnight under a heat lamp, hooked up to an IV. Luckily, I arrived just in time to transfer him and save him from a traumatic and potentially life-threatening night alone.

I am extremely grateful to Scott Fine, Joey's Legacy, and JL Robb for this important opportunity to share how valuable Happy's life was, and briefly explain what I believe went wrong during his final year so that other fur parents can protect themselves and their precious fur children. I am also grateful for the care provided to Happy by the good doctors that we had the privilege of knowing.

Going forward, I vow to all of my current and future fur children to: Remain an active member of Joey's Legacy; stay educated on the risks and benefits associated with titers, vaccinations, medication, and supplements; demand frequent imaging and lab work that meets or exceeds the standard of care; ask for a copy of records after every appointment and check for accuracy and thoroughness; make sure specialists and surgeons are board certified; stay with my fur children as much as possible during appointments; verify that the hospital has a qualified staff for overnight care; get 2nd and 3rd opinions (or more); report malpractice and negligence; trust my gut instinct.

The intense trauma and grief that can result from veterinary malpractice and negligence are extremely difficult, almost impossible, to recover from. The more proactive that you are now, the better your final chapter will be together. I hope that your final chapter never belongs in this book.

First and foremost, HAPPY WAS NOT "PROPERTY." Happy was one of the greatest sources of love in my life, his fur brother Henry's life, and everyone who knew him. His love was perfect and constant. He was a loyal and true "heart dog." He provided affection, comfort, and companionship in unique ways that could never be offered by a human. Days and nights were made sweeter by Happy's smiles, kisses, cuddles, conversations, and fun. He showed extraordinary love and devotion to his family and insisted that we ALWAYS be together. Now, without him, all of that is gone. Our hearts and home are empty, sad, and broken.

This sweet beagle's journey into our lives began hundreds of miles away in May of 2009. He had lived the first 3 years of his life outside and alone, chained to a tree. He courageously broke free and began his search for a real family. Tragically, in the process, he got hit by a car and had to have his front left leg amputated. However, that did not stop him from carrying out his quest for a better life. He was taken in by an animal shelter and received the medical care and adoption services that he needed. His previous "home" was found to be unfit, and his story was quickly posted online. During his rescue and recovery, he won the hearts of everyone that he met. So, it was decided that with a new leash on life, he was deserving of a new name.

With his radiant smile, pawsitive attitude, and outgoing beagle personality, the choice was an obvious one:

His official new name was HAPPY.

Just a few days after the amputation, Happy adopted Henry and me, and made his way across the country into our hearts and home. This time he traveled safely by car with the help of loving volunteers. Happy immediately made our lives better. And for the first time, I was a tripod Mom.

Through the years, I embraced my role as a special needs beagle Mom and did my best to provide Happy with everything that he needed to reach his full potential both emotionally and physically. He would no longer have to sleep outside all alone in extreme weather conditions. He now had full reign of a warm, king size bed full of fluffy pillows and the love of a real family. Our home was proudly furnished with yoga mats, pet steps, extra bowls, orthopedic beds, mountains of pillows, and our favorite – a special needs wheel cart that we traveled 16 hours round trip (on two occasions) to have custom designed and built. All of this allowed Happy the chance to overcome his past and carry on as a joyful, outgoing, fearless tripod beagle. He developed a strong and loving bond with Henry and the two were inseparable. Life together was magical and complete. Until…

OUR FINAL CHAPTER. In May of 2020, I requested diagnostics for a chronic, hacking cough that Happy had developed as well as a mass that had enlarged significantly at the base of his tail. My concerns and requests for diagnostics were dismissed. Instead, a routine exam was performed. To my surprise, Happy was diagnosed with ear infections. He was prescribed medication, and it was also suggested that he receive the Leptospirosis vaccination. I was told that the Leptospirosis vaccination was important and that he should get it. He was given the vaccine and I was not informed about any of the possible risks or side effects associated with it.

Happy's cough continued throughout the summer. And I continued the battle to be heard and receive proper diagnostics for him. At one point in September of 2020, his doctor agreed via email that diagnostics should be done based on his symptoms and past history of a mast cell tumor – a tumor that I had to convince the doctor to biopsy. In October of 2020, I brought Happy in for an exam, expecting the diagnostics for the cough to finally be completed. **Instead, Happy was diagnosed with COPD and prescribed medication with no diagnostics performed. This falls below their own standard of care. The hospital web site even explains that a cough is often the primary symptom of a heart or lung disease; and that lab work and diagnostic testing, such as X-rays, ultrasounds, and CT scans are fundamental in diagnosing a cough. I will never be able to put to rest the fact that I had to plead for months just to get a critical chest X-ray.**

It wasn't until 6 months after my initial requests for diagnostics that they were finally done after Happy began showing additional signs of illness. In November 2020, I took him back for a dental cleaning and surgical removal of the mass at the base of his tail. Yet I still felt very strongly that they were overlooking something serious. I demanded that diagnostics finally be done before beginning the procedures.

Due to Covid-19 restrictions, I had to wait in the parking lot for an update. I received a call from his doctor, and it was one of the most traumatizing moments of my life. She was crying as she told me the devastating news. **Happy appeared to have metastatic lung cancer.** I asked how bad it was and how much time he had left. She said that it was end stage, and she wasn't quite sure, but Happy might have 2 weeks to 2 months to live. When I reminded her how many times I had begged for diagnostics over the past 6 months her response was "I know."

The dental cleaning and mass removal were canceled, and instead additional diagnostics and staging were done. SIX MONTHS AFTER my initial request for diagnostics, which I never should have needed to ask for. SIX MONTHS WASTED that could have been spent fighting cancer together while I worked from home.

The diagnostics and staging were completed, yet the source of the cancer was yet to be determined. It was suspected that the source was masses in his spleen. In December 2020, Happy's spleen and bladder stones were removed and the masses biopsied. The masses were biopsied twice and both times found to be benign. I was told that we would not be able to see the oncologist until February 2021 because of scheduling issues, but that it was okay because they still did not know what the source of the cancer was. WAIT ANOTHER MONTH?

I complained to the hospital about how horribly wrong things had went. After a lengthy phone conversation with an administrator, I was told "I'm not sure if there is anything that I can say that will make you feel better." I continued to raise important questions with the hospital and express my devastation that Happy was never given a real chance to fight cancer. A chance that he deserved. The responses that I received were insulting and belittling. I was told that dogs with his type of cancer do not live long anyway, so it would not have mattered if it was caught sooner. **Yet research and experience show otherwise**. I was also told that now he could eat whatever he wanted to (because he was going to die anyway). **Yet research and experience show otherwise**. Cancer fighting diets can make a difference. I was told that any type of treatment involving chemo or radiation would be wrong. **Yet research and experience show otherwise**. When I asked about the Leptospirosis vaccination, I was told that despite Happy's pre-existing conditions, he should get it. **Yet research and experience show otherwise**.

I was also constantly told that I needed to think about Happy's quality of life and consider euthanasia and was eventually referred to their social worker. I did not need to consider any of this. I had devoted the past 12 years to Happy's quality of life. I always had his best interests in mind and received compliments from numerous doctors (including his own doctor at that hospital) for being "the most dedicated dog mom." Furthermore, there were very competent doctors at other practices willing to continue to treat Happy. So, what I truly needed to consider was possible malpractice and below standard care.

Despite all of the stress, failure, and devastation, I did my best to remain supportive, kind, and respectful to the hospital staff. I continuously tried to give them the benefit of the doubt. I continuously tried to give them another chance. However, it was not enough.

In January of 2021, I took Happy to a university hospital for a second opinion where the source of the cancer was finally determined. Happy was diagnosed with Transitional Cell Carcinoma and it was confirmed by a BRAF test. The university hospital discovered a tumor in his prostate, which they felt had been overlooked by the previous hospital. But again, it was too late. The only option was palliative care. A plan was established for palliative care at the university hospital and follow up appointments were made.

In March of 2021, Happy suddenly stopped using his back legs and seemed to have no control of his lower bodily functions. I was devastated and rushed him to the original ER/hospital because it was closer than the university hospital. Once again, no diagnostic imaging was offered. I was told that Happy was overall responsive and seemed to just be acting stubborn. I was told that he was most likely choosing not to walk. I had never heard of such a diagnosis. A beagle choosing not to walk? He was prescribed Xanax. I had never heard of Xanax being prescribed for what appeared to be partial paralysis. I questioned all of this and asked for more information. The response that I received was "where should we begin?" I gave up and took Happy home.

The next day, I consulted with the university hospital and my holistic veterinarian and inquired about the possibility of Happy having a stroke or cancer in the brain, perhaps both. The doctors all agreed that both were very possible, and Happy started prednisone to reduce any possible inflammation in his brain. Tragically, he never regained normal use of his back legs and lower bodily functions.

In April of 2021, the palliative care sadly turned to hospice care, which due to Covid-19, was up to me to provide for Happy 24/7. Throughout the final weeks, I slept an average of 2 hours each night. I spent much of the time preparing home cooked organic foods, administering medication and supplements, bathing Happy, washing bedding, praying, crying in another room, but most of all, loving and comforting him. It was a great honor to be Happy's hospice Mom.

With the help of my wonderful and supportive holistic veterinarian and an outside hospice service (all accessible by phone), I did my absolute best to provide Happy with everything that he needed to live out his final days with the love, care, and dignity that he deserved.

Looking back on it all, I can honestly say that I have never tried at anything so hard in my life. The support staff helped me cope with the trauma that Happy, Henry, and I had already gone through so that we could focus on each other and live in the moment. However, it was far from easy. I had to reach out to them numerous times. We made our own personalized bucket list together and found ways to make new memories despite our limitations. We were not able to complete everything on the list, but that was okay. We still had each other.

Although the medication, Piroxicam, prescribed by the university hospital, along with supplements recommended by the holistic doctor had helped to reduce the prostate tumor and improve some of the issues, Happy's lungs became progressively worse. By May, there was no room left for air. The chronic cough and condition that I had repeatedly asked for help with one year ago would kill Happy.

On May 3rd, 2021, I made the excruciating decision to set Happy free from his bodily suffering and the suffering caused by potential veterinary malpractice. It was the worst day and year of my life.

I AM SO VERY SORRY, HAPPY. I am so sorry that they did not listen to my repeated concerns and requests for proper diagnostics. I am so sorry that you were betrayed by "bad actors" who claimed that they loved you and would help you. I am so sorry that you were given a vaccination that most likely harmed you. I am so sorry that you were not given a real chance to fight cancer. I am so sorry that they failed to take accountability. YOU DESERVED SO MUCH BETTER.

I hope that you somehow know that we will ALWAYS love, miss, and cherish everything about you. I promise that we will continue fighting for you. Your pain and suffering will not be forgotten or minimized in any way. I am immensely proud of you for all that you were and all that you did. You were so extraordinary and perfect.

THANK YOU for the gift of YOU. Thank you for giving us the best days of our lives. Thank you for your truly unconditional love, loyalty, and devotion despite all that you went through. Thank you for fighting so incredibly hard and courageously. Thank you for lighting up the world with your beautiful, HAPPY smile. You will always be our hero.

I am the luckiest person in the world because I got to be your Mom. Rest in peace, my precious son.

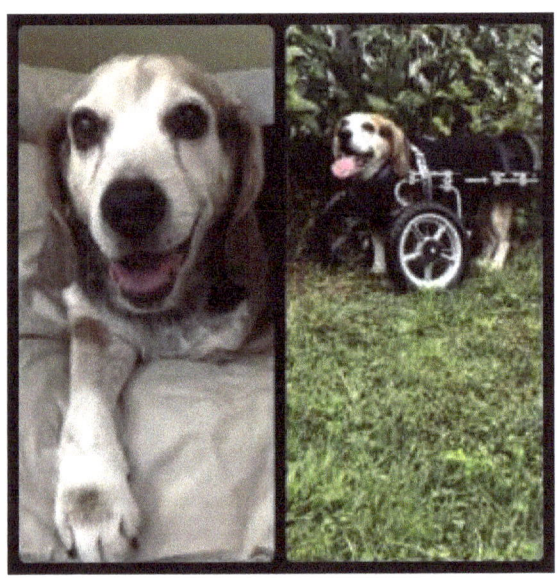

Chapter Thirteen

HARPER'S STORY
Brittany Quaas-Clark

My kitty Harper died on 10/30/17 at 5:30 PM at the age of six due to, I believe, the negligent actions of her primary veterinarian's clinic with whom I had boarded her. In order to fully understand the scope of this preventable and tragic outcome, I wanted to tell you of Harper's medical history prior to her boarding. On 7/1/17 I had taken Harper to her primary vet that she had been seeing for the duration of her life located in South Eastern Wisconsin. Not only does this veterinarian practice there, but he owns the business as well. I brought her in to be looked at as I was concerned about her recent breathing activity. After being evaluated by her vet, he informed me that he believed she had Pleural Effusion. This meant she had liquid forming around her lungs which was making it hard for her to breathe. The vet also informed me that she was possibly diabetic. In order to help her breathing the liquid needed to be tapped immediately, so he recommended that I take her to the local animal emergency room.

From his clinic, I immediately drove her to the emergency room which was a few miles away, where she was admitted and treated. After the procedure and an overnight stay for monitoring, I was able to pick her up the next morning. The treating vetcrinarian there had referred me to see an internal medicine specialist at a different location. Between her emergency hospitalization and our next appointment, I did some online research and built Harper an oxygen chamber to make her as comfortable as possible.

Our appointment with the specialist occurred on 7/12/17 where the liquid around Harper's lungs was tapped again. At this time she also needed multiple tests. Based on what the specialist saw, he believed that she was being affected by Pleural Effusion and high blood sugar. His concerns at that time were Idiopathic Chylothorax and Lymphoma. After this visit, I started to administer Rutin with her food as well as giving her Octreotide injections. Harper's diet was also changed to try and help her high blood sugar. After another appointment and liquid tapping with the specialist on 7/24/17, he recommended that I get a consultation from a college veterinarian hospital for a possible surgical correction of the Chylothorax. He had also wanted to wait on starting to administer insulin, as we needed to deal with one medical issue at a time. An appointment soon followed on 8/3/17 at the college hospital which verified the specialist's suspicion of Idiopathic Chylothrax. At this appointment the liquid around her lungs was tapped again and they taught me how to start administering the insulin.

I opted for Harper to get the surgery on 8/11/17, which was followed up with a hospital stay that lasted four days. Up front I was informed that this was a risky, expensive surgery, and there would be no guarantee that it would correct her issue. It consisted of four procedures: Thoracic Duct Ligation, Cistern Chyli Ablation, Subtotal Pericardia, and the insertion of a Pleuralport. I was sent home with special syringes and pumps if we needed to tap the liquid around her lungs through the port.

    Upon multiple follow up visits with the specialist, it appeared as though the surgery was a huge success. Her breathing was back to normal and at this time the port implanted had never needed to be used, as no new liquid had accumulated around her lungs. Less than a week before her death on 10/24/17, she had another follow up appointment with the specialist and he had stated that: "Harper looks GREAT today!" in his report. The only item that still was of concern was her diabetes, which was possibly brought on as a result of the stress from her other issues. We were making progress on finding the right balance of food and insulin, and she seemed healthy and happy. Since the time her primary vet saw her on 7/1/17, Harper had not gone back to see him, however he was apprised of her status as updated records were sent to his hospital throughout the process.

Due to Harper's diabetes, I wanted to ensure that she received the proper care when we had to board her. I chose to kennel Harper with her primary vet as he knew her history and I thought it would be a better option than a "general kennel". The first boarding at his hospital occurred on Monday October 7th through Wednesday October 9th, 2017. We were out of town, and I wanted professionals to take care of administering the insulin, rather than a family member, friend, or an unfamiliar kennel. There were no issues during the stay, other than that when I picked her up the tech had mentioned she was "a little finicky with her food, so we weren't able to give her some insulin". I didn't question it, as I trusted them, and no one seemed worried about this isolated incident. The second time I had to board Harper with them was on Saturday October 28th and I was going to pick her up on the evening of Monday October 30th, 2017. In her six years of life prior to her medical issues, I had never boarded her so this was not a regular occurrence.

I arrived at 9:00 AM on Saturday so that she could be evaluated prior to her kenneling. At this time the vet on duty, but not her primary care provider, proceeded to get her up to date on her yearly vaccines. Less than 48 hours later, I received a phone call at 8:20 am on 10/30/17 from her primary vetcrinarian stating that Harper was found unresponsive in their kennel. She was cold and found in a state of hypoglycemic shock at 7:15 am and we were told that they had been doing CPR on her since that time. The vet basically told us he could not further treat her condition at his clinic, that the only other option was to try and transport her to an animal emergency room a few miles away. He wanted to obtain our permission before taking the risk of moving her. Harper survived the transport and arrived there at 8:40 AM.

My Husband and I were five hours away and were racing to get back as soon as we were notified of her condition. We arrived at the hospital around 2:30 PM. It was presented to us at this time that she could either be transported in order to be ventilated at another location with the proper equipment, or be euthanized. Without knowing how long her brain was deprived of oxygen and without being able to put down the $5,000 up front deposit for the transport, we were left with no choice. At that point all we knew was that she had suffered hypoglycemic shock and not the depths of neglect that had caused it.

The following day, my Husband and I went to Harper's primary veterinarian to get answers and to collect her belongings. We were met by a manager and a vet tech who couldn't, or wouldn't, answer any of our questions. They informed us that the vet was not in the office. These two workers were apologetic and genuinely sincere with us, more than what we received from the actual vet. They provided us with the boarding documents from both stays, and upon evaluating the documents we saw that she had not been given her insulin since 8:20 AM on 10/29/17.

Apparently, the attending kennel worker was given instructions to not administer any insulin if Harper did not eat and to instead call one of the vets for further evaluation. I asked how long they would have given her to eat, and they told me an hour and then the food would have been removed from the kennel. Harper did not have her food or insulin for over 23 hours. She had been left unattended for 14 consecutive hours despite the admission forms I had previously completed, clearly stating that she required insulin every 12 hours. Instead of this kennel worker coming Sunday night at 8:00 PM(as her schedule was to receive the insulin at 8 AM and 8 PM prior to boarding), they chose to have her try to feed and administer the insulin to Harper during the assigned pick up time the hospital has on Sunday's. They are only open from 4-5 PM on Sunday's for other owners to get their pets from the kennel. After this visit, and leaving with more questions than answers, we were asked to return the following day in order to speak to Harper's primary vet, who was conveniently out of the office for our first visit. We left with her empty carrier, empty insulin pen, and no idea what had happened.

On 11/1/17 we made our way to the hospital for another meeting that was scarcely more informative than the first. All that her vet chose to tell us was that the kennel worker "did not follow protocol" by failing to notify one of the vets if Harper did not eat. A major concern that he could not answer was why the insulin pen was returned to us empty, when there should have been about 54.5 units remaining, or about a two-week supply for Harper. The vet had made the statement that he "didn't even know that Harper was being boarded with us this weekend". The boarding report that the kennel worker completed made matters worse, as many critical details were absent. We also saw, for the first time, the report from Harper's previous stay. It showed that out of four meals she was to be fed, Harper had only eaten two. I asked the vet if the attending kennel worker had contacted a vet during Harper's first stay and he said he "did not know."

Bottom line is that they knew of Harper's medical history and made no indication that they would be unable to handle her condition. Upon further review, the boarding records from her last stay were not fully completed by the staff, and seems to indicate a pattern of negligence rather than just a single incident with tragic consequences. Multiple boxes, pick up info, and the special instructions area were left empty, despite these issues and expectations being clearly laid out ahead of time during boarding. I believe they broke multiple codes and torts based on my interpretation of the law, as well as, in my opinion, ethical failures in the handling of the aftermath.

I truly believe that negligent retention, training, entrustment, and/or supervision were all factors that lead to her death. There is no evidence that the kennel worker followed the protocol to notify the veterinarian, during the first boarding on 10/9-10/11/17, that Harper was not eating. No one bothered to review her boarding records after her first stay, at which point they would have seen this and hopefully corrected the employee. or procedure and thus prevented a tragedy. This negligent behavior repeated itself during Harper's second stay which I feel resulted in her death. If negligent retention, training, entrustment, and/or supervision had nothing to do with it, then the kennel worker made a conscious decision not to follow protocol twice in one month. This could be considered willful disobedience, disregard, or negligence on her part, in not following his/her work duties.

We were not notified that an unlicensed, uncertified worker would be taking care of Harper. If I knew that, I would not have chosen to kennel her there. Based on what medical professionals told me, she should not have gone into hypoglycemic shock due to a lack of insulin, but more than likely was given a deadly overdose. This would explain why the pen was empty upon its return, despite containing two weeks of doses just two days prior. Based on their records they had only administered one dose of 1.5 units, so more than 50 units of insulin are unaccounted for. It's entirely possible that the kennel worker, possibly due to insufficient training, did not know the difference between a "unit" and a "milliliter." At some point someone gave her more insulin than what was documented on the boarding form I had completed. This is frightening, especially seeing that the doctor claimed to have no knowledge of this.

As the days passed, I tried to get more information from Harper's primary vet in order to better understand what had happened. I was met only with information regarding his insurance provider and claim number. I hired an attorney on 11/9/17 to represent us and then submitted my formal complaint to the Wisconsin Veterinarian Board on 12/12/17. It was not until 2/3/20 that I learned of the board's decision, which I was told I could not discuss publicly. After months of correspondence between my attorney and the vet's insurance company, they finally submitted an offer to us on 9/4/18. The insurance company then contacted me on 9/24/18 to obtain my decision. On 10/5/18 I formally rejected their offer and that is where this story currently pauses, but it does not end.

There is not one day that I do not feel sorrow over Harper's loss. What hurts the most is that she had survived the surgery and was prospering, only to have been, in my opinion, killed by a negligent kennel worker. Did she blatantly disregard the directions she was given, or was she not properly educated? I wish I could go back in time to redo things but I cannot. The only thing to do is to educate other pet owners by sharing Harper's story. I do not want her death to be in vain, so I created the Facebook Group called: "Harper's Hope & Lucy's Lookout".

Pet owners need to be educated, not only in what questions to ask their vets, but on what to do if negligence was committed against their own pet. Unfortunately, here in Wisconsin, my understanding is that pets are only considered property, and any damages will only reflect the replacement cost of the animal. In my home state of Wisconsin, the law has not yet caught up with the times. Pets are considered equivalent to an inanimate object, rather than sentient beings who have the ability to perceive and feel things. Some states are changing their laws, but not all of them want to consider the change. The ideology on whether pets are property vs. important members of the family cannot go both ways. Veterinarians know that owners will do and pay whatever they can to save their animals, yet when they commit negligence and face the possibility of consequences, the pets should only be considered as property, an item to be replaced.

We love and miss you Harper, I promise your death will not be in vain.

Harper

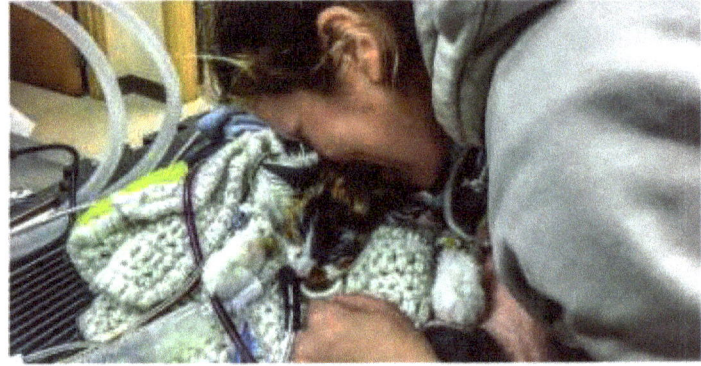

Chapter Fourteen

Hedgehog
Anonymous

    My story is a little different from the ones you've read because I didn't lose a cat or a dog. I lost an African Pygmy hedgehog to a tragic and all-to-common misdiagnosis by a vet who advertised himself and his practice as an exotic pet practice. I can assure you that size does not matter among sentient beings, and the hole in my heart is just as big. The guilt is the same and like everyone else in this book, I am forever changed as a person. This will be a difficult story to tell.

    I'm about to break a few hearts of hedgehog enthusiasts for a moment because I want to be clear up front that I don't support the exotic pet trade. Unlike dogs and cats that have sought out human companionship for thousands of years, hedgehogs don't have a natural relationship with us. Unless you're rescuing one from an already unfortunate situation, I'm of the opinion that they really have no business being in a home. It's actually seen as cruel by other countries to keep them in cages. Hedgehogs haven't been pets for very long and as you're about to read, it can be incredibly difficult to find them the right care. Many people live in areas that are hours away from any vet who has experience dealing with these animals, so that's something to think long and hard about if you or anyone you know is considering getting one.

    In late August of last year I brought my hedgehog to a vet for a yearly checkup and aspiration of a lump he had on his skin. Hedgehogs are nocturnal by nature and very skittish animals, so our 11am appointment was practically the middle of the night for him. The vet who saw him was very rough with him, prying him open with giant gloves as I looked on with some degree of panic. She spoke in a big, booming voice just inches away from his face in the small room, and I had to hold myself back from asking her a second time if she could please keep it down. As such, he was being pretty uncooperative that day, to the point that I didn't allow her to do the aspiration of the lump. I thought he'd already been under enough stress from the visit and frankly, I was upset just watching. Many vets will insist on sedation for a physical examination of a hedgehog but even easier than that, just put them in a tub of about an inch of warm water and they unball pretty much immediately.

He was given a clean bill of health, but I was told that he was overweight. It was recommended that I switch to a different food. I went home and looked at the ingredients of the food that was recommended, and to be honest they were pretty bad. It's a brand that's popular among zoos so I imagine that's why veterinarians recommend it, but it's loaded with fillers. I ended up finding a better food online with a higher protein content, so I went with that. The front desk manager called the next day to ask for my email address because they'd forgotten to at the end of our visit. I took the opportunity to share my experience with the vet we saw and explain that I really wasn't thrilled with the care we received. My boy still needed to get the lump on his skin aspirated, and I was hoping she could recommend someone older or a maybe a little more calming. The front desk manager was very nice and said, "No problem at all – I'll give you our surgeon." I immediately felt comforted because, well, he was a surgeon. Certainly this would a better person to see my animal companion.

At the beginning of September, I brought my hedgie back to see Vet #2 and have the lump aspirated. I explained that he was being uncooperative the week prior because of the noise level in the room and probably the brightness as well. The vet dimmed the lights for us right away which I really appreciated, and it made a big difference in behavior. He aspirated the mass, and at the same time I showed him a photograph of bumps I was getting on my skin when I held him. I'd been taking my hedgehog outside on summer evenings to walk around since the weather was warm enough, so I thought maybe he picked something up. In showing the photo to the vet I asked, "What is this – does he have fleas or something?" The vet said, "It looks like mites." "Oh, can you recommend something topical for that, like a shampoo or something?" I asked.

"Something topical is not going to work for mites because they burrow under the skin," he said. "We'll give him a shot of ivermectin, which is an antiparasitic." "An injection for something like bugs? That seems pretty extreme. I really don't want to inject him with anything if we can help it. Can we at least do a skin scraping first to be sure he has mites before we give this stuff to him?"

"We'd have to knock him out for that, and that could kill him," he said.

"Is that my only option?" I asked.

"We have an oral version we can give him instead if you want, and you can make another appointment for seven to ten days from now to give him the second dose."

I didn't feel right about making him ingest something to get rid of bugs, but I also didn't understand the science behind it either. At the least, I felt like it was the better choice of the two. The vet called me a couple days later to give me the results of the aspiration, and fortunately it was benign. I was really relieved. I took the opportunity during the phone call to ask him about the ivermectin.

"Is there anything about this medication that I should be worried about?"

"Nope," he said.

"So, there's no side effects or anything that should be any kind of cause for a concern or anything?"

"Nope," he said again.

I got a bad feeling about it – probably because I wasn't comforted by his one-word answers. I did an online search for hedgehogs and ivermectin and came across absolute horror stories from owners and breeders who had experience using it. Ivermectin is in the classification of macrocyclic lactones, which are bacteria derived from soil microorganisms. As I understand it, it paralyzes parasites once they ingest the blood of the animal you're giving it to. I read that it was toxic to the point of being potentially fatal if a hedgehog is given even a single injection because it's incredibly easy to overdose for their size, and the oral version has the potential for neurotoxicity because it crosses the blood-brain barrier. I also read posts in public forums from veterinarians who said they'd seen rats die from it and would only use it as a last resort *after* a skin scraping determined it was necessary. That was enough to freak me out. I was scared for him and felt incredibly guilty. I asked the vet twice if there was anything about this medication that I needed to know, and my concerns were all but dismissed.

I learned that the product Revolution is selamectin, and that's a lot safer for hedgehogs. I called the hospital back to speak with the front desk manager again and ask if they carried it, and they did. At this point, I was doubly upset because they had something remarkably safer, and it wasn't even offered as an option. I didn't even know there was an oral version of ivermectin until I balked at the idea of an injection. After reading how dangerous it could be, I never went back for the second dose and tried treating the mites on my own by sprinkling the inside of his cage with diatomaceous earth for the next few weeks. That was causing me some worry as well because I didn't want him breathing it in, so I was trying to be as careful as possible. I had a conversation about the mite issue with a friend of mine who used to be a veterinary assistant. I told her I was still getting bumps on my skin weeks later, and we ended up having a light bulb moment. She said, "You're probably getting HIVES. The fact that you had to show the vet a photograph because the bumps disappeared a half hour before your appointment should have been the first indicator they weren't bug bites – you were having an allergic reaction." It's common for people to get "hedgie hives," and it was pretty unbelievable to me that this wasn't even suggested as a possibility – by a surgeon, no less. I was angry and also scared for my animal companion because I didn't know if the ivermectin had done any damage. As soon as I started doing a better job of washing him off after going outside, I stopped breaking out altogether.

About a month later, I started feeling like something wasn't right with my hedgehog. I wasn't sure because they're only awake for about six hours a day, and most of the time that was late at night while I was sleeping. For about a week or two I noticed he was eating less and getting him to drink water was becoming an issue. I was witnessing what I perceived to be mobility issues. He seemed to have a hard time getting himself off the ground, and he started falling over to one side. There were some issues with constipation that I was trying to trouble shoot with organic pumpkin baby food. I also just started giving him more live insects over the kibble, so there were too many variables for me to figure out what was going on at the time. Was constipation making it harder for him to move? Did he breathe in the diatomaceous earth? Was it the ivermectin from September? I did an online search for "exotic vets near me" and came across Vet #3. We went in for the physical examination, and I asked for an x-ray in case he'd hurt himself. I watched the vet check his heart, eyes, and lungs but there was no attempt at palpation. After he came back from the x-ray he said, "I don't see anything, so what I believe we're dealing with is Wobbly Hedgehog Syndrome."

Wobbly Hedgehog Syndrome (WHS) is pretty much a death sentence. For all intents and purposes of this story, it's like MS for hedgehogs in that it's a degenerative neurological condition. There's a lot of misinformation about this disease, and it can only be diagnosed from a necropsy. From my understanding, YOU CANNOT DIAGNOSE WOBBLY HEDGEHOG SYNDROME WHILE THE ANIMAL IS STILL ALIVE. If you learn nothing else from this story, remember those words. It's a diagnosis of exclusion, which means they have to rule everything else out before they even consider WHS. Since Vet #3 didn't see anything on the x-ray, he felt that's what we were dealing with. There's no treatment for it, and the only thing he offered was a steroid shot to help get him moving. Admittedly, I'm not a vet. I don't have that education, but I said to him, "From what I know about steroids, they suppress symptoms and inflammation without actually addressing what's causing them. I really don't want to give that to him if we don't know what's going on." He explained that there really wasn't much else we could do for him. He shook my hand and said, "Sorry to meet you under these circumstances. Call me if you need anything." I was devastated.

    I went home and thought about what to do. It didn't make sense to me that it seemed to come on so quickly out of nowhere. The only thing I could think of was the ivermectin that was given to my hedgehog back in September. This was only going to progress over time, and I had to learn how I was going to take care of him. I made a post later that evening in a group for hedgehog owners and enthusiasts, and I said the vet believes my poor baby has Wobbly Hedgehog Syndrome. I was extremely distressed and looking for help from anyone who had dealt with this before – palliative care, vitamins, or dietary changes. A few people shared their experiences with it, and a newcomer asked what WHS was. When I told her what the vet said to me, an admin for the page jumped onto the thread and very coldly said, "WHS is extremely rare. It's just misdiagnosed all the time. You can't diagnose it while they're still alive." As straight forward as that was, I didn't know what she was getting at. I said, "How does that help me? Am I supposed to argue with you?" and the reply I got was, "Just correcting wrong information." Rather than show any sympathy, the comment seemed more about invalidating my vet and what I was going through. This person had no credentials whatsoever. She wasn't a vet, a vet tech, a vet assistant, or even a breeder. I was now in the position of trusting either a formally educated Doctor of Veterinary Medicine or a rude stranger on the internet who at that point had heard and seen nothing of what was going on with my animal companion. Nearly everything I learned about WHS from this thread came in complete disagreement with what the vet said. He told me WHS was common due to the limited bloodlines in breeding. Even though most resources would agree with him, this is NOT true. It's actually rare to the point of nonexistence in some countries. The problem with WHS is that more often than not it is a misdiagnosis, and many things can mimic the effects of WHS. Hedgehogs as animals of prey often hide their illness to the point that they can't even walk, so if you bring a hedgehog to a vet with mobility issues, he's likely to assume it's WHS.

There was a lot of back and forth on this thread, and people were basically telling me that I needed to see another vet. Since this was the third vet we'd seen in as many months, I was NOT ready to hear that. The first vet was physically rough with him and recommended a garbage food for him. The one before this misdiagnosed him with mites and gave him something neurologically toxic without even suggesting that I was breaking out so sadly, I couldn't accept that now I needed to look for a fourth vet. I'm really, really sorry for that.

This was my first hedgehog. I had cats before this, and I grossly underestimated what an unusual pet this was. When the front desk person of Vet #3 called a couple days later, I told them everything I learned about WHS from the chat thread. I was told that it's incredibly rare, that they have to rule everything else out first and on top of that,

symptoms of WHS come on very slowly and typically present between the ages of 18 and 24 months. My hedgehog was almost four years old, and I'd only been seeing these issues for the last week or two.

One of the first things to troubleshoot with a hedgehog that's wobbling is the temperature of their habitat. They need to be between 72 and 80 degrees at all times or else you're running the risk of a hibernation attempt, which can be fatal. I knew that wasn't the case. An inner ear infection can also cause a balance issue. I had actually asked Vet #3 to check his ears during our appointment but was told, "You can really only see so much from looking into their ears," so he didn't. In the chat thread, people asked if I had any blood work done, and I hadn't. All I had done was an x-ray that came back clear. I asked the front desk of Vet #3 to please have him check the x-ray again for anything usual, and let me know the name of the steroid he planned on using so I could do some research in the meantime. I asked for blood work to be considered, and I wanted to be sure the vet checked his ears next time. They called back and told me the x-ray was fine, and the steroid would be dexamethasone.

Watching my poor hedgie struggle to spin himself around or even lift himself up, I decided I was going to come back for the steroid to see if it would help. I didn't think it would do any good, but I hoped. I made our second appointment for the beginning of December and while we were there, something prompted the vet to want to take a second x-ray. Vet #3 said my hedgehog's bladder felt firm and enlarged. He tried to empty it and explained that he was having difficulty doing so. When he asked to take a second x ray, I was confused. What happened to the one from last week? I said to vet #3, "You just took one a week ago – isn't that a lot of radiation for him?" He sort of half-shrugged and said, "I won't charge you for it." He brought me into the back to show me the new x-ray and pointed to a mass in the area of his bladder. When I started getting upset, he said, "I can arrange for an ultrasound and a biopsy of the mass. We would need to sedate him for that, but he might not wake up. Of course, we can't even be sure at this point if the mass has anything to do with his symptoms." I was stunned. I didn't know what to do, and the options I was given were potentially fatal – again. There was no talk of euthanasia, and I didn't know what this meant for us moving forward. I got the impression that doing anything about the mass was elective, and this was now the second vet to tell me sedating him could kill him.

Why didn't anyone have a safe way to sedate hedgehogs? What's anyone supposed to do if they get sick? I pretty much concluded that Vet #3 couldn't help us. I didn't know how to express his bladder. I wasn't instructed how to express a bladder, and I didn't know if this was something that needed to be done for him at home. I explained to the vet that I'd been giving him water baths to help him go to the bathroom. I was massaging his belly during the baths and trying to get him to move around in there. Since hedgehogs need movement to help them go the bathroom, I thought this was the reason he was having trouble. The vet said that we'd see some improvement in the next day or two if the dexamethasone helped him and if so, we could make an appointment for another shot. There was no change at all, which was what I figured. Nobody called to see how he was, and I was doing everything I could think of at home to take care of him – adding CBD oil, probiotics, fish oil, and vitamin E to his food. I was even waiting on a shipment of Ormes from Canada that unfortunately made it to the house too late because of the holidays. He ended up passing away a little over a week after his last appointment. I feel like I failed him.

A couple of weeks after his passing, I made an appointment with an animal psychic – someone who speaks to pet spirits that have passed on and communicates with them while they're in form. The details of the reading were incredible. He told me how old my boy was when he passed, what his play area looked like, and even described some of his favorite treats. I asked the psychic to find out for me why my hedgie got sick. "Towards the end, he was almost completely immobilized. What caused that?" I asked. His response was, "Was he fighting an infection of some sort? He feels... bloated to me." I really didn't know what to make of that. I didn't have any knowledge of any infection. I suggested that the ivermectin had attacked his nervous system because that was the only thing I could think of. The psychic also said, "Were you giving him any kind of like, fortified vitamins or something? Something round and chalky, something similar to blueberries maybe, but smaller than blueberries?" I let it go because I really couldn't think of anything like that that I'd been giving him – I hadn't.

The new year came around, and I felt like I wanted to get another hedgehog. I found one that needed to be re-homed, and within the first couple of weeks he slipped and fell off my bed. He's had a strange gait ever since then. With all new vets, I've brought him in for x-rays twice, ultrasounds twice, and blood work. Feeling a little more confident in the care we'd been receiving, I found the courage around April of this year to request a phone call with Vet #3. I wanted to ask some questions because I didn't believe my hedgehog ever had WHS, and I wasn't convinced he'd gotten the care he should have. The first thing I asked was why we never gave him anything for pain. The vet said, "We couldn't give him anything for pain because we just gave him a steroid, and you can't use steroids and painkillers at the same time." I've since learned that's not true. Steroids and NSAID's are a problem, but you can use painkillers with steroids. I couldn't understand how this man was rationalizing not giving an animal with a mass and a full bladder anything other than a steroid shot. I ran by what the psychic had said to me. "Isn't it possible that the reason he couldn't walk very well was because he had a mass growing inside of him, and he was carrying the bloat of a full bladder?" I asked. "Well, he had some extra weight on him, and bloat would have shown up like gas in his bowels, and it wasn't there," the vet said. I was referring to more of a fluid boat from something like an infection rather than a gas bloat. I guess he didn't understand that, but I wasn't going to push the issue. Looking back at this exchange now, I still can't believe that nothing about my hedgehog's bladder was ever addressed. I foolishly assumed since the vet made no mention of pain management that my animal companion wasn't in any pain. I can't believe how stupid I was for thinking that and how I didn't realize he sent me home with an animal in a state of medical emergency.

I wasn't satisfied from that conversation, so I requested the vet notes. Upon reading them, I was sickened to realize that they painted a completely different picture than what transpired at our two appointments. The first thing I noticed was that "Hedge Hog" was written as TWO WORDS. If there's any doubt that this vet is inexperienced in dealing with these animals, you can start there. The notes from our first visit say that a mass was suspected. I can tell you with one hundred percent certainty there was NEVER any mention of the possibility of a mass at our first visit, to the point of me actually being confused when he wanted to take another x-ray a week later. If you remember, I even asked the front desk if he could check it again – why would I do that if I was told about a mass? I truly believe to cover his ass, he blamed me in the notes, saying I was warned that an x-ray wouldn't be clear without sedation and I made him take one anyway. No such conversation took place. I asked for an x-ray, and he took an x-ray. There was no talk of sedation for anything at our first visit. The vet defaulted to recording anything regarding his abdomen as normal because he never bothered to palpate him, despite an enlarged bladder in the x-ray. His ears were never checked as I've said, and their appearance was also recorded as normal.

The report card from the second visit was left half blank. There were twelve spaces for entries – skin, teeth, urogenital system, etc., and half of them were left completely blank. More specifically, anything at all having to do with his abdomen that was recorded as normal the week prior was now blank. I was blamed in the vet notes for turning down any and all testing that would have led to a conclusion other than WHS, but the vet talked me out of testing him for anything. He just kept telling me he could die if we even tried. The notes said I turned down blood work. I specifically asked for blood work, and I was told, "There's no blood test for Wobbly Hedgehog Syndrome." Vet #3 must have misunderstood what I meant because he wasn't willing to consider that he was wrong, or maybe he didn't want me to find out that he was wrong. Either way, an email exchange later confirmed his feelings by saying that "aggressive" testing (meaning any at all, I guess...) would only have proven him correct and caused "undue stress" to my animal companion. To this day, he's convinced my hedgehog had Wobbly Hedgehog Syndrome. That's what he says, anyway.

I asked for my hedgehog's x-rays at the same time that I asked for the notes, but I only received the notes. I sent a second email requesting the x-rays and instead of giving them to me, I received a response saying, "We sent them to you in an email the same day we sent the records. Some computers have trouble opening them. Did you not get the email?" I tried opening that email from three different sources – my phone, laptop, and tablet. I even forwarded it to a friend to have them try on their computer, and there was nothing attached. I then reached out with a third email attempting to obtain the x-rays. This time, they came directly from Vet #3's email address rather than the office's email address. When I saw them, I wanted to vomit. The first thing I noticed on the x-ray was the word "UNKNOWN" next to the word "Species." I understand that it could have been a new machine or program, but this wasn't exactly a vote of confidence. Looking at the images from the first visit, it was completely obvious that not only was a mass visible, but his bladder looked like it was about to burst. No wonder he didn't want to drink his water. I didn't know any better at the time, but I know what a normal hedgehog x-ray is supposed to look like because of the one I have now. The fact that my animal companion lived for another three weeks in this state of agony without being given anything for pain still gives me nightmares almost a year later. For weeks, I was massaging his little limbs like an idiot thinking I was helping him because I was told he had a degenerative neurological condition. All I can think about is how much he was hurting and how he couldn't tell me. It's almost too much to bear at times.

The second x-ray was even worse. While he wasn't sedated on either day, he was so full of urine that he couldn't move and lay there completely straight and sprawled out for the imaging. His bladder was even bigger at this point, and so was the mass. It was impossible for him to ball up, so any talk of the vet not being able to examine him is complete nonsense. He was flat like a squished bug for two weeks because all he could do was swing his arms around, and it breaks my heart thinking about it. I was doing everything I could for him, propping him up with towels to keep him from rolling over and feeding him by hand. This vet couldn't have been any lazier trying to assess my animal companion's health. My gut was screaming at me that something else was going on, but he just wasn't having it. He was so sure of himself, and he told me that everything I read in the online thread was incorrect. I'll remember this man's name and regret ever walking into his office for the rest of my life.

After seeing the x-rays, I realized what the issue was, and I realized what made sense that the psychic had said. I made the mistake, in this same time period, of using clumping litter for him in his litter box. You can't use clumping litter for hedgehogs because they get urinary tract **infections**. I didn't know any better because the bag said it was nontoxic and made specifically for small animals. I went on vacation towards the end of September and asked someone to watch him. While I was away, they sent me a photo of him, balled up and turned with his belly facing the camera. He had a piece of litter stuck in the sheath of his penis like a cork in a bottle. I said to the person watching him, "You need to get that out of there as soon as you can." I was told, "I'm at work right now. That picture is from last night." (!!) That meant my animal companion had that piece of litter stuck in his penis all night long, and that's probably what gave him a UTI. Neither the psychic nor I realized that what he was describing in the reading was actually the litter. They were **small, round, BLUE and gray pellets**.

If my vet would have had the common sense to do even a urinalysis, an antibiotic could have been offered, which likely would have taken care of my hedgehog's inability to express. Maybe he had stones at that point, or a catheter would have been needed. I won't try to hypothesize whether the mass would have been operable or not, but I will tell you that if I wasn't unnecessarily scared into thinking he could die from sedation, I would have let the vet test him for everything under the sun. Not only that, but the mass could actually be seen without even touching him. I didn't realize this at the time but when I look at videos of him, I can actually see the mass protruding from under his quills. You wouldn't have even had to touch him to realize that he had a growth there. NONE of this is any excuse why nothing was offered for pain. If this meets even the basic standards of care or the oath upheld, I have officially and completely lost my faith in veterinary medicine.

I tried so hard for my boy. I worried so much. I questioned so much. I did my own research, and I have such shame about myself for allowing two different vets to scare me into thinking testing him for anything could kill him. At the end of the day, both of them were completely wrong. The hedgehog I have now was brought to a different vet for his x-ray, and when they came out to the car to take him, the first thing the tech said to me without prompting was "We have a very safe gas we use for exotics." As soon as I heard that, my heart broke all over again. I wondered why it was so easy for one place to sedate while two others told me he could die. I would say that's probably because neither one of them were board certified in exotics, and they weren't confident in their abilities to sedate such a small animal. Even though the web site for the animal hospital that employs Vet #2 touts him as "one of the nation's leading experts in exotics," he's not board certified. I'm sure he's been a veterinarian since before the additional certification came along, but that's no excuse to me. If he's one of the nation's leading experts in exotics, wouldn't you presume that he's board certified in exotics? It's necessary education – go get the necessary education. Maybe he'd find out he shouldn't be giving ivermectin to hedgehogs so owners don't have to figure that out from online searches and strangers on the internet. Maybe he would learn how to sedate hedgehogs safely, as a surgeon. Or, maybe the real reason he didn't want to sedate him was because he didn't have time, and it had nothing at all to do with the anesthesia. I'll probably never know.

One of the most important things I've learned from this horrible experience is that vets can legally advertise that they treat exoticswithout being board certified with the additional and very necessary education. Despite advertising as an "exotic pet care practice," Vet #3 also wasn't board certified in exotics. Somehow, that's legal – it would only be illegal if he said he was a specialist. I even called before we ever went over there to be sure that they saw hedgehogs, and they said they did. They've actually since changed their web page, swapping out the word "exotics" for "pocket pets." That's a really tragic loophole for a vet to make money off unsuspecting clients who believe they're paying for expertise in the care of their animal. At the least, there should be a disclaimer on his website so people aren't misled. I certainly was. I was also pretty disgusted to learn that he has a video online teaching veterinarians how to make more money through marketing strategies. Since my animal companion and I had to learn this lesson the hard way, I'm now only dealing with vets who are board certified in exotics. Even still, I've had four of them tell me that the hedgehog I have now probably has WHS, even though I've explained to every single one of them that he's only had these mobility issues since he fell from my bed. He's also almost four years old, and I am completely baffled to hear professionals who went to school for exotics attempt to diagnose this while my animal companion is alive without so much as an x-ray, as one of them did. I don't understand how I explain to someone that I have an animal that's walking awkwardly since they took a fall, and that means they have a rare neurological condition. That doesn't make any sense to me. With this type of animal, I've dealt with a total of eight vets – the one that passed away saw three, and the one I have now has seen five.

This has affected me in ways I can barely articulate. It's taken a tremendous toll on my mental health that my beloved animal companion was deprived of a peaceful passing because I was ill informed and told that doing nothing was the best course of action. It's my fault – I had people telling me I needed to find another vet. We actually had an appointment with one of the top four animal hospitals in the country a couple weeks before he passed away, and I canceled it because I was afraid I couldn't afford it. It was right after our first appointment with Vet #3, and I let somebody talk me out of it. I don't know that I'll ever forgive myself for this and somehow, I am going to have to find a way to make peace with it.

There's nothing that any of us wouldn't give to go back in time and fix these tragedies. I understand that no one goes into veterinary medicine to hurt animals and for most of us, a screw up at work doesn't cost the life of someone's family member. That's a lot to sign up for – imagine the moral injury. I keep in mind the high suicide rates for this profession as a way to hold onto my compassion. Mistakes do happen, but what really puts it over the top is being blamed for it after the fact and reading scrubbed paperwork because I didn't think to ask for it at the time. If you need a vet who is board certified in exotics, search for one in your area on aemv.org. Remember to ask for the vet notes, test results, imaging, etc. to be emailed to you as soon as possible. It can be incredibly difficult to think straight when you're in a place of fear, worry, and vulnerability. I had choices at every turn, and my fears put me out of touch with my instincts. That's really been the hardest lesson I've had to learn from this, and it cost my poor animal companion his life. In the beginning stages of my grief, I looked to the counsel of rabbi Steve Leder who speaks extensively on the topic of suffering and how it leads to transformation. I'm paraphrasing, but the most important message for me was this: "Nothing will ever be worth it, but we can make sure it wasn't worthless." I hope with all of these stories, some greater good comes from this and positive changes can be made – legislative or otherwise, for the sake of our four-legged family members and for our peace of mind.

Chapter Fifteen

JOEY'S STORY
Scott Fine

Joey, our beloved dachshund, died at Daniels Parkway Animal Hospital at 6880 Daniels Parkway in Fort Myers, Florida on June 21, 2017, at 4:42PM. Joey was brought there on June 19, 2017, presenting with GI symptoms. He received an injection of a drug called Convenia. Joey returned the next day. Labs were performed on day 2 by the owner and it was determined that Joey had renal dysfunction. According to Zoetis, Convenia is contraindicated for dogs and cats with renal dysfunction. Joey stated overnight on day 2. We received a call on day 3 that his prognosis was poor, and we had to decide. We decided to end his suffering.

I filed a complaint with the Florida Department of Business and Professional Regulation in September 2017. In June 2018, I received a letter from the Florida Board of Veterinary Medicine's Probable Cause Panel who found probable cause to move forward with a formal complaint. Count One was 474.214 (l)(r), essentially practice below the standard of care and 474.214 (1)(ee) essentially recordkeeping violations. At the final hearing in December 2018, the Florida Board of Veterinary Medicine dismissed Count 1, the more serious count and retained Count 2, the recordkeeping violations. The vet received a $2,000 fine and 1 year of probation. Joey's case was the third filed against the vet since 2012.

We will never get over this. The negligent vet has caused irreparable damage to my wife and me.

Be forewarned. Most veterinarians are caring and compassionate. Just watch out for the arrogant ones.

Chapter Sixteen

Katina's Story
Joan Clarke-Marsh

If you love your pet, don't ever take them to this Out of Hours corporate

We visited this UK Out of Hours corporate on the evening of 15th April 2018 due to a shoulder injury on our 14 and a half year old, otherwise healthy female cat.

I had called for her evening meal, she did not show until about 15 mins later, very distressed, in pain and unable to stand on her right front leg.

The vet stated that 'K' had possibly suffered a slight RTA or an altercation with another cat, since she had some swelling and a slightly damp patch over her right scapula.

At no time were we informed of the need for blood or urine tests. 'K' was injected with medication to 'sedate' her, an antibiotic for possible (bite?) infection and an 'anti-inflammatory' (turned out to be the Nsaid meloxicam) to ease her pain.

We were relieved to be told that 'K's' injury was likely fairly minor, she did not need an x-ray since the vet didn't want to sedate her, having already suffered enough trauma, besides she thought it unlikely that 'K' had broken anything. The vet then stated that our main problem might be keeping 'K' indoors long enough for the scapula to heal properly after the medication had worn off.

We were asked to take her to our regular vets should either an abscess develop or if we felt that she might need an x-ray after all.

'K' was totally 'stoned' for over 24 hours, remaining in only the most comfortable position, eyes open but pupils massively dilated.
We had been given no warnings of any side effects which might occur, so naturally assumed she would be fine once the medications had left her system. We assumed wrong.

On the 17th as instructed, we gave 'K' her second dose of oral meloxica

By that evening, having been assist fed and syringe hydrated, (having lost all interest in food) 'K' suddenly started drinking copious amounts of water. We became increasingly concerned that she had neither urinated nor defaecated since her injury.

By the 18th we managed to secure an appointment at our usual vets for that same afternoon, the vets first comments were "Why ever haven't you bought this cat in sooner, it's in Chronic Kidney Failure" and "it's got a heart murmur".

This came as a complete shock to us, since only 6 days earlier (12th April) 'K' had been given a clean bill of health at her annual check up and booster vaccinations.

We objected that 'K' couldn't possibly have 'chronic' K F, she had displayed none of the usual symptoms prior to her injury.

Our vet revised his opinion to 'acute K F'. The diagnosis was confirmed after blood and urine tests.
When asked what had caused this, the vet replied 'Poison', I asked specifically 'what poison?' and he replied 'probably Rat Poison!!! (meloxicam?)

He recommended we "put 'K' to sleep", or placed on a drip but his prognosis was likely death in any case. We declined, because she was still responding to us. Also our two sons needed to be involved in making such a decision, since she was their pet too.

Turns out this particular brand of meloxicam has been implicated in both Acute Kidney Injury/Kidney Failure and Liver Damage in felines.

We brought 'K' home to be syringe fed with the aim of feeding of her own volition. This was not to be.

By the evening of day 7, 'K' was refusing food altogether. She started to turn away and 'switch off' before finally being put on a fluid drip at our regular vets, for most of day 9.

That evening she was taken back to 'Vets Now' where bloods were taken. By now 'K' had crackles on her lungs and 'fluid overload' together with general organ failure.
We had to make the extremely painful decision not to let 'K' suffer any longer and soon thereafter she was put to sleep.

Still reeling from the loss of our beloved companion, we cannot comprehend how our beautiful cat, could have had a clean bill of health on Thursday, an inflamed scapula on Sunday, 'Acute Kidney Failure' and a Heart Murmur by the following Wednesday (3 days after her first meloxicam injection, 1 day after the second) having to be euthanised (due to organ failure and fluid on her lungs) by the following Tuesday (a total of just 9 days)

Our query is this. Why would a qualified veterinary surgeon at said corporate give a 14 and a half year old cat a drug contra-indicated for use in renal impairment without first analysing blood or urine for pre-existing kidney problems? Particularly in view of the fact that she was an elderly geriatric feline?

We feel let down, angry and guilty for ever trusting this Out of Hours corporate with our treasured family pet.

We trusted the vet at this corporate, we relied on her professional knowledge and training.
Little did we realise that our much loved pet would end up being euthanased for what started off as a mere (albeit painful) shoulder sprain.

Chapter Seventeen

Lady Bird's Story

Mindy Berube

Lady bird was a three-year-old English cocker spaniel. She was given to me after I spend months training her for her former owners. She had become sick on a Friday that nothing of it dogs get sick I became concerned when it lasted all weekend and I took her to my vet. She was given meds I was told to come back for a checkup a few days later at that point they sent her to get an ultrasound done to see what was going on with her belly. This particular vet made a snap judgment about me and my ability to pay her and for lady's care told me to surrender her. She never sent the diagnostic information to my vet she waited more than 10 days to do so. When my vet received it was too late to save her, she suffered a horrible death as what she had was an obstruction and needed immediate surgery. There isn't a day that goes by that I don't miss her she should still be with me. She was a happy girl full of life, full of love and brought joy to the people that met her.

Lady Bird

Chapter Eighteen

Lightning B. Ware
2010–2016
Jodi Ware

...gone in a flash but illuminated so much

More than 10 years ago, a yellow stray puppy excitedly bolted toward me in a parking lot. We named him Lightning Bolt which became more fitting than we would know, for in life and in afterlife, his story helped shine a light to mitigate similar risks to others.

I've thought long and hard on what chapter of Lightning's story to submit for this compilation. Two short perspective pieces of mine were published in veterinary journals in 2018, so I will try to avoid being redundant. [1,2] I will also spare you the long version because it's complicated. Instead, I will offer some important insights I've gleaned along the way regarding veterinary 'innovation'. I will preempt with a couple of disclaimers: 1) my experience is specific to the United States where I reside in Texas, and 2) these points are to the best of my recollection and understanding after years of trying to maneuver through the minefield of veterinary care. I hope what I share will help readers more carefully approach health care decisions where their beloved companions are concerned.

- Protection from less than quality veterinary care is astonishingly absent. State veterinary boards are the principal, if not sole, governing bodies with the authority to enforce action against violative veterinary licensces. Yet, they are stacked with board members from the same profession who tend to be biased in favor of the very

---

[1] Ware JR. In favor of standards of care. J Am Vet Med Assoc. 2018 Aug 1;253(3):264. doi: 10.2460/javma.253.3.264.

[2] Ware J. Veterinary trials and tribulations. Vet Rec. 2018 Aug 18;183(7):228. doi: 10.1136/vr.k3564. licensees they are in place to regulate and notoriously lenient on even the worst offenders.

- Board certification (not to be confused with veterinary board licensure) is an extra step that some veterinarians take to become more specialized. While I am generally a proponent of using board-certified specialists for specialty care in pets as is routine for humans, I'm afraid these licensees may be especially insulated, since clients may lack the confidence to question their care in the first place, not to mention those who serve on (regulatory) veterinary boards may revere them. What's more, even if questioned, specialists could convincingly claim that departures from recognized norms represent specialty (or a higher than standard of) care.

- Federal laws protect human and *laboratory* (but not *companion*) animal research subjects.[3,4] This can result in a whole host of issues. Victoria Hampshire, veterinarian and then Director of Advanced Veterinary Applications, U.S. Food and Drug Administration (FDA), outlined some of them nearly two decades ago.[5] Fifteen years later, concerns regarding the lack of research protections for companion animals and their guardians were reiterated.[6] Still, nothing is being done—which is quite troubling given the fact that most consider pets to be family members and would never intentionally expose them to rogue research. Dr. Hampshire eloquently stated, "Key aspects in the prevention of consumer fraud during the consent process are relevant

---

[3] Federal Policy for the Protection of Human Subjects ('Common Rule'). U.S. Department of Health & Human Services Office for Human Research Protections website. Reviewed March 18, 2016. Accessed October 3, 2020. https://www.hhs.gov/ohrp/regulations-and-policy/regulations/common-rule/index.html.

[4] Animal Welfare Act and Animal Welfare Regulations. United States Department of Agriculture Animal Care Blue Book. Updated July 2020. Accessed October 3, 2020. https://www.aphis.usda.gov/animal_welfare/downloads/AC_BlueBook_AWA_508_comp_version.pdf.

[5] Hampshire VA. Regulatory issues surrounding the use of companion animals in clinical investigations, trials, and studies. ILAR J. 2003;44(3):191-6. doi: 10.1093/ilar.44.3.191.

[6] Walker RL, Fisher JA. Companion animal studies: slipping through a research oversight gap. Am J Bioeth. 2018 Oct;18(10):62-3. doi: 10.1080/15265161.2018.1513587.

facts about just how new the procedure or drug in question really is and the chances that the animal in question might not benefit from such a new procedure." By my view, 'new' includes in the hands of the treating veterinarian, meaning inexperience should be disclosed.

- To further compound matters, unlike veterinary drugs, veterinary devices do not require FDA approval before they are sold to veterinarians who then use them in patients. Quite literally, an implant can be put inside your pet with no demonstrable safety, efficacy, or quality control whatsoever. The FDA also exempts manufacturers from post-marketing surveillance, meaning no formal mechanism exists for tracking adverse events associated with veterinary devices (and, in fact, reporting is not a simple task should a caregiver wish to do so). The pet-loving public trusts veterinary health care professionals who trust the claims of researchers (some of whom are veterinarians themselves, pioneering new treatments) and manufacturers. Call me cynical, but these are the very entities that stand to benefit, not to mention they likely suffer from various biases that have been well described in the veterinary literature.

- Some veterinarians become 'key opinion leaders' and partner with manufacturers on side jobs such as research, education, consultancy, and product promotion. These types of conflicts of interest may not be apparent to the public. Going back to Lightning, the surgeon and soon-to-be spokesperson for the new and unproven orthopedic surgery that he used in 2013 (not to mention the new and unproven supplement that he later prescribed in 2016 for treatment of late surgical complications) did not disclose any conflicts (to me or to the public at large in subsequent presentations and publications). Mere months after Lightning's surgery—when the procedure was still being tweaked and specific implants were not yet commercially available—the surgeon began seeding it via short implant company-sponsored 'certification' courses. (Such courses vastly differ from the board-certification process that specialists undergo.[7]) These courses have been sold to both specialists and general practitioners with claims of technical ease and rapid healing. To be clear, this major, invasive surgery involves cutting the tibia in two with a saw and putting it back together with implants, while modifying the joint architecture to certain specifications and

---

[7] AVMA Policies: Distinction between the process of board-certification and earning a certificate. American Veterinary Medical Association website. Accessed October 3, 2020. https://www.avma.org/resources-tools/avma-policies/distinction-between-process-board-certification-and-earning-certificate.

paying careful attention to the surrounding structures. It absolutely does not seem like something the inexperienced should return to their clinic after a 1- to 3-day course practicing on plastic bone models and cadaver limbs and add to their repertoire. And, certainly not before any one construct has been proven to be safe and effective in prospective, controlled clinical trials. However, a participant's investments in the course and special instrumentation might result in reluctance to abandon. "There is also the risk that a surgeon's enthusiasm for a given creation will blind him or her to its flaws, bold confidence sliding into perilous hubris."[8]

- Expensive, risky and unproven interventions may be marketed with catchphrases like new and improved, cutting edge, innovative, novel, state of the art, new gold standard, or similar lingo in an effort to appeal to vulnerable people aiming to do their best (and willing to pay premiums) for their companions. Notably, for the few who carry pet insurance, exclusions for these types of treatments generally do not exist. In other words, payers don't necessarily impose limits on experiments or extremes. This may sound great on the surface, but it can lead to unchecked use of interventions that have devastating effects, including repeated treatments to try to correct problems—and ultimately culminate in death. On a related note, it is my opinion that pet and caregiver burden are all too often overlooked.

- For many reasons, outcomes of new treatments in pet patients who aren't enrolled in bona fide controlled clinical trials are rarely captured, especially in the longer term. This means that negative results may not be realized for extended periods of time while more and more animals are put in harm's way.

- I firmly believe that decisions for major elective interventions (eg, cruciate surgeries, joint replacements, many cancer treatments) should neither be made in haste nor without second opinions. It is worth taking time to understand the diagnosis, prognosis, level of evidence, risks and benefits of potential treatments (including doing nothing)—from multiple perspectives. This is especially important when emotions are running high, putting pet parents in jeopardy of not fully comprehending what treatments entail. For

---

[8] Groopman J. Do some surgical implants do more harm than good? The New Yorker. Published April 13, 2020. Accessed October 3, 2020. https://www.newyorker.com/magazine/2020/04/20/do-some-surgical-implants-do-more-harm-than-good.

instance, I was told that Lightning would undergo a 'minimally-invasive, arthroscopic cruciate repair' (which I understood to be like that used in humans). It was quite the contrary. I realized this afterward, given the significant pain he was suffering, and the incision revealed when the bandage fell off. Regrettably, it would be a long time (only after chasing many unsuccessful remedies) before I began to understand that he had been treated with an unorthodox (and long failing) intervention (Figure).

- On a related note, veterinary informed consent may be viewed by some as more of a contractual commitment for payment and legal release than a two-way exchange that benefits all parties in the veterinary triad. Pets, of course, cannot execute a contract or consent, so we humans are their surrogates. We must be fully informed by veterinary professionals in order to effectively share in the decision-making process. As part of informed consent, supportive written materials can help augment the discussion, but so can various online resources, such as support groups that can be accessed during the pause and second opinion seeking that I previously advocated. Information exchange should be a constant from diagnosis to treatment (or lack of treatment) and beyond. The point is, diagnostic test results including copies of x-rays and other medical images, details regarding treatments (and/or supportive care) administered and monitoring thereof, as well as longitudinal follow-up should be continually furnished.

- Caregiver placebo effect can be problematic in veterinary medicine because our pets cannot speak to communicate the safety and efficacy of a given intervention. As common sense as this may seem, it is important to consider when weighing treatment options and especially when monitoring outcomes.

Fortunately, evidence-based medicine, standards of care, shared decision making, veterinary informed consent, and ethical study conduct are among many areas with recent calls to action. I applaud those who are working hard to put protective measures in place for pets and (all of) their caregivers.

Acknowledgements

I thank friends (old and new) and family who have supported my advocacy, but especially my husband and boys who lost not only Lightning but a little bit of me along the way.

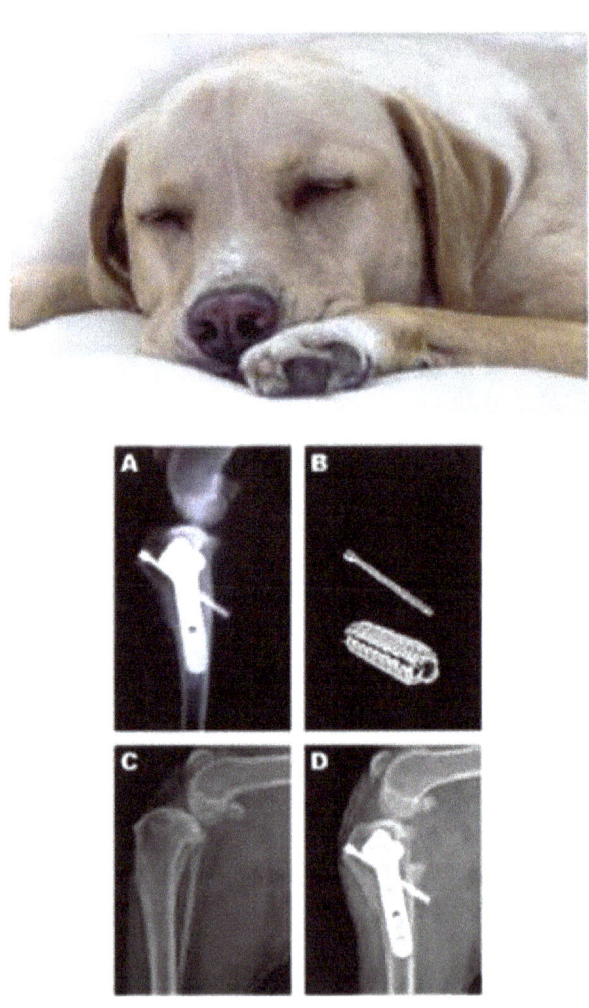

A, February 5, 2016 radiograph taken by my general practice veterinarian after Lightning went abruptly and severely lame (the first time I recall seeing an x-ray).
B, Diagonal bone-cutting toothed and cannulated headless compression screw tip meant to reside within the confines of the bone.
C, July 24, 2013 pre-operative radiograph retroactively obtained in 2016 via medical records request.
D, July 26, 2013 post-operative radiograph retroactively obtained in 2016 via medical records request.

Chapter Nineteen

Lincoln's Story
Susan Lask

In short, lincoln was a spokesdog for shutting down Puppy Mills. he met with senators, Mayors and attended numerous

events and court cases against animal abuse and for animal rights. i have written numerous laws for animal rights,
and one very famous one that passed the legislature in NYS as teh first law prohibiting puppy mill dog sales in
a New York State town.

You can see the videos and my work at my Face Book page @SusanChanaLaskEsq and a short tribute to Lincoln at https://www.facebook.com/SusanChanaLaskEsq/photos/a.225255494211362/4932157410187790/

also posted on Joey's Legacy page where I add the Vet Hospital issue. I did not publicize it in Lincoln's tribute
because it makes me sick to repeat it, no less I didnt want that negativity on his tribute.

The rest of the story to Lincoln's tribute is that on my birthday, January 26, he attended a dinner party with my close friends in Florida. He was happy--even laughing with us. He shared my dinner and a few licks of birthday cake.
We all enjoyed that dinner. At 1 AM lincoln's breathing rate increased as I constantly monitored him due to his having congestive heart disease. Now, I had the best cardiologists and medicine for him, and he was well taken care of. Was he sick-- yes. Did he have an incident before-yes. But he did not have to die ALONE at the hands of calusa that night.

I drove him to the only hospital in the area that was open at 1 AM--Calusa. His breathing was find by the time I arrived, but the Vet Tech met me at my car and said "He doesnt look good". He was senior and he was fine, but i wanted him checked and I told the tech to be careful with him. They would not allow me inside of the hispital with lincoln,. claiming covid as an excuse;however, and as you'll see later, they let me in for hours after they killed him.

Furst, Lincoln and I have never been separated. That is my choice- that is how we decided to live our life together. Calusa never asked anything about our history, and that's important because you can't take a dog that is so bonded like Lincoln and separate them at a time of sickness. It doesn't work, and the dog will give up. They just took him from me, then called me as i waited in my car for an hour in their parking lot and said it would cost close to $6,000 because they wanted to keep him in an O2 cage for days and they gave him lasix. he never had lasix, and my regular vet's plan was to keep him off that. Nor did he ever stay in a cage for any time without me-no less, an O2 cage. i later discovered Calusa throws companions regularly into their Oz cagse and many of them die. Why? Well, in Lincoln's case proves they threw him in there for 4 hours without any monitoring, observation, nothing. At some point he was scared and alone, and he had a breathing attack in their O2 cage. Noone was there watching him. The vet etch later admitted he found Lincoln in distress during his rounds. Rounds means sometime in an hour or two hours, he walked by and saw my dog dying. Something that could have been prevented if they ha dtheir eyes on him. Worse, their notes, that I obtained the next day, in capital letters, states that I wanted Lincoln returned to me after they said they would keep him in a caseg. they refused. the notes then state "Owner" will wait in parking lot after they told me to leave. i wasn't l;leaving. The notes last state, "Owner" wants notification of there is any change in Lincoln.

If Lincoln was that seriously ill, which he was not, they hsould have given me the option of euthanasia and I would have done that. I had the right to make that choice. If he was that ill, they should have been observing him every minute. The notes show they dropped him in the O2 cage and after that absolutely no monitoring of him. in fcat, as I waited in my car from 1 AM to 4 AM, whenever I saw a tech leave the premises, I pleaded for contact with Lincoln. The big favor they did was send me the attached pics of him in the O2 cage. Clearly he was fine. And more clearly, I know my dog and he was scared to death being alone. He may have given up after 4 hours of being ignored and scared, especially in his delicate condition. And the vets should have taken a more holistic and compassionate approach and accounted for the fact that I wanted him back as I told them he has never in his life been separated from me, and he needs to know I am there.

At 5 AM my cell rang in my car and a tecxh yelled "Lincoln is in CPR, what do you wnat us to do?" I told her let me in that hospital. I was at the door and they never opened it, and then the tech showed up EIGHT MINUTES later. I was banging desperately on the door to see my son. She cruelly yelled at me "You do not have to bang on the door", when she wrongly left me in distress by not letting me in for 8 minutes. I arn to the bacj to find Lincoln's dead body with a plastic tube down his throat and blood by his mouth. The Vet yelled "do you want us to continue cpr?", but they weren't even doing anything. He was dead. I responded "He's dead, what are you doing?". Next I heard, do you want us to give him a shot, (i guess to finish off the dying process). I said yes, stop this!.. And that was the end.

I had a full blown breakdown there, where I fell to my knees screaming Lincoln's name because I hoping that his spirit was still there to hear me. the fact is, clearly he died awhile ago, and the vet never called me. They had him on the table for a mocked up CPR , and they didn't let me in for 8 minutes after they called me. Lincoln died alone, without seeing my face. Without hearing my voice. Our life plan and plan for his death was completely ruined by the callous Calusa Vet hospital that ended up billing me $16,60 for killing me and Lincoln--killing our dreams together of how we planned his life to end.

Incredibly, they refused to return my companion and refused me to stay with him using CovId as an excuse, but as soon as they killed him I was led into a separate room where they brought his dead body to me and we could be together--in face of their CoVid excuse. I was there for over an hour with him, until 6:30 a.,m My friend arrived to be with us. We asked to peak to the Vet--she refused to speak to us. All i got was from that same vet tech who took Lincoln from me four hours before was "He was a fighter, he really tried to survive". That was more devastating as now I'm left with the image of Lincoln suffering. yes he wanted to survive. There was no reason for him to die like that. He wanted be with me, and if he fought then I know if I was there he would have calmed down. I know because I raised him for 15 1/2 years and we were soul mates--that's just how it is when you love your companion not as a pet, but as your family. Indeed, they never returned Lincoln's belongings to me--a red towel he loved that I gave them when they took him from me (see picture). There's so much more, and it was all completely traumatizing what they did--not even a condolence card.

Later I called the hospital manager and wrote her what happened. She confirmed there was a lack of communication and they should not have traumatized me more by yelling at me for knocking on the door as they made me wait another eight minutes. Then I never heard from them again. No explanation. No apology. They just charged my credit card $1,660 --so I will have to sue them to hold them accountable.

I left with Lincoln's dead body and took him myself to a private crematorium. I would never leave my companion alone anywhere, even at death.You can pick up the rest of the story from https://www.facebook.com/SusanChanaLaskEsq/photos/a.225255494211362/4932157410187790/

That story is proof that Lincoln's love and soul was real, and that negligent vets that robbed us of that are inhuman.

 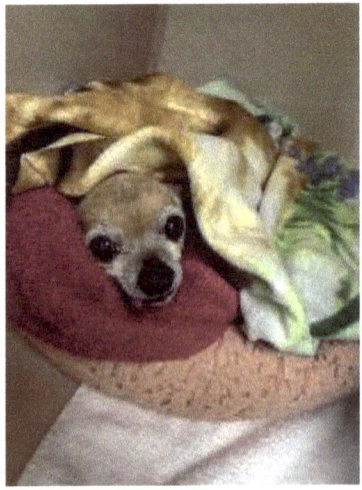

Chapter Twenty

Kayden: My Pet's Story
Lisa Gruccio

I have sadly received my response from your review. I was truly hopeful that my case was going to be the one that will make a difference. However, after joining awareness groups that are all around the country, I have learned that the bigger problem isn't so much the Vets. It's the governing body that is that issue. You see, I have discovered that they are not truly regulating the industry for the betterment of the animals and their caretakers. Like always, everything in this country is about the bottom line. I have realized your organization is also run in this matter. There have been many of us who have this discovered it and one has even written a book about the failures of systems like the Board of Vets across the country. There are tons of cases that have been documented. Perhaps you have read Joey's Legacy. I do know that Ron DeSantis now has a copy of that book filled with stories about failures. I also have friends who have recently had dinner with him. Perhaps he has had time to read it, or maybe he needs to simply be educated as to what the bigger concerns are. I am sure this has been a problem that has been under the radar for some time now. But not much longer!!!!! I love to spread awareness!!

I do know that the Florida Board has been in the newspapers before. I am excited about this, as this is going to make it easier for a news reporter to pick up the story about the failures of the board and how they lean heavily to make sure the "good ole boys" club is taken care of. My media experience should come in handy. It's been a while since I have been connected, but I am sure I can jump in the saddle really quick. After all, NOBODY likes to hear about animal mistreatment, and when a blind eye is turned, that is even worse excellent story material, with another bad guy to focus the attention on.

I have hired an attorney. I will be pursing this further. Sadly, your lack of action has led me into become an activist and I truly thank you for providing me with a focus on where I can make an impact. I have been praying over both of you since I learned your names. Every night I ask for the Lord to guide your hearts into stepping up and DOING THE RIGHT THING. I ask him to guide your moves daily to make sure you are doing God's work in protecting his creatures. I felt lead to do this for you both because of the failures I have learned from others. But because of the circumstances and the overwhelming amount of evidence that I presented to you both about the bigger picture and the bigger problems at that facility you chose to ignore the opportunity to investigate. Which is truly shameful. You are not in this to protect anyone but yourselves and your colleagues and the tax paying citizens need to be made aware of this. Our dollars are not being used to truly regulate this industry and that is why it is so bastardized. It's because you turn your back. It's not too late to actually make a difference on this planet. You are in a position of power to do so. I know the Lord above gave me a voice for a reason. He also kept me on this earth after many, many physical cardiac recoveries. It is so sad that your hearts are so harden that you couldn't even recognize that. You can change this. You truly, truly can. You can work with me to make this better or you can fight against me to continue to protect the ugliness in this world. Some people believe in Karma. I can only imagine how heavy you must feel going to work daily and knowing you are being used in a bad, bad way. I know what that is like. I worked in television for years. It's a dark, dark place. However, I got out because it broke me physically knowing that I was a cog in the wheel of evil doings. Do you feel that way? I bet you do. Kind sucks doesn't it.

I will continue to pray for you as you have lost your way. The dollar is not your God. You cannot take that with you when you die. But your deeds on this earth and how you protect God's people and his creatures will MATTER MOST. I forgive you for not doing the right thing. I hope you can forgive yourselves. I hope my words ring deep into your heart, if you are allowed to still have one doing what you do for a living. I know you can change. I know you can seriously make difference. Its why you are here…. remember that…. don't let the dark steal your light….

Thank you for the SPARK to ignite my journey to help stamp out darkness in places where it needs to be shined on. God Bless You Both….

I look forward to meeting you both someday!!

God Bless You…..

James 4:17 New King James Version (NKJV)

17 Therefore, to him who knows to do good and does not do *it*, to him it is sin.

Chapter Twenty-One

Major's Story
Sheryl and Timothy Blanford

Major (Dog) Adopted 09/11/2008 4 year old rescue

My husband and I adopted Major from our local rescue / shelter. He was an owner surrender because the couple was going through a divorce. He was a German Shepherd Rhodesian Ridgeback mix around 70lbs. He was 4 years old when we adopted him.

He was our first dog as a couple in a new home with a fenced backyard. We were given his health records and a big bag of Science Diet Adult Chicken and Rice. (I still have the note on my wall from when I called ahead of time to see what food I needed to buy him, but they were giving us a bag from the shelter attached to the vet. How nice and convenient.) We brought him home and let him slowly get acquainted with our 3 cats. We had no issues since Major could care less about the cats. We played and we spent the day with our new dog.

Fast forward to 4 weeks later and it is time to give him his heartworm preventative pill and flea and tick drops on his neck and back. So we give him his pills and drops. That night we notice he is not feeling well and he has started to itch. We knew he did not have fleas so we called the vet and they said give him some benadryl. So we did. He continued to itch and not feel good. We kept in contact with the vet. We were going to take him for a walk to see if he would feel better. We went to hook up his collar to the leash and he yelped. I was stunned. What did I do? I looked at him and his back and his collar were all fine. I thought maybe his collar pinched him. He wears a nylon collar all the time. So I removed the collar and found his fur and skin were "burned" in little sections under his collar. We never saw it since he is a big dog and we bought him a big wide collar. We took him to the vet and the vet said the flea and tick meds "could" have done that to him. I was stunned. Why didn't you tell us that? So we got meds and cream to heal his neck from the vet. A week later he was healing slow and steady. Spots were going away and fur growing back.

We went back for the follow up after 2 weeks and he was looking better around his neck. We now addressed the crazy itching and constant scratching since his heartworm pills. Vet said well he could be allergic. That pill has flavorings in it along with the poisons. That is the first time he mentioned poisons. I guess I was clueless about what magical things kept bugs off my dog. Sadly we were both clueless, my husband and I.
So the vet said we will look for something different next month. Keep giving benadryl every 4 hours. So we did.

In 2 weeks it was a new month and it came time to give him everything again. We called the vet and asked now what do we do? He said come in and get this all-in-one drops. I said well that does not sound good since the last stuff burned my dogs neck and the other stuff he is allergic to. What else can we do? The vet said nothing. We only have options of chemicals. I said well it is winter and we will wait until spring and figure this out again.
Well spring comes around and we decide to look into natural things for our yard and not give anything to the dog for flea and tick or heartworm meds. We live in Illinois west of Chicago so it does get cold and that lasts into spring. So we decided to get Major tested for heartworm instead of giving him any meds. We kept him in at dusk and dawn and never went walking except around town on the sidewalks. This worked for years. Never anymore poisons and never any bugs.

We continue every year getting him all his vaccines and the rabies vaccine too. Not thinking that since we stopped the outside chemicals, we should stop the vaccines. I never thought about stopping the poisons being injected into my dog / dogs. I never knew there could be a connection to illness from vaccines

Now fast forward to time to get his vaccines at age 9 years old. Vet suggests he gets Rabies and a combo vaccine to PROTECT him from everything since he is getting older. Of course I want to protect him from Everything, right? So he gets the combo vaccine and Rabies same day of course because I don't want to come back and pay another vet visit bill to get other vaccines. Just do it all at once. (Now knowing how horrible combo vaccines can be to some dogs that can have all types of bad reactions, also not to do rabies vaccine the same visit as other vaccines, Spacing them out would have been better, Titer testing would have been even better.)

Within a few days after vaccines we were outside playing ball with him in the backyard and he never misses the ball and he missed catching the ball. We were shocked. We know he is 9 but he is healthy as a horse. Just went to the vet and the vet agreed. Ok maybe Major had the sun in his eyes, right? It happens to ballplayers all the time. So we call it a night and go into the house and he trips coming into the house. We are like whoa, slow down and thought nothing else about it. This goes on for a week. We take him back to our vet and the vet says… He is BLIND. In a matter of 2 weeks he went blind. The vet called it SARDS. Which can come as an extreme bad reaction or otherwise a result of over vaccinating. The name SARDS is a very vague name too.

Sudden Acquired Retinal Degeneration Syndrome. Vets label it an IDIOPATHIC illness which means they do not know how it happens per se. Some vets label it as an autoimmune disease and where do those come from? Over Vaccinating?
So now I have a blind dog that can not have anti flea/tick meds or heartworm meds or any more vaccines from the vet or he could possibly die. I am so glad I listened to my vet.

NOT!

Well a good thing I stopped listening to my vet about my MAJOR dog. He lived another 3 years. He was fine being blind after the first few weeks. He adjusted very well. I had 2 other dogs at the time about the same size. I had a girl dog that was 90lbs and another male that was 100lbs. All 3 played ball in the backyard. We had to retrain Major to get the ball differently after going blind. We would bounce the ball (a deflated soccer ball) off the fence. He would hear a thud and go searching for it. We used a happy YES YES YES to help him get closer and a quiet no no no when he was cold and nowhere close. He was a happy dog even though he was blind.

I had to make the hardest decision of my life and send my Major to doggie heaven in 2016. He was tired and ready. He will be a dog I will never forget. Major went to heaven in August in 2016 on my (Sheryl) birthday
RIP Major

Mommy and Daddy love you and will always protect our other dogs better because of you. Xoxoxo. Sheryl and Timothy Blanford Romeoville, Illinois

Major

ROMEOVILLE, ILLINOIS

Chapter Twenty-Two

Nina's Story
Debra Malone & Family

In September 2018, I was visiting the Bergen County Animal Shelter in Teterboro NJ, after dropping off donations. I already had 3 rescue pups at home, but I liked to visit the shelter and say hello. In the largest cage, I saw the tiniest little Chihuahua with the saddest eyes, little Nina. On her cage hung a sign that read she needed a hospice home due to the severity of her medical conditions. She had been at the shelter over 6 months, arriving with 40 or so other dogs from a hoarding situation. They estimated she was about 8 years old and the volunteer at her cage said she would likely be put down soon, as she was not really adoptable. I knew in my heart at that moment that wasnt going to happen, because she was coming home with me. The fact that the nationwide "Clear the Shelter" event was that weekend made it seem like fate. Nina came home and thrived almost immediately. She did just fine getting around with the luxating patella of her back legs. We addressed her bad teeth, fatty tumors and weight issue and with love and a safe home, her stress melted away and she came off all heart meds. We were all so happy. She was joyful, always. "Smiled" all day long, sweet little tail wagging. I had a connection with Nina unlike any I've ever had. She never barked at all, just made sweet squeaky noises and eye contact with me, but I always instinctively knew what she wanted. I feel like God brought her to me to help get me through the tragic death of my mom 5 weeks after her adoption. Nina never left my side. She was truly the happiest part of every single day.

On Friday September 18, 2020, I took Nina and my 3 other dogs to a new Vet, after my Vet of 20 years retired. It was meant to be a well visit, nail trim and meet & greet. After looking online, reading reviews and checking the BBB, I decided to try one a few blocks away from my house, the Animal Hospital of Hasbrouck Heights & the owner Dr Mia Frezzo, 180 Boulevard, Hasbrouck Heights NJ. That decision would set in motion a tragedy that would leave Nina dead by Monday September 21. The Vet techs used such force holding down my 8-pound girl, they dislocated Nina's hip & ligament completely on one side. The Vet examined Nina thoroughly and told us Nina's knee had "popped" out during the nail trim due to the Luxating Patella, but with an anti-inflammatory injection and rest, she should be fine. I went home devastated, because I had never seen Nina's leg in that position before, or her in such pain. When it became obvious overnight something much more serious had happened, we went back the next morning and demanded an X-ray, after they ignored the message we left. The X-ray showed the severity of the injury. Dr Frezzo told us she was "sorry for the inconvenience", but we would have to take Nina to Blue Pearl or Oradell Animal Hospital and have Nina sedated to "rotate" the hip back in, something she didn't do at her facility. She whined about how she never had such a "freak" accident at her practice or seen anything like it in 23 years, on and on. We went back and forth with her, yet she never once offered ya any help or to pay for the thousands of dollars she knew it was going to cost to address the injury. We left desperate for help and after 4 hours at Newton Animal Hospital, we were told it was not possible to address an injury like that with just sedation, she needed emergency orthopedic surgery. We spent 2 agonizing days, as Nina suffered unable to move, calling over 30 Emergency facilities in 3 states, looking for anyone with an orthopedist on call that could do the surgery. By the time we finally found a surgeon Monday September 21, Nina's heart rate was erratic from all the stress and pain she suffered for 3 days and she died shortly after being put under anesthesia. I will never forgive myself for taking Nina to these people or get over that my sweet baby waited her entire life to be loved, went through so much to get healthy, only to be robbed of her life and family like this. This Vet never called one time that weekend or Monday to ask how Nina was & called the police to remove us from her office the day after she died on Tuesday, because we challenged the blatantly fabricated medical record of the visit they handed us. She went on to offer free nail trims and raffle prizes if people would go online and give her a good review, after she became aware of the bad reviews about Nina's case. Today, Saturday October 10th, as we protested her practice, she drove into her parking lot laughing at us. I will fight every day to make sure they are held accountable for what they did to Nina and warn as many people as we can so that Nina's death is not in vain. I'm grateful for this book and all the other families like ours, fighting to expose these heartless Veterinarians.

__Nina__

Chapter Twenty-Three

Noah's Story
Tish Ott

I hope our story can be of help to anyone who finds themselves and their beloved pet in our same situation. My name is Tish and my canine companion was Noah, the most lovable, kind, gentle 4 year old, healthy 3 pound black merle chihuahua you could ever meet. He was breathtakingly beautiful on the outside with a soul to match on the inside. Noah had never been to the vet other than his puppy shots, neuter and yearly check ups. Never was sick a day in his life. Our terrible nightmare began on August 8, 2020 when he had some nausea and would not eat and I took him to our current vet of 2 and a half years at the time. It all began on August 8th, Saturday and tragically ended on August 16th, Sunday. I am speaking out because I want to be the voice for my innocent boy he had no voice, he could not cry out for help. I owe this to him to keep his memory always alive and to all the animals that may be put in the same tragic situation.

August 8th he was at my vet presenting nausea and no appetite, she told me not to worry at all.

August 10th, he began to worsen in the middle of the night in which I took him to the local ER. They did extensive blood work and x rays and since my vet was opening in about 2 hours, I was going to continue treatment immediately over there. Took him, and the vet went with the pancreatitis diagnosis and bean treatment, I did not find out til days later that the x rays had shown possible obstruction, not clear. So I was under the assumption we were treating a tiny chihuahua for pancreatitis. He stayed from 8 am to 7 pm for treatment, iv fluids and anti-nausea meds. I picked him up at close and due to the pandemic, everything was curbside. He was very weak and would not eat at all, but they told me pancreatitis can be rough on these little guys.

August 11th, I dropped him off at opening, picked him up at the end of the day and he was very lethargic, I questioned everything to the vet techs in the a.m. and p.m. same answer, give it time. I took him home and he was so weak, no food or water, they told me not to worry because he was on iv fluids.

August 12th, when the tech came out, I told her he was not pooping at all, not eating and so weak, same answer, give it time, problem was I trusted them and I had never experienced pancreatitis with any of my babies, but I told her I think he needs to get an ultrasound from a specialist because something is not right. He went in for his daily all-day treatments, they said he ate a tiny bit, a little better, however when I got him home he was not lifting his head, not eating and no pooping. I was very concerned.

August 13th, 4th day at the hospital, I called before coming to clinic and said I was so concerned about a dark green vomit he produced, tech took it in and told me the vet said it was diarrhea, but dark green I am wondering? Ended up being vomit, they also gave him an enema which was not the right protocol for what was really taking place. I picked him up and still felt he was so off, they told me give it time. Each night I would take him home and just rock him and cuddle him praying to God he would get better as they said he would. Through all of this I heard very little directly from the 2 vets that were caring for him, mostly communication as techs would bring him out.

August 14th, 5th day, 11 hour stay in hospital, and he was till barely eating for me and very lethargic. People were telling me pancreatitis can take a toll, it can take time to get better, be patient. The owner of the practice would be there on Saturday and had not been there the entire week, so I was looking forward to speaking to her in the a.m.

August 15th, Saturday, So once again I dropped him off at 8am and spoke to tech, first time I had been inside in days. I told the tech he is so sick, what has his temperature been each day, my God, there were no temps taken, really? I had her take it while I was there and he was in hypothermia, I almost flipped. Doctor told me they would warm him up and continue all protocol for pancreatitis. I told her to call me at work immediately if he gets even worse, I left there hoping things would maybe begin to upswing. I received no phone call the entire day and when I went to pick him up at close, the vet told me he was significantly worse, why wasn't I called like I asked. She appeared somewhat frantic, she proceeded to show me blood work she drew, x rays she took and pulled out her phone and showed me the dozens of text messages back and forth between her and the other 2 vets that treated him all week, really??? It took this long for them to become concerned? She brought him out and he was in bad shape, they called the specialists for an ultrasound at the specialist 45 minutes away, I grabbed him and bolted with him to the car, probably drove close to 100 miles an hour on the highway trying to get him there. Wait until you hear this, as I am driving I get a text message from his vet stating, Hi Tish, this is Dr. so and so, do you think Noah might have a blockage in his stomach??? SERIOUSLY????? you are asking me? I asked the tech days ago for an ultrasound. He was an indoor dog, but it was possible, piece of a toy, anything really. I never responded I was so shocked. He had the ultrasound, sure enough he had a blockage. They did not have the specific surgeon for this issue so then I had to transport him to a very well-known vet surgery center and ER in the area. They took him immediately and the surgeon had to come because it was the middle of the night, early morning Sunday. The surgeon was amazing and after examining him told me what he would have to do, surgery would take a few hours, I told him do whatever you have to do to save him. It was a very serious situation.

August 16th, Sunday morning, the surgeon finally calls, Noah, tiny weak Noah made it thru the big surgery, but he said it was the worst-case scenario he had mentioned to me he could find before going in. He removed the foreign object but at this time could not even tell what it was, and his colon was proliferated in many, many places, but sepsis had set in because he was misdiagnosed, and that toxic object was in his intestines so long. He said he is in recovery awake from sedation, maybe you will be able to come by a little later. A few hours later the ER doctor called me and said Noah had a stroke, is paralyzed and has gone blind during recovery, he is actively dying. I could not breath, I told him to tell him to wait for me I was coming. We bolted in the car, and he was alive when I got there, he waited, but was in so much pain. I put my body next to him and told him how much I loved him as I kissed his face, he knew I was there. We euthanized him minutes later to take him out of this horrendous torture. My boy was gone, my beautiful innocent, precious angel succumbed to sepsis because of the vet clinics misdiagnosis and the lack of urgency to check for a foreign object.

August 19th, I met with one of the vets because I wanted to know why???? When I asked why didn't you follow up on the x ray stating possible obstruction and her answer was I went with the pancreatitis diagnosis that was on there too, I'm sorry and that was it!

Early September, a friend told me of a group called Joey's Legacy-Vet Mal Victims. I was in contact with the founder Scott Fine who could not have been more compassionate and helpful. He put me in contact with a vet who read my story and said I may have a legitimate case. Then Scott gave me the name of a top attorney who handles injustice towards animals, and he said I had a case and we won the case against the vet. I got justice for my beautiful boy, I owed it to him to not give up the fight, I wasn't going to. And this book, what an honor, now his story is forever printed and told and perhaps the story of his unfair death can help others in the future, a dog or cat that may have the same symptoms. I want to be the voice for these animals that cannot speak and cry out for help.

It was an honor and a blessing to spend 4 years of my life journey with this incredible little guy that taught me how beautiful unconditional love is. Thank you to all of you reading our story.

Noah

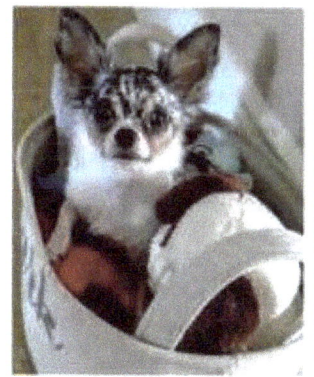

Chapter Twenty-Four

Ollie's Story
Jeremy Cohen, Attorney

Ollie's Plight

The mission when I opened Boston Dog Lawyers in 2016 was to be a law practice focused on the rights of pet owners. It was my understanding that there were plenty of legal advocates for the rights of animals and certainly legislative lobbyists that were far more connected than I. I have worked hard to stay true to our mission, not because I don't love animals but because I am working in a very neglected area of the law that needs our attention. I believe that if the firm expands to animal rights and animal welfare, I am risking the longevity and legacy of a law practice dedicated to pet owners' rights. Lobbying and legislating just weren't for me. Until . . .

I learned of Ollie's plight while he was still alive, clinging to survival after being mauled at a doggy day care facility in western Mass. Nearly $20,000 later, he ultimately lost the battle for life; however, what he is accomplishing through his death will be the reason he ends up so famous.

Ollie's owner is a client of ours. Like most of us pet owners, she brought her dog to a daycare believing that after so many years in business, they had all the safety measures necessary to keep her dog safe. Surely, they would keep big dogs and puppies like Ollie separated. They would have adequate staffing ratios and well-trained employees. They would have the tools necessary to break up a dog fight and of course keep accurate records of what dogs were visiting at a particular time. And, of course, they would be properly licensed and inspected by the town and the state within which they operated. To all of these assumptions I can declare *no, no, a thousand times no*!

Most states do not regulate boarding facilities and doggy day care centers. It is a wild west right in the middle of our cities and towns' and injuries and deaths are occurring at an unacceptable rate. Our clients, Ben, Gabby, Lily, Miley, Pebbles, and Suki have all suffered at the hands of day care facilities.

The theme through these cases is that all had to be hard fought to compel the pet businesses to take accountability.

As a result of the courage of our clients who have been great teammates in these fights, we have found some successes as we are on a mission for accountability. Now, outside the courtroom we are striving for similar results.

I am part of a 15-member team trying to get "Ollie's Law" passed. The legislation is now drafted to start regulating doggie day care and boarding facilities in Massachusetts. While a bill is presented every year for this to the state legislature (and fails), it has never been the product of a task force like this one. The goal is to have businesses who care for our pets, be licensed at the state level and be subject to easily understandable regulations and requirements. Those who push back will reveal themselves to have agendas that are simply incompatible with a healthy lifestyle for our pets. A bill like this should not take courage to pass yet it will require it. It will take hundreds of hours of telling Ollie's story and of pressuring legislators to take it seriously.

At Boston Dog Lawyers, we are the regulators in the absence of regulators. Unfortunately, like many lawyers, we tend to be called upon only after something bad has happened. It is time to get out ahead of it. We now offer free safety training sessions to doggie day cares which include a client of ours sharing their story and an expert of ours sharing their knowledge. You, too, can become a regulator by having the courage to seek information before you entrust people with your dog's life. Pet owners should feel empowered when interviewing a day care manager to decide whether their pet will be safe there. Feel comfortable asking some form of the questions below.

- Do you have a fire safety plan and has your staff practiced it?
- Does someone stay overnight with the boarded dogs?
- What is the experience level of the staff?
- Are you affiliated with a nearby vet in case of emergency care?
- What is the fewest amount of employees working at any one time?
- If someone calls out sick, do you call for a substitute worker?
- When was Animal Control last here and why?
- How many dogs have been injured on the premises this year?
- Show me your tools for breaking up a dog fight.
- Show me your current declarations page of your insurance policy.
- How many injury claims by clients in the last 3 years?
- Do you hold any staff trainings and are they documented?

- o   Show me where you keep dogs of different sizes separate.
- o   Is your AC/Heating system working? You sure?

Then, call the local animal control officer or police chief and ask if they have received any complaints about the facility or had to go there on a call and whether they would bring their own dog there.

We must be diligent when it comes to doggie day cares because right now, the *law* is not.

Ollie

Lilly

Chapter Twenty-Five

PINTA'S STORY
Maribella Perez

My Little Companion, Pwetty Girl, Princi. My little Girlie, My best friend called her Pinturia!

My feisty Jack Russell Terrier!

Aug 19, 2003 - Jan 01, 2020

She was 16 years old with diabetes and blind. Perfect hearing.

I took Pinta to her vet, Dr. Steve McColman on Dec.9, 2019. I noticed slight stuffiness in her nose and being diabetic, any sort of irregularity, I immediately took her to the vet. He stated her lung airways clear and gave her an antibiotic for her stuffy nose. He did blood work and stated all looked good except for some elevation of her liver. This also occurred when she was diagnosed with diabetes over 2 years ago. He prescribed Denamarin. It cured her back then. Otherwise, "All looked good." the Dr. said.

On Dec. 25, 2019, Pinta didn't eat all day. I immediately took her to LeadER Animal Specialty Hospital in Cooper City, FL. This is the hospital I took her to for all Emergency after hours care. Let me go back…

On May 29, 2018, I took her to LeadER Animal Specialty Hospital due to a mass on her belly that grew over time. This hospital was recommended by Pinta's vet. One day I noticed it was getting hard for her to breathe and she stopped eating. I called and was given an appointment with a surgeon. Dr Jason E. Horgan. She needed surgery 'today' and I thanked God for him because I knew if she didn't get it removed that day, she was going to die. It was a successful surgery.
I used to recommend this hospital to everyone. They were expensive but had just about all you could need for any type of emergency. I trusted this hospital implicitly since that day Dr. Horgan performed her surgery. He didn't delay and that saved her life.

On Dec. 25, 2019, Pinta hadn't eaten all day, and I observed a slight stuffy nose. It was at 1:30 am, Dec. 26, 2019, when Dr. Kate Spahn did a CBC and told me if next day she still hadn't eaten to bring her back within 24 hours. She gave her an antibiotic shot and gave Mirtazapine, an appetite stimulant.

Next day, still being Dec. 26, 2019, Pinta did not eat, was drinking well, and was not dehydrated. When I got to ER, I could see she was stressed. This was a 45 min drive at 10 pm. She hated going to vets, any kind of vets. She gets nervous and anxious. Being blind, she starts pacing back and forth and slightly bumping into things, but she is smart, she slow paces and she remembers her surroundings after a few round about turns and bumps.

Dr. Spahn tells me she has small amount ketones, suspect early DKA and she will be placed on IV fluids. I agreed to admit her into the ER. When she was placed in the cage, the first thing I noticed is they had many animals to tend to. Christmas time and most of the cages were full. The nurse was cleaning the cage beneath Pinta's and was out of breath and appeared tired.

On Pinta's first day there, I spoke to Dr. Phillips by phone and he told me all her meds she was getting and what they were for.

On Dec. 27, 2019, Dr. Clay Phillips mentioned her glucose was high, moderate ketones. She was not eating but was barking a LOT. They placed a urinary catheter. She barked 4 straight hours! I was concerned as I could see she was extremely anxious and agitated. I asked him to give her a tranquilizer. He said he needed her awake to try to get her to eat and it would outweigh the benefits to monitor her and if sleeping, she wouldn't eat. I uneasily agreed for 2 days. She was always barking when I saw her and at night when I called the hospital to check on her.

I also noticed that up on her cage where her name tag is located, it said, diabetic, blind, deaf in both ears.

I spoke to the nurse to correct that, as she was NOT deaf. She said ok but didn't do anything. My son actually had to have Dr. Phillips come over and he didn't look too pleased to have to do this now, but it was important because Pinta responded when talked to. Yes, even with her mild dementia. (I had not been aware of her having mild dementia, he mentioned he saw signs.)

Dr. Phillips told me that some of her electrolytes were elevated.

Blood had started to collect in the catheter from constant pacing and every day thereafter, I asked them to flush it out every day when I visited until her last day of her life, blood is in the catheter.

On Dec.28, 2019, when I went to visit Pinta, she was barking, panting, breathing heavily, shaking and I felt she might have a heart attack! I asked her nurse to bring her to a private room. It took me 90 min. of petting and talking to her to calm her. Then she fell asleep.
I told Dr. Phillips she had been given a tranquilizer by her vet and I wanted her on it. He was adamant saying that wasn't a good idea.
I knew she would not eat if she was not relaxed and was anxious. It would relax her and she would sleep 3 or 4 hours. She had recently been given it after our move to another home.
This conversation took place daily with Dr. Phillips. One time he was talking to me about it then said, "We've already been through this conversation", he was agitated and then abruptly said he had another patient to tend to and left the room!
Next day, same thing, she was out of breath, barking, panting, shaking! I had her nurse bring her to a private room. Mind you, the blood is in the catheter from her pacing.
I talked to her and pet her to sleep. At one point, Savannah, her nurse came in and said to me that without the Dr's permission she couldn't give Pinta anything to tranquilize her. Savannah was aware of these episodes and would bring Pinta in a small cart into the room for me to calm her down.

The actual paperwork of her hour-by-hour daily list and her clinical summary are difficult to interpret. I notice they change shifts every 12 hours. I can see she had Dr. Sandra Buckweitz on a shift as well as Dr. Kate Spahn.
On her last day she had Russell Miller DVM, who is now at Creekside Pet Care Center, TX.
The rest of the times it was Dr. Phillips.
None of them noticed the agitated state Pinta was in?

I only encountered Dr. Phillips when I visited Pinta. I went every day. On Dec.29, 2019, It is noted under Assessments: Diabetes Mellitus. Some Dementia, Anxiety. It is acknowledged she has anxiety, yet nothing is given to help this anxiety.

She was syringe fed baby food. I saw she slowly ate through syringe but by next day stopped.

Dec.30, 2019, Dr. Phillips mentioned that her ketones were gone and I could take her home the next day Dec.31.2019. But her electrolytes were out of range. She still was not eating nor with syringe.

I said, "If she is not eating and her electrolytes are elevated, she will die. Her vet is away on vacation for 2 more days. She will die at home." He agreed. I requested to let her stay until her vet came back. He agreed. Then he suggested placing an NG tube.

On Dec.31, 2019, they inserted the NG tube and I felt relieved thinking maybe this nutrition would get her strength up, maybe help her electrolytes. I felt optimistic.

1. I expressed daily concern that Pinta was not given some sort of tranquilizer to calm her. There are notes written she has anxiety. I understand some barking for 1-2 days but when it reaches the point of tremors, panting, breathing heavily, shaking, you realize this is NOT a normal situation. She is suffering. This is an elderly blind dog. ALL the time, I feel she is treated as a young dog. I found out after she died and I researched the effects of anxiety, barking, shaking, panting, will also affect her glucose, electrolytes, mental condition and can cause a variety of other things. Why allow an elderly dog bark and pace out of the norms?

2. Her glucose records show high then low, then high daily. Dextrose given. Her glucose was not under control. It's known STRESS is a contributing factor to elevations and high elevations can cause seizures.

3. A few days earlier, Dr. Phillips had told me she would be able to go home within 2 days as he noticed the DKA almost gone. I agreed. Two days later he said, "Because of her electrolytes, let's wait." I agreed. Now, why was he willing to let her go home Dec. 31 in this condition? She was not eating and electrolytes abnormal. That's when I requested her to stay more days.

4. The Doctor started her on the NG tube feeding which is a tube inserted thru her nose that carries nutrients and medicine to the stomach. I realize later that as she is already stressed, Pinta can experience further significant stress and discomfort and certainly try to remove it as she does with her catheter. No mention was given to administer either pain med or tranquilizer.

5. Along with her NG tubing Pinta is given 2 other meds. One of those meds I have found out is not FDA approved. I've recently seen reports showing animals have DIED from this medication. She was given 2 injections of Metronidazole, one on Dec.31, 2019 at 4pm and one on Jan

1, 2020 at 4am. She had a seizure on Jan. 1, 2020. This medicine should have been discussed with me in detail. I would not have approved the Metronidazole medication that is still not FDA approved! I don't know how her body would react to it.

6. Why concerned that a tranquilizer will knock Pinta out and she won't eat and yet 2 of her meds given daily has a side effect of decrease in appetite and now I wonder why she was not given Mirtazapine to increase appetite. This is the med given for her when I initially brought her to the ER for not eating.

7. Why suddenly decide on giving her daily full lab work rechecks on Dec. 31, 2019, when I had asked previously about doing more extensive lab works and this was not considered. Daily full lab works detect more accurately what all her current levels are.

8. I have spent endless hours researching all electrolytes mentioned that were affected. Mild hypernatremia, (Imbalances in water and sodium that occur from either water loss or sodium gain, often in the presence of inadequate water intake and makes them thirsty) Mild hypokalemia (low potassium in blood) and Mild hyperchloremia (Too much chloride in blood)

9. Since they put in catheter from day 2, how does one know the actual urine water output vs. the blood that was constantly in her catheter and how would this affect her.

10. The ER was pretty full of animals, did they have an adequate number of medical personnel, I wonder.

11. On day 6, going onto day 7, her medical records show a constant barking throughout the day. It's written 12-x. Panting is also written. Her glucose levels for Dec. 31, 2019 through Jan 1, 2020 show very high levels during the 12-hour shift. Vetsulin was given 2-x at low dose units. I was giving her 5.5 units at home, they were aware of this. She had fever at 11:00am. Nothing shows anything is given for fever nor discussed with me when I arrived. All this, they allowed.

On Jan. 1, 2020, at 11:00 am, I received a phone call from Dr. Russell Miller saying Pinta had a seizure and to come quick!
I got there around 12 pm. It is a drive of 45 min. Dr. Miller said this was not a good sign and that he gave her diazepam and I should consider putting her to sleep.

(After she passed, I looked up articles regarding seizures) Quote: "Several seizures in a row or a seizure that lasts longer than 5 minutes is considered an emergency that can be life threatening. More than 3 seizures in a 24- hr. period is also an urgent matter that requires a trip to the vet right away." No where did they say euthanize after a first seizure.

While he is talking to me in front of her cage he says "Oh, she is having another one!" I didn't see anything. He said, "It's a focal seizure, a nose twitch." He pulls a syringe out of his pocket and administers a dose of diazepam. He told me this was her third seizure. Her medical records show 2-x he gave Pinta diazepam.

I asked him what can be done besides the diazepam? "Nothing" he says. "Whenever she gets a seizure, we give diazepam. There is nothing else that can be done. She is suffering."

I said, "No, I want to wait and see if her body relaxes and responds with the diazepam."

He leaves me standing in front of her cage. I'm praying, begging for guidance, crying. I tell Pinta,
"THIS is what it took to get your tranquilizer, my little girl" This, the first time I see her actually sleeping peacefully.

I always prayed I never wanted to be placed in a position to put her to sleep. I remember seeing a lady at my vet's office holding her dog and crying. After some time, I asked my vet what was wrong? He tells me she had to put her dog to sleep. I feel so sorry as I'm in the next examining room with Pinta all hyped up and I am just hearing her cry. She was alone.

After a long while, Dr. Miller comes and takes me in a room. I'm sitting there and every so often, he comes or sends the nurse to see me. Every time I ask, "What else can be done?" "Nothing" he says. He comes back and again, I ask, "What can be done? Are you sure? There must be something. I don't want to put her to sleep." I asked so many times. "There must be something that can be done. Let me wait and see what happens."

He tells me"You know, there are hospitals that when there is nothing more that can be done, they give the dog to its owner and the owner takes the dog home." I just looked at him. "But we don't do that here."

I say to him "That is a hurtful thing to say. That is not appropriate." He semi acknowledged and looked away.

I know he is rushing me. I feel it. Whatever for? If I wanted her to stay more days, then let it be.

Eventually I believed there was nothing else that could be done for her. That she is mentally gone. She will not be the same. He told me this. I truly regret not staying there longer, even overnight. I'd always thought my Angel would die in my arms when the time came. Not put her to sleep. I got there at 12pm and 3pm she was put to sleep. They wheeled her in a small cart with her catheter still on her. I braced my arms around her. She was breathing comfortably. I regret not picking her up. I regret not waiting for another day. I regret believing him. I regret ever having taken her there.

Under Plans section in her medical records, 01/01/2020 at 9:17am Russell Miller, DVM, wrote:

"Discussed w/owner need to correct the hypernatremia (potential cause of seizure vs. neoplasia) P needs advance imaging and is not currently stable.

P suffering currently getting diazepam and needs long-acting seizure meds. Advised either further treatment or humane euthanasia because p is suffering.

O elected for humane euthanasia."

1. Why is the time 9:17am when I got there at 12:00pm?
2. Diazepam was given at 11:00am and at 12:00pm

Never did he say she needs long-acting seizure meds. Never advised further treatment. Only euthanasia. He misled me.

I also asked about doing a necropsy. I wanted to know what had caused her death. He said "No," (he advised not to get, saying it wouldn't reveal anything) "and this is Jan 1, no one is going to come down since no one is open." Months later, I enquired with a lab that does necropsies. A necropsy can always be done. No-one can pre-determine what it reveals. If it's a holiday, the body would be picked up the following day.

Dr. Russell Miller doesn't begin to realize what he did by rushing me to euthanize my girl after having had 2 seizures. He took away my chance of seeing what was going on with her. Most seizures do not have a detrimental effect on the brain. The nose twitch, he gave her diazepam. I did not see a nose twitch. I was standing there. Did it actually happen, I question this.

The diazepam is a tranquilizer. Had she been left to finally rest as she so desperately needed, she would have responded one way or another and they would notice abnormalities or whatever else presented itself.

Was she given diazepam as soon as she had her first seizure or was she seizing for minutes before he noticed? Her nose twitch was so minimal, I didn't see it. These things I now question because of his urgency to euthanize her. He knew I didn't agree nor want to euthanize. She was sleeping peacefully with the diazepam. I believed and trusted in him.

Dr. Russell Miller had no respect what I, the owner wanted for Pinta nor respect for my own piece of mind. I had signed the form to provide Emergency Stabilization to Pinta. In the event that CPR is required, I authorized them to YES, give her CPR. My intention was always to allow her to live no matter what.

My allowing this euthanasia has devastated me beyond words. I live with guilt. It has left my heart crushed and shattered to pieces. There are no words to describe it. I feel she was 'taken' from me. I have dreamt it, Taken.

(I recall after taking Pinta home from her mass surgery on May 31, 2018, her left leg was swollen. I called the hospital and asked if she had a fall or something happened while there. "NO." I was told. Something must have happened in that ER to have her leg swell up. I put ice on and off for several days before the swelling slowly went down. She had a catheter placed on her during her stay. At home, it slowly seemed her urine was starting to change in color.
By June 15, 2018, I noticed blood in her urine. Red blood. I went to the hospital and was told, "Urinary Infection" The Dr. gave her an antibiotic injection. I believe this was caused by the catheter from her ER stay during surgery. Infection took place.

I looked at Pinta's notes from that initial surgery today. I quote, "On 5/30/18 it is noted patient awake, moaning, vocal paddling to try and stand up, once you talk and touch her, she settles down."
She is blind but not deaf and whoever attended her that day, I express intense appreciation, because Pinta can hear and is responsive. This is the kind of treatment that makes all the difference!!!)

I understand Pinta may have died and complications may arise even with the very best care available. It is for this reason I brought her into the ER the same day she did not eat. I never let any condition escalate.

After about a week, I spoke to the Medical Director personally. (I found out he was Dr. Horgan, the doctor that saved Pinta's life the day I brought her in for her surgery in 2018)
I couldn't get over the fact that her death could not have been avoided. He's looking at her records and going over Physical Exam: based on her medical records of Dec.27, 2019.
He goes over a written note by Dr. Phillips. Under the heading of Neurologic: Not really mentally appropriate. Barks at times and then is very quiet at times. Dr. Horgan tells me, "Neurologic means something in the brain, like a meningitis." I asked what could have been done to confirm. "Spinal tap."
Our conversation continues.
I ask Dr. Horgan, "Can electrolyte imbalance be caused through glucose?" "Sure, Dr. Horgan says. "You give insulin, give the fluids, monitor the electrolytes, keep stable as possible. That's how it works. I've done this for many, many years."

I tell him, "Calm her down, that's really a concern I had. She was barking a lot, I asked Dr. Phillips to give her something to calm her down. He was against it. She was so upset; she was shaking and I'm sure that's going to affect her electrolytes." "Of course." he says. "And her glucose?" I ask. "Absolutely" he responds. I continue, "He didn't feel it was the right thing to do to calm her down. Every time I saw her, she was barking and whenever I called to check in on her, I was told most of the time that she was vocalizing/barking." He asked, "Did she bark at home?" I responded, "Never."

Pinta was nervous and anxious since I brought her in to the ER. Being this upset will cause her to pace and being blind, she can't see her surroundings- makes it all the worse. She paces when nervous, she paces when in pain. When she had her mass surgery in 2018, it's written in her chart, she was pacing. Adding to the pacing is her excessive barking. I would expect it to cause her to also tire out and act inappropriate.

When initially seen on Dec. 26, 2019, Dr. Spahn had written: Alert and appropriate, cranial nerves intact, normal gait.

I believe had she been able to get rest, she would have reacted much differently than Dr. Phillips notes and her chances of survival been a lot better.

Final Thoughts and Advice:

I have read many sites that ER's and vets do not treat elderly dogs right. There are too many to include all. I looked previously at the reviews on Yelp for LeadER Animal Specialty Hospital, I saw a very negative review on Jan.6, 2021, and there are negative reviews throughout. I see they are not there anymore. Other negative reviews come and go. Interesting to note.

Another site, "The entire staff needs to be trained on how to handle a senior dog with dementia and especially one showing such obvious distress."

On another it says, "I took my senior to 3 vets and all they talked about was quality of life, instead of trying to get her better. They didn't even care because my pets were old. It seems as if the vets only want to take care of young animals and have no concern for the elderly ones."

1. All who read this story, please be aware and cautious after your pet reaches maturity. In my experience, Vets will NOT tend to them as the elder pet needs to be treated.
Based on my experience I will never again trust in an ER they will get proper treatment, nor due care. And compassion to your elderly pet, very slim to none.

2. I advise if you are not satisfied with the treatment your pet receives to have them write it in the medical records. This provides notice to the next Dr. on call of your situation and focuses more attention to your concern. It also provides evidence if something should happen to your pet.

3. Another recommendation is speaking to the Head ER Dr. if you don't feel comfortable with medical procedures being given to your pet. I found out later there was a Head ER Dr. and had I spoken to her, I feel Pinta would have received better care.

It has been over a year since my little girl was taken from me. I believe she suffered needlessly for 7 days. Tortured, I will say. Barking hysterically for hours while no one listened.

I am devastated, depressed, and my heart, broken in pieces. My life is not the same.

I miss her dearly. I think of her all the time and how she must have felt in a strange place and scared. Barking all the time for attention, feeling sick and most likely in pain.

I love you, my little companion. I miss you, my Angel.
I used to sing to her all the time. A little made up song. "Pinta's such a pwetty girl, yes she is, yes she is."

They say Pinta had mild dementia. When I talked to her she responded. Her ears twitched. I'd say, "Let's go for a walk" and up she was. Slowly, but she got there.

Bless you, my Pinta.

Pinta

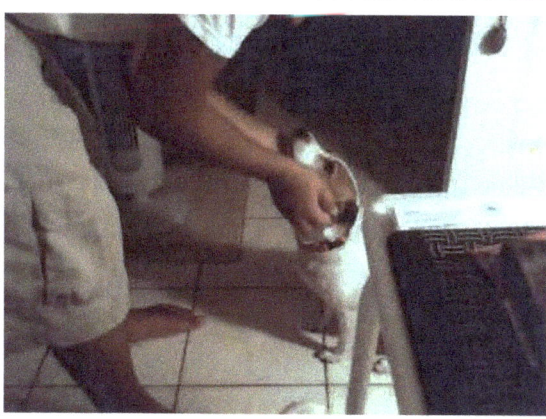

Chapter Twenty-Six

PRESSLEY'S STORY
Susan Stranger

The morning of June 10th, 2020, Pressley, our sweet little boy Chow mix, age 6, was not his usual energetic self. He'd thrown up the night before, but seemed fine after. He got up a couple times throughout the night for some water and to go pee. When he didn't want to eat that morning my 21 year old daughter, Kaycie, offered to take him to the vet. We didn't think it was going to be anything serious. The plan was for her to drop him off and then come back for me. Things quickly took a turn for the worst.

The first vet she took him to had noticed something we didn't. There was a pale yellow tinge to his eyes. She advised my daughter to get him emergency care and my daughter did just that. It was only about a ten minute drive, but by the time she had gotten him there, he had become acutely lethargic. They took him back right away and stabilized him. He was given fluid, antibiotics, and antinausea meds. She called to let me know what was going on and was going to pick me up while they ran tests. She called them from the parking lot to let them know she'd be right back, at which point they suggested she take him for an abdominal ultrasound and said he wouldn't be much longer. When he came out, he was active and happy again. She decided to take him for the ultrasound on her way back since everything seemed ok.

After dropping him off, she went back to her place to wait, a less than 5 minute drive away. About an hour later, she received a call back saying he was fine and ready to be picked up. She called and relayed the message. We were on the phone less than a minute when the vet called back, now saying he was spontaneously bleeding from both sides of his nose and it could indicate liver failure or clotting issues.

She switched back over to me in tears telling me what they said and that he might not make it. I remember hearing her crying, saying over and over again "I don't know what happened; they just told me he was fine."

She was there in probably less than five minutes, according to her estimate. When she got there, she saw no blood anywhere on him or on or near his nose. No wet fur indicating he had been cleaned off either. Surely my dog would've sneezed or pawed his nose. I just don't see how it's possible to stop a spontaneous double nosebleed in such a short period of time with no evidence of. This was all unbeknownst to me at the time. My daughter didn't question her and took her back to the E.R.

The ER vet cut right to the chase with my daughter, gave her a $4,800 estimate --the cost of keeping Pressley alive. He needed some more tests and a life saving plasma transfusion, possibly several at additional costs. She let them know she was going to have to talk it over with me and came and picked me up. When we got there, they allowed us to come in and meet with the doctor. The first words out of her mouth were to my daughter asking if she had a chance to go over the estimate with me. She told them she hadn't and let her break it to me. I got the estimate before I even knew how he was doing, or what was wrong with him. So, I asked and the answer I received left me with more questions than answers. I was told he had "hepatitis" and by hepatitis, she said she meant liver inflammation, not the viral kind humans get and the cause unknown. Four possibilities were presented: an acute poisoning, chronic liver disease turned acute, a bacterial infection or leptospirosis. I couldn't understand why with four possibilities, each having a different treatment plan, how it was determined a transfusion with a 50/50 survival rate was his only hope. How is nothing but inflammation able to be determined from a complete blood count, urinalysis and physical exam? The way it was described, it didn't even sound like a diagnosis; it sounded more like a symptom to me. How the hell can I make an informed decision based on that? I didn't like either option. I felt he had the same 50/50 odds at home with the given causes and decided if he was going to pass, I'd want him to be comfortable, surrounded by people who loved him. She was clearly bothered by my decision. She left and slammed the door on her way out to bring Press in. I was expecting him to be rolled in on a bed with an IV or something, the way his condition had been described, but he came leaping up on me when he saw me, all happy wagging his tail. He didn't resemble a sick dog in need of a life saving plasma transfusion, not that night anyway, hopefully not any night. I thought plasma transfusions were for critically ill patients or emergencies. I still didn't know what was wrong with him, but the Doc had to get one more last nasty dig in before we left and screamed "You take him home tonight, he will bleed out and die!" She put his discharge papers and antibiotics on the counter before slamming the door again. When we were about to walk out the front door, the receptionist came running up behind us and handed me a list of crematory services. Probably part of their training and routine to distressed pet parents who decline service.

When we got home, I started looking over his discharge papers. There was 10 different issues written under his "Problem & Assessment" list; 11 if you count the one that was hidden behind a staple I found two weeks later. I hadn't been told about any of them, only his hepatitis and was clueless at the time as to what any of them meant.

I went through the same thing with the ultrasound report. Couldn't understand any of it, but could tell his gallbladder was affected. It was moderately distended and filled with a good amount of bile sludge and an emerging mucocele. I didn't know the clinical significance of it or how or if it was related to his hepatitis, so I called them hoping to gain a better understanding. The response I got was anything but helpful. When I asked what it meant, I was told in a very nasty tone; "IT MEANS YOU NEED MORE TESTING!" I was at a loss for words and said the first thing that came to mind; that he seemed to be doing fine. Wrong thing to have said because I was told "Well, that's what happens, and then a week later, they take a turn for the worst and die!"

I literally had nowhere else to turn for answers or deciphering his lab results that I'd already paid for. I had very little money at the time to pay anyone else. Even if I did, I wouldn't know who to trust. These negative experiences changed my whole outlook not on the industry itself, but in humanity as a whole. Perfect example of why I like dogs better than most people.

I read and reread his discharge papers and blood count using reputable websites for reference. Although his sonogram states a mucocele was present, his discharge papers say the complete opposite. So I have two different vets, one a radiologist had interpreted the results of and the other a liver specialist who said no mucocele was present. I didn't think either of them had been 100% forthcoming about everything, so I didn't know what to believe, but don't think they can both be right. In fact, his gallbladder wasn't even mentioned in his discharge papers. I don't know how it couldn't be relevant; it might not be but had no one to answer any questions I had.

His diet in his discharge papers reads "whatever diet Pressley would like to it." I took that to mean she doesn't care and there was no hope for him anyway. When I started learning what was on his paperwork a little bit better, I realized just how little care was actually put into it. His urinalysis had the results of his bloodwork mixed in with it. In fact, the only thing I felt she put care into was describing the plasma transfusion as a possibility, and if indicated, which was not at all what she had told me and my daughter.

He didn't show any other signs of illness besides that first night, and over time, his jaundice cleared. I remained hopeful that it had been an infection or a toxin that had resolved. Then, in late October, I saw the telltale sign of orange colored pee and my heart sank.

During the course of the summer I had managed to find a vet I felt optimistic about and brought him in right away. It pained me not to be able to go back with him but was very detailed filling out his paperwork and even verbally told the two vet techs who came out to the car, he was on a very specific human grade organic diet. They told me they'd take good care of him before taking him back. The vet brought him back out when he was done and gave me hope in what I had thought was a hopeless situation. She wrote him a script for Urso a bile flow enhancer saying it could help him and to call if I had any questions. When we got home, my dog got sick and vomited up a huge amount of cat food (I could tell by the smell) and then a huge amount of dog food. I was devastated besides being mad as hell. As I began taking care of him, my friend who'd gone with me called them up to confront the situation. I was expecting a denial or maybe to hear he hadn't been watched, but heard her through the phone in a heavy Southern accent, clear as day say "Well, he was hungry!" I couldn't believe they were defending their actions or even admitting to it. Neither one of them saw a problem with it and the one had been a vet tech for twenty years!

Pressley passed a few weeks later on November 19th, 2020. I later found out the medication prescribed was contraindicated if an obstruction was present.

I've been going over his results for over a year now, hoping to find some sort of answers and if anything, learn about the disease that took my boy's life. On the one year mark of when he first fell ill, I believe one of those answers might have come.

He had cholestasis, or a slowing of bile flow, which resulted in a blockage or near blockage somewhere in his bile duct(s). Why this had never been mentioned, I don't know. The vet who confirmed it also told me it wasn't anything significant. I don't understand how it could not be or why it would've been left off of his report since it was in his blood work they drew. Everything I've read says it absolutely is important and an emergency. Why couldn't this have been presented for more testing to find out where it was and a treatment plan for that put in place? I don't understand how that and his gallbladder are just dismissed. Wouldn't the sludge in his gallbladder and the distention be evidence of impaired bile flow? Perhaps there's answers that when explained would make sense, I really don't know. I've had to accept I may never know and that some questions will likely remain unanswered.

Press was my first and only dog. I had originally got him for my daughter from an ad on Craigslist advertising him as a purebred Corgi. I took the two hour drive to go pick him up, which ended up being more of a rescue than anything. Four puppies about two months old were penned up in the hot Florida sun, with no food or water. All of them had fleas, eye and ear infections, and from what the "breeder" told me, survived off scraps of bologna. I remember when I picked Press up for the first time, my lifelong fear of dogs melted away. I had tears in my eyes when I held him that day and remember telling him he was rescuing me.

In Memory of Pressley Stanger 08/20/2013- November 19, 2020

Chapter Twenty-Seven

RANGER - My Big Red Dog

Joette Gaccione Tindell

Anyone who knows anything about dogs recalls the children's book and television series "Clifford - The Big Red Dog!" It's a beautiful story about a young girl named Emily Elizabeth, and her humongous, enormously big, red dog. He makes Birdwell Island a better place to live with his kindness and assistance to others. He is a friend to all and is always by Emily Elizabeth's side to lend a faithful paw, or ear. Clifford is so huge because the love she has for him makes him grow so big! He charmed children into adulthood adoring dogs and, singing the theme song at the top of their lungs, they declared their overwhelming love of Clifford, the Big Red Dog! He even had his own major motion picture, "Clifford's Really Big Movie" (2004), dedicated to the late "Three's Company" television star, John Ritter, who was the timeless voice of Clifford. This dog was truly something special!

Which brings me to *my* "big red Ranger" - the first owner-assisted, program-trained, mobility service dog in Central Florida. He was a 101 pound, fire engine red, flat-coated golden retriever, and he was amazing! Even at birth, he was nearly four times the size of his littermates! He was purchased as a "buy one get one" on the side of the road, and my husband picked him out for me. Such an easy going, laid back temperament and incredibly smart with a huge heart that matched his size, he was definitely a keeper from the start!

Certified at the highest level of qualifications, Complex Level for Unpredictable Environments, by Delta Society's Pet Partners Program to provide Animal Assisted Therapy (AAT), Ranger volunteered with therapists to assist children with their physical therapy at Florida's Celebration Hospital/Advent Health and was the leader of the first dog team at Nemours Children's Hospital Lake Nona, Florida. He was dedicated to encouraging and assisting children with orthopedic disabilities to walk. Ranger loved his job, and everyone loved him. He was so charming and gentle, this "big red" giant would win the hearts of even those who were terrified of dogs.

Everywhere we went, we were stopped for photographs - even in the middle of Orlando's notorious interstate traffic! At rest areas and gas stations while traveling on vacation, we would return to our car to find Ranger sitting behind the wheel, patiently waiting for us in the driver's seat with onlookers gathering around him to take pictures, waiting to meet him. At our local Barnes and Noble Bookstore, a professional Brazilian girls' soccer team could be heard exclaiming "Oh! Que Lindo!" as they posed with Ranger for photos and gave him much loved belly rubs. At Sea World, the dolphins in the nursery pool were infatuated with him, swimming up in a group to interact with him through the aquarium glass. Iconic theme park characters truly enjoyed Ranger at their meet and greets, excited to have *their* pictures taken with him. Especially fond of Sea World's Christmas reindeer character, Clarice, from the movie "Rudolph the Red-Nosed Reindeer," Ranger would nestle into her fur when she hugged him, while waiting for his photo op. At Hollywood Studios, Toy Story's Woody and Jessie jauntily escorted him on their way backstage through the park, and Pluto had a heyday with his fellow canine friend! Even Walt Disney World's beloved Santa Claus adored him so much he called Ranger back to his side for a private photo after our family visit. To the surprise and amusement of many park guests, Ranger enjoyed the gentle theme park rides alongside me. To the delight of the neighborhood children, he had an open invitation to their birthday parties. And on hot summer days, when the ice cream truck could be heard merrily rolling down our street, Ranger could be found with the children gathered around him as he waited his turn in line for a special frosty treat. Every afternoon like clockwork, come rain or shine, Ranger retrieved the mail, receiving a much appreciated pat on his head from our friendly mail carrier in exchange for his service. And at home, he patiently enjoyed playing dress-up and tea parties with our sweet little girl, listening to her countless "storytimes" while curled up together inside their blanket fort. Always seeking to comfort others, Ranger was a friend to all, regardless of status or creed. A dear friend of mine put it best when she described Ranger's personality, "Ranger is not a dog – he's a person in a fur coat!"

He was such a Central Florida phenomenon, a canine celebrity to everyone we encountered. Ranger by day became "Knightro" by Knight, having volunteered at the University of Central Florida's School of Medicine. It was only fitting that he was acknowledged by the UCF Knights Football Team as they celebrated in their first National Championship Parade at Walt Disney World. And he loved every minute of it!

Most importantly, he was *my* dog. My beautiful, beautiful Red Ranger whom I loved so dearly and to whom I owe so much. I was diagnosed with a very severe and debilitating form of Meniere's Disease, with recurring vertigo, dizziness, severe nausea, hearing loss and imbalance as well as a very painful autoimmune disorder, both of which affect my ability to live a normal life. No longer able to work as an elementary school teacher certified to help children with varying disabilities and exceptionalities, I became medically disabled, isolated, and dependent on the care of others at home, especially during episodes of debilitating vertigo or painful flares in my condition.

Ranger changed all that for me. He brought the world to me. He alerted me to changes in my blood pressure and fluid shifts just prior to a Meniere's attack. He brought medicine to me, opened doors for me, and retrieved objects that I could not bend for or else I would fall from imbalance. He assisted me up and down curbs, and brought the phone to me to call for emergency help. He watched me all through the night, guiding and supporting me lest I fall. He never took his eyes off me, ever. Worth his weight in "gold," Ranger intently performed his most important task whenever he braced for me. After falling from sudden vertigo attacks or dizzy spells, I used him as a support to lift myself up from the ground once I recovered. He would tense his body, plant his paws firmly on the ground, and stiffen his massive back, and holding himself impeccably still and rigid, he would allow me to use him as a brace to raise myself up from the floor with only his assistance. In public, he would stand guard over me while I was incapacitated until the vertigo episodes passed. His mere presence lessened the negative perception those of us who are disabled often face by others, because people were suddenly enamored with him, his sweet disposition, and his array of assistive skills. He calmed my anxieties and fear of falling by just being next to me. My "WonderDog" who wore a service vest as his cape! I was able to participate in life again because I had Ranger with me... Always.

But now he's gone. And I can barely write about it. So here it is, a short narrative of how my Ranger died, how I had to struggle against a vet's superiority mindset, and how they were wrong, but in the end Ranger died anyways. And with that so did my world. It's a dark and scary place for me now; I can't go places because I can't go alone. I fall often, and I am limited once again in even the smallest part of living that most of us take for granted. I didn't want to believe it, but it is true…and although nothing will bring him back or ease my heartache, maybe somehow this narrative will open the minds of others to make a change in how all medical practices, including veterinarian practice and the pharmaceutical companies they use, need to be held accountable. He was more than just a living, breathing, assistive device; my walking brace and gripper - he was truly my very best friend.

How was I to know that a simple treatment would tumble down to steal his life away from me? That a highly regarded veterinarian's indifference would nearly cost Ranger his life? That even after exhausting every effort to save him, I would lose him forever?

In October 2020, Ranger has bloodwork drawn during his exam at our vet's office. He is deemed healthy with an excellent report. My husband asks our vet about Ranger scratching at his ears lately, wondering if it could be a food allergy. Assuming the cause is environmental, our vet prescribes Apoquel to provide relief. We are concerned to use it, at first, because Ranger has never taken any regular medications. We ask for a more holistic approach, but our vet assures us Apoquel is safe. We later learn that Apoquel is a powerful immunomodulatory drug that suppresses the immune system in response to allergies. With many adverse side effects, this drug is not without risks and is more harmful than what we understand it to be.

Unbeknownst to us, in 2018, the FDA, Center for Veterinarian Medicine, Division of Surveillance issues a Warning Letter (N141345) to the manufacturer Zoetis for (1) failure to accurately represent the risks associated with the use of Apoquel in their promotional materials and on their website (2) misbrand the drug by making false or misleading representations about its safety, (3) contradict the important safety information and risks associated with the use of Apoquel, and (4) failure to reveal facts which makes its distribution violative. The Center for Veterinarian Medicine requests that "Zoetis immediately cease its dissemination of Apoquel promotional items and materials that fail to accurately represent the risks associated with the use of Apoquel, or, in the alternative, cease the distribution of the drug itself."

As of December 2020, Zoetis revises Apoquel's product insert and updates their manufacturer's website to include that Apoquel not only increases susceptibility to infections, makes existing cancers worse, but in addition to many other adverse events, new benign and malignant "neoplastic conditions" were observed in dogs treated with Apoquel … New, cancerous tumors. Cancer.

However, the most concerning side effect, not listed by the manufacturer but rather by Pet Dermatology Clinic in July 2019, is their observation of bone marrow suppression. Their website notes that, although rare, "Bone marrow suppression is the most concerning side effect" seen in pets on Apoquel. "No outward signs were seen in these dogs who had bone marrow suppression, only changes on bloodwork were discovered. This is why we recommend bloodwork at the 2-3 month point after starting Apoquel … Other allergy medications do not cause bone marrow suppression, even at extreme doses."

Hindsight is 20/20, and we are pet parents, not vets. Had we known this information, we would have never, ever agreed to put our wonderful Ranger on Apoquel.

2 months fast forward.

Playing and working, Ranger is outside with me enjoying a game of fetch with a stick, and as he slowly approaches me, he suddenly collapses at my feet. My husband races him to our vet's office. Our vet is not there, so another vet attends to him. This other vet prescribes steroids and a broad spectrum antibiotic, but does not perform any bloodwork. He tells my husband Ranger's condition can be only one of three things: an infection, an autoimmune disease, or parasites (worms). He says this course of medications will work on all three, and since Ranger has been on heartworm preventative for so long, bloodwork is unnecessary. He advises us to come back on Monday if Ranger isn't doing any better.

Ranger isn't doing any better; he is rapidly deteriorating. Due to Covid restrictions, and the Christmas holiday weekend, we cannot get him into the ER. They have no availability. First thing Monday morning, Ranger is seen immediately by our regular vet who performs bloodwork. He returns with a shot to euthanize him. He says Ranger is severely anemic; his organs are shutting down and he doesn't know why. He says Ranger's red blood cell count is at 9 percent ... and at 8 percent nothing lives! He says he is surprised Ranger is even alive, that it must be by sheer will-power and love for me. With a heavy heart, he delivers the news that Ranger needs to be euthanized to forgo the pain and suffering of his organs shutting down and the imminent seizures that will follow. He tells us, "It is time."

I'm sobbing on the floor, laying across my dog's body. My husband's mind is racing....Anemia, anemia, anemia. He then asks our vet about getting a blood transfusion for dogs. Do they even do that? Our vet's office doesn't have the capability to do them; they are a small, low cost facility. However, the University of Florida's Small Animal Hospital in Gainesville does! Although he is worried Ranger will not survive the trip, our vet makes the referral to UF, and helps lift Ranger onto a gurney and then into our car. He tells us, "If Ranger starts to run into trouble, just turn around and come back here. I will wait for you. Now hurry!" We know if we need him, our vet is there for us. He will fax the referral and records to UF ahead of us. He will pray for Ranger.

Nearly 2 hours later, we make it to UF. They are waiting for us. The gold standard of care. They inform me they require $4,800 of their estimate to be paid up front to initiate care, in case Ranger needs surgery. Without full payment he cannot be evaluated or treated. At registration, there is a sign to "Apply Now for Care Credit" to help with veterinarian expenses. We pay what we can in cash and emergency credit, and then I open a new Care Credit Card for $3,600, which they charge up to the limit, saying they will reimburse to the card what they don't spend on his care.

The ER Vet at UF is kind, compassionate, and knowledgeable. He asks us if Ranger has accidently ingested any rat poison, which, to our knowledge, he has not, but we share he has recently lost weight. We inform him our vet is treating Ranger with Apoquel to address possible allergies that are affecting Ranger's ears. He speculates Ranger's anemia could be from Apoquel, and in his opinion, "Apoquel is a horrible drug!" He states Dermatology will take a look at Ranger's ears. My husband requests a fecal test for worms because it had not been done at our vet's office. The ER Vet assures us that UF will run all the necessary tests, including the standard fecal exam for parasites, because, in his opinion, it could be anything. Even Worms.

But they don't test. Ever.

Ranger receives great care initially and responds well to the blood transfusions. When we inquire about the results of the fecal test for worms, we are told that it has not been done yet. They are transferring Ranger's care from ER treatment to Internal Medicine with an Oncology consult as it is more appropriate care for him. They suspect cancer, although they have no bloodwork or bone biopsy to prove it. The ER Vet is off rotation now and our point of contact is now a second UF vet in Internal Medicine.

The Internal Medicine Vet is opposed to performing a fecal test for parasites, even though it is very inexpensive and, if it is worms, easily treatable. He refuses to listen to our request for another blood transfusion, but instead is going with his "leading diagnosis" of unconfirmed AML Leukemia, rarely diagnosed in dogs. He also refuses to acknowledge that Apoquel can cause anemia, bone marrow suppression and new cancers in dogs. He orders a bone biopsy to confirm his diagnosis, but the anesthesiologist refuses to continue to anesthetize because Ranger has developed a new heart arrhythmia while under her care. She is concerned she may lose him as he is too unstable for the procedure. The Internal Medicine Vet then refers Ranger to Oncology.

During this time, I recall a few weeks earlier Ranger chewing on a piece of dead rat! I know, it's gross, but it did happen. We knocked the carcass piece out of his mouth with a small stick, so I remember it well. Because it happened a few weeks prior to Ranger's collapse, I didn't make the mental connection. It's important because our neighbor had a professional exterminator company treat for a rat infestation at their home. Yikes! And the dying rats had travelled to our yard, apparently looking for water. We discover that the chemical agent used by the pest control company contains an anti-coagulant, which causes anemia in rats. And hence, if ingested by dogs, could cause anemia in them as well. The antidote is Vitamin K for dogs, but no one carries it - trust me on this one, except the hospital. We share this newly recalled information with the Internal Medicine Vet, but he chooses to not believe our report.

We are contacted the following day by a 3rd UF vet. She is the Oncology Vet who eventually becomes our advocate for Ranger. After speaking with her, she states they will have a conference to plan his chemotherapy. The next day, however, we are contacted by the Internal Medicine Vet, instead. He informs us they are not going to proceed with chemotherapy because - it is extremely expensive and it won't give him much more time, anyway. He is discontinuing treatment, informing us that Ranger will decline quickly and, unfortunately, Ranger cannot be released to us for hospice care. The Internal Medicine Vet is recommending euthanasia. We plead for him to reconsider, but are denied. Again, we ask him to order the fecal test for worms, but he again refuses saying it is not worms. Again, he dismisses the possibility of our poisoned rat report. He continues to disregard any information or concerns we ask him to consider. He is transferring Ranger's care, with instructions to euthanize, to the next shift. Since no one is allowed in the hospital, I can't be there with Ranger to comfort him when he passes…I won't even be able to say goodbye.

Later that evening, we receive a call from the Oncology Vet. She shares with us how everyone there loves Ranger, saying, "He's such a sweet boy." She apologizes for the inevitable decision to euthanize and informs us, without treatment support, he is deteriorating rapidly. Because she knows my desire to be with him when he passes, she informs me that my window of time for this is very small ... and is now. She indicates that she would like to release him to us immediately to go home with pet hospice instead of euthanasia at UF. She is afraid that if we "wait too much longer, he will not be able to go home." My husband requests a blood transfusion to help ensure Ranger will make the trip home to pass away, rather than die alone in the hospital without me or during the car ride home. As a Hail Mary pass, he also asks if she could have him tested for worms or parasites, as we were told it was routine practice when Ranger was first admitted to UF, but it still has not yet been done. Additionally, I ask her for Vitamin K in case the anemia is from the rat poison exposure, of which she states she is unaware of the incident. To ensure this incident is documented, I write everything down and ask the staff to add my notes to his intake file. She says she will present our requests to the faculty for their decision. Later, the faculty concurs with the oncologist, but agrees to only one unit of blood transfusion, and we are to pick him up in the morning.

The next morning, the Oncology Vet calls us to inform us, to her surprise, the one unit of blood has really perked Ranger up! He finally ate well and is eager to go home! At checkout, we are instructed to settle our bill of the additional fees incurred before they can release Ranger to us. We discover we are being charged for a dermatology consult for his ears that has not taken place. We inform the Oncology Vet and she contacts Dermatology on our behalf. Ranger's ear are then evaluated and treated for a bacterial infection in his ears, rather than allergies. He is discharged with Vitamin K supplements, high dose steroids and a new heart medication for the dangerous arrhythmia he developed while there. He nearly runs to us when he sees us and we walk him out to the car with him pulling on his leash. He is so happy to be with us and go home.

It is a long drive and he is worn, so we spend the night at a good friend's house along the way to help break up the trip for Ranger. He eats well as she cooks homemade liver and other iron rich foods for him. He is bright eyed and exploring, enjoying his stay and special meals. With the New

Year's Eve holiday safely behind us, we begin our travel home. A few days later, we attend an appointment with a very knowledgeable, holistic vet in Ocala. There, Ranger receives acupuncture with vitamin B injections and herbal medicine. In discussing Ranger's condition, the Holistic Vet provides us with information about the success of treating cancer with the dog dewormer, Fenbendazole. The following day, as we are driving Ranger to establish him at a new vet's office who can provide both blood transfusions and chemotherapy near our home, I receive a cell phone call from the Oncology Vet at UF. She asks if we are nearby. Can we come back to UF? She states she had ordered a fecal test for worms just as Ranger was being discharged ... and it came back positive!

Positive for Rare Whipworms!!! Ranger has a large whipworm infestation and needs immediate treatment with Fenbendazole!

Because we are now very far away from UF, she will have Ranger's medical records forwarded to the new vet's office right away. She sends me an email regarding the new finding of whipworms to expedite his treatment, recommending Fenbendazole. Yet, when we arrive at the new vet's office, we are informed they have not received any records nor returned calls from UF. I share the oncologist's email with the new Office Vet and she confirms that Ranger, indeed, has a large, rare whipworm infestation. She prescribes Fenbendazole, which we purchase there, and recommends we continue his treatment with a different high dose steroid, Prednisolone, because it is more readily absorbed in dogs, Vitamin K therapy on the rare chance he ingested rat poisoning, and the heart medication to control the newly diagnosed arrhythmia. She also adds a liquid iron supplement with Vitamin B to help counteract Ranger's anemia.

We thank God! Ranger does not need to be euthanized! He shall live and not die!

After researching many success stories of using Fenbendazole to treat cancers, including AML Leukemia, we are hopeful and decide to continue Ranger's treatment with a specific protocol, using the brand, Safeguard, even though he may no longer have worms. We purchase it for a fraction of the cost at Tractor Supply Co. Although the evidence of its effectiveness is anecdotal, Ranger's bloodwork for leukemia and subsequent anemia continue to improve as long as he is on it. Whenever we discontinue dosing him with it, however, his red blood cell count rapidly decreases and he is deemed anemic again. It appears to us Fenbendazole is effective against the suspect leukemia. Out of an abundance of caution, the new Office Vet recommends he remain on the high dose steroids while waiting for his red blood cell count to increase to the threshold needed to initiate leukemia treatment with Palladia, the only anti-cancer medication in the US approved for dogs, also produced by Zoetis (the manufacturer of Apoquel). Vitamin K is discontinued as it is no longer indicated. We continue to supplement with iron-rich foods and liquid Vitamin B with Iron. At home, my beautiful, big red Ranger continues to improve. His bloodwork continues to improve. His health and weight continue to improve. He is thriving. In light of this, and without a bone biopsy, the thought of AML Leukemia remains a distant diagnosis, or at least one we will defeat.

4 months. I have four more beautiful months with my Ranger.

Then, one morning in April, Ranger appears to be a bit lethargic and somehow just not really himself. Worried he is becoming anemic again, we bring him to the new Office Vet for bloodwork and a possible blood transfusion. We are relieved to find out that his red blood cell count has not decreased. Even though he is somewhat anemic, he is not "anemic enough" to warrant the blood transfusion. However, he has not yet reached the threshold level needed to start treatment with Palladia. The Office Vet recommends we order Palladia, the anti-cancer drug for leukemia, for the following week, although she is not sure if he will need it or not. While Ranger is in the back room having bloodwork drawn, his nails are trimmed for the first time in his life. We hear him crying out incessantly, which is unusual for him. When he is returned to us, he is tender-footed and favoring one paw, which we are told is normal. By the time we get to the car, he is limping. On our way home, we pull over to a quiet nature preserve nearby the vet's office, but now he cannot stand or walk. We immediately contact the vet's office, but are told we will have to wait for a call back. No one calls back. Then their office closes. My husband gathers my gentle giant up in his arms and lifts him into the car. For the remaining ride home, we feel the dread of uncertainty weighing heavy on our hearts. That night at home, Ranger winces in pain and trembles whenever his shoulder area is touched. What happened? Did the nail trim create a pathway for infection? Was his front leg accidently strained while trimming his nails? Did they try to lift him and he somehow got hurt? Or is it something else? (I don't know, but he never walks again.)

Within these two days, he takes a downward turn, *fast*! Because he can no longer stand or walk, he drags himself across the floor on his stomach, searching the house to be with me, which he has never done before! He becomes anxious if I am out of his sight and constantly calls with a gentle "Woof, Woof" for me to stay right by him. Then, during these small hours, he slowly stops eating and drinking. By the end of the second day, he is vomiting brown bile and laying very still. Barely able to lift his head, Ranger looks to me for help ... My beautiful, big red dog was dying. But why?

We race him back to the new Office Vet. Ranger has a fever and is dehydrated. She explains that, unfortunately, it is possible the four months of high dose steroids have lowered his immunity and he has contracted an infection, however, she is not sure what kind it is. Although his present bloodwork shows his red blood cell count has improved again, and Ranger is no longer severely anemic, he now has extremely elevated liver enzymes and a severely enlarged liver. She shares that at his initial visit, they were only expecting him to live through the weekend, based on the information UF provided. She continued to treat him with high dose steroids because she truly believed the unconfirmed AML Leukemia would kill him before the effects of the steroids would. She never expected him to live past the weekend, let alone four more months! She believes the effects of the steroids have caused irreparable damage, bringing him to this point...she doesn't know what is wrong, but recommends treating him with IV antibiotics and fluids. She's hoping to support him enough to help him feel better, so he can go home with us. We consent to treatment.

After a long while, nearly 4 hours later which seems like an eternity, and multiple reports that he's doing fine and resting comfortably, we are offered to take a break away from their facility and come back for him at the end of the day to take him home. We don't leave because we want to stay near to him in case of an emergency. It is nearly closing time for their office. Suddenly, the vet tech approaches us and, with great urgency, rushes us to the back room to see Ranger and the Office Vet who has been committed to his care. Ranger's condition has rapidly changed. He is suddenly struggling to breathe and the Office Vet is worried he has septicemia, which she fears will quickly progress into septic shock. She informs us he needs immediate ER care because her office is not equipped to handle the change in his condition nor monitor him overnight. She has the shot to euthanize him and places it on the table. While the vet tech makes prints of his paws, I notice Ranger has a faraway look in his eyes. The Office Vet explains it is because he is concentrating on breathing, possibly from developing a pulmonary emboli. Her office is closing, but the ER Clinic across the street has just opened for continuum of care. We choose to take Ranger to the ER Clinic to try to help him. Placing the shot in the pocket of her lab coat, the Office Vet advises me that now is time to spend with him and leaves to write the referral. When she returns, she hands us his records with the ER referral and crawls into his cage to say goodbye. With tears in her eyes, she hugs him, whispering, "Have a safe journey, Big Guy."

Time is of the essence - Ranger is disconnected from the IV drip and fluids. As the two techs, who have been incredibly kind to us and Ranger, lift him with great care, up and out from the large bottom kennel to place him on the gurney for transport, the one tech becomes unstable with Ranger's weight, awkwardness and his sudden flaccidity, and losing balance, she nearly drops him head first. Once Ranger is placed securely on the gurney, my husband races alongside the techs to help load him into the back seat of the car. While my dog is dying, we overhear the receptionist calling another client to inform them that their prescription for Apoquel has been filled and is ready for pickup. We are in disbelief.

On the way over to the ER Clinic, Ranger's head tremors slightly from side to side for a brief moment. I wonder if this a seizure. Once there, we are directed to drive around to the side door of the building for someone to meet us. I climb in the back seat and, holding Ranger's head in my lap, stroke his velvety head, reassuring him that he is a good boy and telling him how very much I love him. His head starts to slightly tremor again, until I softly call his name with the command "Ranger, Watch Me" and he sees me. He knows I am there. Two nurses from the ER Clinic come rushing out of the side door with a gurney, but as they lift him out of the car and onto the gurney, he passes away ... looking for me ... Always.

As I cry out in shock and despair, the nurse places her stethoscope to listen to his heart again and states she hears a faint heartbeat, though irregular and weak, she assures me it is there. He is still alive! She asks me to quickly decide - Do I want them to take Ranger in to try to save him? Do I want them to resuscitate if he passes away? I tell them no, to leave him with me because that is all he ever wanted. She places the stethoscope against him again for a third time and says, "He's gone."

Had he already passed away? Did he try to come back for me? Or was it just an echo, a remnant heart beat that she heard? Oh God, the uncertainty! I will never know. As I stand there in the parking lot alone, with my Ranger on a gurney beneath a canopy of trees, I can finally hug on him because I don't have to bend to reach him. I bury my face full of tears in his fur, and thank God that when Ranger passed away, he did so softly and gently ... just like my Ranger was.

My big red, gentle giant.

His red fur glistening as fading sunlight streams softly from the heavens, ethereally between the leaves of the trees touching him.in this sanctuary. My child lays wildflowers on him. It is quiet and still. It is all I have. I stay with him this way until it is time to take Ranger on his last road trip home.

My beautiful, beautiful, big red dog! I tried so hard, but neither love nor money could save him. It's such a convoluted tale for such a simple, straight forward dog. And now I know ... I know that new cancers, "malignant neoplastic conditions," were observed in dogs after receiving Apoquel as noted in Zoetis's Post Approval Experience. I know Apoquel causes anemia, a decrease in red blood cell production, as reported in the safety information link on Zoetis's website. And I know Apoquel has been observed to cause bone marrow suppression according to other clinical studies. I know Acute Myeloid Leukemia (AML) is a malignant neoplastic disease causing cancer of the bone marrow, evidenced by anemia with a decrease in red blood cell production. I also know Apoquel is an immune modulating medication, thus it suppresses the immune system, which increases susceptibility to developing serious illnesses and infections, including parasitic infections, per Zoetis's package insert, which may explain the rapid onset of severe infection that became Ranger's collective downfall and led to Ranger's passing . And I know Ranger had also been diagnosed with and successfully treated for rare whipworms – a parasitic infestation that causes life-threatening anemia when the host is severely infected, which is most likely to occur with a weakened immune system, as noted by the Veterinarian Centers of America (VCA), the largest animal health network in North America. Additionally, he was prescribed long-term, high doses of steroids which, like the immuno-suppressant drug, Apoquel, are also known to lower one's immunity to infection. And, at one point, he was taking both Apoquel and steroids together, of which the safety of combing these medications has not been evaluated, per Zoetis's Apoqeuldogs website. I now know that AML Leukemia is a very rarely diagnosed cancer in dogs. And to treat this "malignant neoplastic condition," the same company that makes Apoquel produces the antidote,

Palladia, the only anti-cancer drug approved for use in dogs by the FDA, which is what they were going to prescribe for Ranger. Knowing what I know now, Apoquel should have NEVER been given to my dog.

Instead, the very first vet should have tested for parasites. The University of Florida's Small Animal Hospital should have ran a fecal test for parasites as part of their initial workup as they indicated they would, without us having to request it numerous times, only to be denied. The second UF Vet in Internal Medicine, with his presumptive "leading diagnosis," should have pulled his head out of the sand and listened to our concerns to appropriately address them. And, since he was the UF Vet presiding over Ranger's case, it was his responsibility to have practiced due diligence by taking the opportunity to correlate the medical implications of the medications prescribed, the effects of parasitic infestation, and Ranger's resulting condition, and if finding any significance, report it accordingly. He was so superior in his mindset, we were made to feel that we were a bother and an inconvenience while advocating for our dog. Unlike our long time family vet at the low cost clinic who referred Ranger to UF for blood transfusions in our desperate attempt to save him; he embodies all the good qualities a good vet could possibly have and be. As does the top rated Oncologist at UF, who went out of her way to go around the obstinate Internal Medicine Vet who knew everything and who stood in the way of helping our dog. The Oncology Vet attentively listened, truly cared, and was invaluable in Ranger's care, even outside of her own department. She not only gave Ranger the honor and dignity he deserved towards the end, but also the opportunity to live ... She is a hero in a tainted system.

Most importantly, EVERY VET should have done their research about Apoquel and its role in cancer, bone marrow suppression, and immunosuppression. Zoetis should have been forthright and provided a factual risk assessment so veterinarians and their clients can make informed decisions. Apoquel has not been tested on dogs receiving corticosteroids. Prednisone is a corticosteroid and systemic immunosuppressive agent. Again, Ranger had received both. And yet, misinformation still abounds all over the internet, even existing on veterinarian websites purporting the safety of concomitant use of Apoquel and steroids, which is a direct contradiction of the manufacturer's newly revised informationals and an ignorant and reckless assumption by educated professionals responsible for the direct care of our pets. Somewhere down the line, someone should have told us that they were only treating my dog for the weekend, not for his life. Someone should have told us the truth.

But none of it matters. It doesn't change the heartache or the loss. I can only hope that his cautionary tale may help someone else, or become an agent of change in the accountability of this time- honored profession of veterinary medicine. So this is why I share...

I lost my best friend on April 9th of 2021. He was nothing short of amazing. I am so completely lost without him. I am utterly disconnected from society now without his four paws beside me - I miss him. I miss him. I miss him. I miss him. He is gone And there's nothing I can do to change this.

My beautiful, beautiful, "big red dog." My helper, protector and friend. He walked me through this world of uncertainty and pain with such grace and precision. He made my life beautiful and all those whose lives he touched. He was a trailblazer who set the path for the owner-assisted service dog training program in the state of Florida so others could experience life more freely and fully. I love him so much. He was one of a kind. And he was mine.

I buried him with tears streaming down my face, desperately singing at the top of my lungs, Clifford's theme song with the words, "I love Ranger! My big red dog!" Like an inconsolable child, longing for something I'll never have again ...

My dad always said, "Dog is just God spelled backwards."

I thank God for the gift of my Ranger. He was such an incredible blessing in my life. He taught me how to walk by faith when he showed me how to live. When my time comes to pass, I hope and pray my Ranger is there waiting for me, because it won't be Heaven to me without him. He truly walked me through the valley.

"Yea, though I walk through the valley of the shadow of death, I will fear no evil: for thou art with me…" Psalm 23

Thank you Ranger for keeping me safe with the whole of your life. 🐾🐾

Always my Ranger-Danger, his Big Guy, her Everest, and our Gruff.

*** My one and only Star Buck … keep watching over me ***

Miss you, Buddy

Chapter Twenty-Eight

Sassy: The Crown Princess, Baico Dolce
Juliana Micklos

February 12, 2009 - January 17, 2021

Loving YOU changed my life
Losing YOU did the same

And so, The End Is The Beginning with this Greek Tragedy which was born out of the owner's Business acumen based on Greed that overshadowed his entire operation from hiring incompetent veterinary technicians (according to his advert: HS or equivalent) and recently graduated Veterinarians with either poor mentorship or apparently none. Or the owners' method to pay doctors-production based -compensation, encouraging them to sell ALL services, including euthanasian and cremation for commission. And by doing so, Impacting Ethical Decision-Making in Veterinary Medicine!

And the Death Angel said, "she has a Perfectly Formed Heart!"

And then she made it STOP!

On January 17, 2021 I took my Great Dane, Sassy, to Mountain View Animal Emergency Hospital in Hagerstown MD when she was experiencing Upper Respiratory Distress. The moment that I did, her life was in JEOPARDY! I will now explain how horribly wrong their care and treatment was.

1 I was given the name and location of this hospital by one of Sassy's veterinarians who stated if there is an emergency, Upper Respiratory Distress from what she believed Sassy was presenting from her symptomatology, Laryngeal paralysis, (known as lar par) this is the closest location for you to take Sassy. And so the day came on Sunday. January 17th, it was cold outside which was impacting her respiration and had led to the second worse day of my life, the first

being the passing of my daughter through malpractice. My Sweet Girl, Sassy got me through this tragic loss, she was my companion, my best friend. I was very concerned about taking her as she was terrified of being in a strange place and especially without me. Sassy had suffered life-threatening separation anxiety because it significantly exasperated her respiratory condition which I made known to the Techs. Last summer her condition was so severe when she last went to her veterinarian, she had collapsed outside and was gasping for air and had to be sedated. When Sassy collapsed this time earlier that day when she went outside, I desperately wanted to get her help, I just couldn't lose her and for the first time four of the men in the neighborhood gathered together to lift Sassy while she laid on her dog bed into the van. I thought finally she'd get the life-saving oxygen and life-saving steroids' in a hospital setting, she needed them, like NOW. I had texted her veterinarian on Friday evening that she needed a prescription for steroids' but it would be better if she received them now.

Unfortunately when we arrived around 4:30pm like a Bad Omen Sassy's Stress and Anxiety was heightened the moment we pulled into the parking lot at Mountain View Animal Emergency Hospital. The Techs that descended upon our van were unprepared and wanted to force my Great Dane to jump out of the van!

2 Prior to our arrival I had made multiple calls explaining to the receptionist whose job description I found out was to have clear communication with the staff and that included the techs! I had explained that it took four men to load my Great Dane into the van while she was laying on her dog bed because she had collapsed and couldn't walk from breathing difficulties!

After Sassy was already experiencing anxiety and fear the Techs finally listened to me and retrieved the gurney, they had again no idea what they were doing and thereby making it that much worse for Sassy, heightening her anxiety! With laryngeal paralysis, stress compounds the problem. So much so, that keeping your dog calm is as important as keeping your dog cool. The "perfect storm" for these dogs is the combination of environmental stress, heat/humidity, and respiratory distress. They obviously lacked knowledge, experience and skill causing me to become nervous about her going inside...but she needed oxygen and steroids especially since they heightened her stress level, she was scared, but I thought it would be different once she got inside.

When Sassy entered the building by gurney, at Mountain View Animal Emergency Hospital in Upper Respiratory Distress, presenting Dyspnea and Cyanosis, (there was a concern for her having respiratory failure,) therefore I stressed that I wanted Sassy's condition STABILIZED, oxygen, steroids' x-ray to rule out aspiration pneumonia, ECG to rule out an enlarged heart! I had explained to the Intake Tech while she was receiving Sassy's medical history from me, that Sassy was being treated by her regular veterinarian for undiagnosed Laryngeal paralysis. Laryngeal paralysis in dogs (lar-par) is one of a handful of TRUE veterinary emergencies when seconds count for quick assessment and stabilization. Laryngeal paralysis occurs when the vocal folds are unable to abduct (open) in response to exercise or respiratory demands and eventually progresses to periods of severe respiratory distress.

3 I was told by the Intake Tech, that Sassy was in Triage and that she would be STABILIZED and the tests would be run. At this point I was able to feel hopeful.

Quick, accurate physical examination skills are critical skills to master assessment of the patient in Triage and are an essential element in critical care. Careful handling, minimizing stress, and rapid and focused treatment are crucial in the management of all patients in respiratory distress.

But that NEVER HAPPENED! Sassy wasn't assessed and treated as Critical Care even though she suffered from Upper Respiratory Distress! Sassy should've been treated with steroids, corticosteroids for reducing inflammation and swelling and other medication or fluids after what should have been her receiving a rapid and correct assessment in Triage. Steroids, I later found out, were in the Veterinarians notes as a Treatment Plan, they were never administered after assessment in Triage when that treatment was vital to her survival when seconds to minutes count according to the Standard of Care as stated in the MERCK MANUAL VETERINARY MANUAL. Not to have done so was a prime example of Incompetent! Negligence!

I didn't know until it was too late. It was when I saw my sweet girl four hours after I had first arrived at Mountain View Animal Emergency Hospital, that they left out life - saving steroids! Therefore she couldn't receive the life - saving oxygen, because of continued airway obtrusion from a narrowing airway due to inflammation that became more severe when she continued to struggle to breathe, try sucking on a straw! That's what it was like for her to breathe! The harder she tried to breathe the more inflammation and swelling that occurred. The outcome is death, and the process is painful. In conversation the veterinarian stated she was PANTING. And in the same sentence she used the word comfortable. She can't breathe! NO!

4 She's not comfortable! *PANTING...In animals with upper airway obstruction, there may be minimal to no movement of air over the surface of the tongue, considerably restricting their ability to thermoregulate. The higher the body temperature becomes, the more they attempt to pant, resulting in generation of even greater swings in airway pressure, and further worsening of the airway obstruction. Extreme hyperthermia can have serious consequences including disseminated intravascular coagulation and shock.

Sassy should have been STABILIZED...without Steroids as she had laryngeal edema which was causing airway obstruction. she wasn't PHYSIOLOGICALLY able to receive the oxygen she needed, (which the oxygen they only provided briefly while she was having the ECG and X-ray), SEALING HER FATE! HER BEING AT MOUNTAIN VIEW ANIMAL EMERGENCY HOSPITAL WAS HER DEATH SENTENCE AND AN EXCRUCIATING ONE AT THAT...TORTURE!

And so in conversation over the phone, due to Covid 19 no one was allowed inside to wait, I sat in the van in the dark while the veterinarian explained in a soft and monotone voice, how perfect Sassy's organs are and that she had a PERFECTLY FORMED HEART! I was so happy to hear this wonderful news. And then she continued that cortisone would make her comfortable and I am thinking to myself, I already requested a prescription to be called in, OK, no big deal, so far so GREAT! I was HAPPY she was STABILIZED and had received oxygen and steroids' and her Heart was Perfectly Formed...I expected to go home with medication. but then I lost hope when she stated that Sassy can't live without oxygen outside of a hospital setting! What place offers Life-Support for a dog?

5 She didn't stop talking, she went from one diagnosis to the next until she came to lar par and suggested from where the sound came from it would be lar par is. I interrupted and told her there is tie back surgery! However she emphasized that the surgery comes with life threatening complications of aspiration pneumonia and that the disease progresses regardless and stated multiple times in HER EXPERIENCE SHE NEVER SAW A GOOD OUTCOME! And then she discussed humane euthanasian. I broke down and cried.

I assume they stabilized Sassy, as I was told she would be, they ran the tests I requested, her organs were in excellent condition but that she could only remain stabilized in a hospital setting, and she was going to die? I had no idea that they started treatment with oxygen but stopped and disconnected her oxygen nasal catheter tube from the tank, put her in a cage, not an oxygen cage but just a cage to suffer hypoxia, low blood oxygen, and bring her to the brink of death! AND Sassy was never tested to find out if she actually had Laryngeal Paralysis and if she did what did it originate from? Hypothyroidism?

"If laryngeal paralysis is not treated, a respiratory crisis can emerge. In this situation, the patient attempts to breathe deeply and simply cannot, creating a vicious cycle of anxiety and respiratory attempts. The laryngeal folds become swollen making the obstruction in the throat still worse. The patient's gums become bluish in color from lack of oxygen and the patient begins to overheat.

For reasons that remain unclear, fluid begins to flood the lungs and the patient begins to drown (as if the laryngeal obstruction wasn't lethal enough).

The patient must be sedated, intubated and cooled down with water in order to survive. As soon as intubation is effected, the patient can breathe normally, oxygen can be administered and the crisis can be curtailed if it has not progressed too far. "

6 Of course, eventually the patient will have to wake up and be able

to survive without medical equipment. Corticosteroids can be used to reduce the swelling but ideally one of several surgical solutions is needed.

And the Death Angel said, "she has a Perfectly Formed Heart!" And then she made it STOP!

And so, The End Is The Beginning with this Greek Tragedy which was born out of the owner's Business acumen based on Greed that overshadowed his entire operation from hiring incompetent veterinary technicians (according to his advert: HS or equivalent) and recently graduated Veterinarians with either poor mentorship or apparently none. Or the owners' method to pay doctors-production based -compensation, encouraging them to sell ALL services, including euthanasian and cremation for commission. And by doing so, Impacting Ethical Decision-Making in Veterinary Medicine!

The veterinarian had recently graduated from College, an obscure college in January of 2020, she saw Sassy on January 17, 2021.

Sassy was euthanized after 9pm because her alveoli in her lungs filled up with fluid, she suffered low blood oxygen to the brain and went unconscious with my arm around her neck.

I felt the last beat of her Perfectly Formed Heart, and since, I haven't been the same.

Juliana Micklos (Sassy's Parent, Guardian, Companion)

 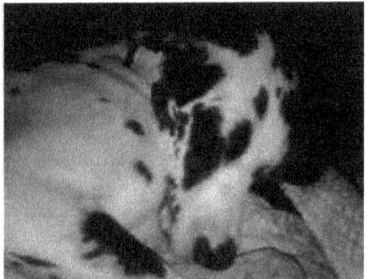

Chapter Twenty-Nine

SHILOH SKYLAR RAYNE'S STORY

Robin Lawson
Shiloh Skylar Rayne

(Birth) 05/10/16 - 01/27/2017 (Death)

This is a tribute to my Beautiful Heart Dog - "Shiloh Skylar Rayne"

"My ANGEL With a Purpose" - (A Negligent & Horrible Loss of a Beautiful Life & Soul)

https://www.facebook.com/justice4shiloh/

Public Record: IN THE CIRCUIT COURT OF KANAWHA COUNTY, WEST VIRGINIA

Lawson, et al. v. Good Shepherd Veterinary Hospital, et al., Owner/Veterinarian - Stephenson

CIVIL ACTION NO. 17-C-597

West Virginia Laws for Pets: MUST BE updated! Out with the Old Laws, and In with the New. That's my mission in Shiloh's name. I promised Shiloh that her tragic death would not be in vain, and a promise I will keep.

After she lost her life, I have found there is a HUGE need for stricter animal laws to be put into effect and stiffer protocols placed in every Pet Professional's place of business to better protect our pets. Shiloh's perpetrator (Veterinarian) had none in place when needed at such a crucial time in her practice. This pushes me to fight even harder!

Another weak spot I have found in our legal system, is that we as pet parents must continue to fight to ensure that our beloved Pets are considered Family and NO longer considered to be JUST a worthless piece of Personal Property, in a Court of Law. Our pets have NO Voice, so We MUST be Their Voices for change.

Truth is, whether it be in a court of law or the way our current laws in WV render and consider her and all animals worthless, she will never be worthless and just a lousy piece of Personal Property in my eyes. Considered useless, disposable and not worthy of their life in most court systems and the present laws in place both nationally and across the globe are pathetic. Shiloh was and will always be my God given child and the love of my life, so she is worthy!

Two words that I never want to hear again in my lifetime, and they are "Personal Property." When someone says, I am sorry but your pet is only considered Personal Property, it literally makes me sick, and I want to regurgitate.

For the record, this is NOT and has never been about revenge, this is solely about CHANGE. Lobbying to implement stricter laws, and to update our outdated laws to better protect our pets. I will work hard to change our West Virginia laws from old and outdated ones to new and current ones. My hope is to make a change no matter how long it takes, whether it takes months or years, to get them put into effect and a new law named after my girl. "Shiloh's Law" in her honor. Not only am I doing this to carry on Shiloh's legacy, but the need is great for all of our fur children in the future years to come.

Rewind a few decades of my life and it will explain how I became a Parent to many fur-babies in the years ahead of me. I had a complete hysterectomy performed, due to acute endometriosis when I was a very young 26-year-old woman. Fearing the surgery and knowing what lie ahead and what was in store for my life and future regarding not being able to conceive children was starting to grow dim very quickly and it overwhelmed me. As time passed, in no time it became apparent that God had other plans for my life and parenthood, and HE made it known rather quickly. Instead of blessing me with children that have 2 legs, 2 arms and skin, he blessed me with children that have 4 legs and fur. Moving forward after surgery, HE quickly showed me my purpose in this life. It would be that HE would lead me to mothering precious fur-babies that HE would eventually place in my life. To protect and love just like a mother does her human children. With Shiloh being one of many I had mothered over the years, I can't help but feel like during this incident that happened, as a mother I failed her. I should have never taken her to a Veterinarian that took an Oath to "Do No Harm, in turn she was killed while in her care.

God blessed me with Shiloh to love and protect her. I promised her that I would be back later that day to pick her up from this local Vet's office, and I didn't mean I would be back to pick her up in a cremation urn 3 days later when promising her and when making that statement before leaving her. It was my obligation as a Mother to protect her. She was my daughter!

I promise I will never stop fighting for Justice for all, and to ensure that all animals are safe while in the hands of any and ALL Pet Professionals. Shiloh's life mattered and so do all family pets that have experienced malpractice, negligence, and abuse of any kind.

Together, we as Pet Parents that have lost our beloved will stick together and Get it Done! No matter the time or cost.

This story you are about to read pertains to a routine spay by a local Veterinarian that turns into a Pet Parents worse nightmare. The death of my beloved pet, who was my heart dog and was taken way too soon. She didn't even get the chance to enjoy and excel in life. Sadly her life was cut short by a negligent act that was very much preventable and should have never happened. It was a cut and dry case of reckless negligence at its best, by a licensed Veterinarian that took an oath, "To do NO HARM."

Side note: Good news is, Shiloh DID get her much deserved JUSTICE in court. The fight with the Vet is over and Justice has been granted. Shiloh won her battle!   Now it's time to lobby and get these laws updated.

Here is Shiloh's heartbreaking story. (Her nightmare began the evening of January 25th and lasted through the afternoon of January 27, 2017) that would sadly end in the death of Shiloh's short, beautiful life.

Quick visual regarding the night before, leading up to her nightmare. As she laid on my chest and me flat on my back the entire night before her procedure, it was as if I was being told from a higher power that this would be our last night together and to savor the moment. The feeling was both heavy and overwhelming for me. A mother's intuition if you will. I could not shake this unsettled feeling that continued to haunt and come over me the entire night no matter how hard I tried. I would will it away and it would return. I would try very hard to divert my thoughts as I continued to pet her not wanting her to feed off my nervous energy and feelings, while giving her tons of hugs and love and holding her ever so tight the whole night. To her, I was her safe haven, but little did she know she was mine. I called her my Saving Grace from the Lord above, for many reasons I won't go into. She, her Creator, and I knew and that's all that mattered.

The entire night I was constantly checking the time on my wrist watch not wanting morning to come, knowing I had to be without her by my side the following day. We were inseparable. No sleep at all for me and I'm still wide awake as 4 a.m. is clearly approaching. At this point I'm praying and talking to God about these feelings I continue to have and the way I was feeling, as I continue watching Shiloh sleep peacefully and feeling every breath she took. As a protective mother and one that has always been very protective and intuitive about my fur children, something just felt very unsettling the whole night. Something wasn't right about taking her to have the procedure the next day, and I was driving myself crazy wondering why I couldn't shake this terrible feeling that I felt. It was so very heavy on my chest and heart. A feeling I can't describe. Though after many years as I relived that night over and over in my head and would try to analyze those thoughts I was having that night, I can without a shadow of a doubt give a word to the wise. When you feel like something is wrong or you just don't feel right about a situation, always always always follow your gut feeling and listen to your heart. It will save you a lot of unnecessary grief. We as parents always tend to know first hand when something is not right and feels out of sorts. My goodness, how I wish I would have listened to my inner voice speaking and could turn back the hands of time. I would have done things so different. I would repeatedly tell myself that night I was just overreacting and that she would be fine. That it was just a simple routine spay, and to shake it off because there was nothing to worry about. Yet another part of me felt and kept tugging at my heart strings saying, no don't take her there, just cancel her appointment. By now, my emotions were obviously all over the board by morning to say the least. The sun was rising, I was getting more nervous by the minute, but it was now time to get my girl ready to go and be dropped of for her surgery. I'll always feel like I failed her as a Pet Parent when the reality is, that the system is broken and failed my baby girl.

If only I knew what that dreaded morning of January 25, 2017 had in store for my family, my life, and Shiloh's life, my God how I would have done things different. This day was about to change our lives forever and our life as we once knew it, would never be the same.

I can't stress enough about how crazy nervous I was leading up to this day. As most pet parents tend to be, due to any and all complications that can arise while under anesthesia. We worry about anything that could go wrong during any medical procedure performed whether it be our human family or family pets. I literally called their office on 4 different occasions within a 2-week period, prior to her scheduled surgery day, talking to staff to get all the specifics. What to expect before and after her procedure, including instructions for prep the night before and morning of her surgery. I wanted to know every tiny detail and complications if any, from beginning to end. Anything at all pertaining to and regarding Shiloh's spay procedure once it was completed and the healing process would begin. What to expect and what to look for out of the ordinary after bringing her home. Just a concerned parent at my best and making sure that my girl's care and procedure would go as flawless as possible. Yes I know, you can call it crazy, but I am a very protective pet Momma and I proudly own the title.

Morning arrives, I suck up all my fears and try to shake of the nervousness to act tough about Shiloh's surgery for her sake, when all the while I was literally falling apart inside. I'll never forget, how sunny and crisp that January morning was when we dropped my baby girl off around 7:15 am at the local Veterinarian's office. Remember I got zero sleep the night before, as I held my girl ton my chest the entire night, so by now I can't even focus like I should. I don't do well with no sleep. I kissed my girl over and over and gave her lots of tight hugs like only a pet momma could relate to, reassuring her that she would be fine and only away from me for a very short time. I kept holding her in my arms not wanting to let her go when dropping her off at their office that morning. I told her we would be back to pick her up as soon as her procedure was completed, the sedation had worn off, and she could safely be released from the Vet's care and return home later that day. That Momma may not be at the Vet's office with her during her spay procedure, but that I would be there in spirit and bring her home as quickly as they would allow.

After leaving her there and as the day goes on, I'm on pins and needles with worry. All along thinking I would have her back in my arms later that evening. Lord knows I couldn't wait to pick her up and get her home as that adorable, healthy, playful, loving, and spry widdle baby that she was when I dropped her off that dreaded morning, other than her having sutures from the spay procedure performed. Boy would I ever be wrong. Things were about to take a very tragic turn and would begin to spiral out of control in the blink of an eye. It would unfortunately be the last time I would ever hold my girl in my arms again, and little did I know that my world was about to be turned completely upside down for the rest of my life, and my heart was about to be shattered into pieces. The happy life I once knew, was about to be a thing of the past and was about to change forever. In fact, it would be one of the most painful places to be in my entire life where you begin to feel an overwhelming feeling of sadness, you're scared, have regret, and guilt. I can't explain in words to this day how I felt. I will just tell you it was horrible.

Keep in mind that I only live two streets back and 6 blocks from her the Vet's practice/facility where Shiloh was dropped off, because it comes into play numerous times as this story unfolds. I have no doubt in my mind living so close, that I could have saved her life when they let her loose had I been notified immediately from their office and not an hour later when I called them and found out the truth and what had taken place.

This is a short version behind the story and facts as to how this reckless tragedy happened.

I take my fur baby Shiloh to the vet for a routine spay, dropping her off at 7:15 am on Wednesday morning January the 25th, 2017.

I called three times in the course of the day to check on Shiloh, as I'm like any other mother of a fur baby that worries and wants to make sure my baby girl is okay and doing well from the surgery. I needed to know how she was progressing for my own peace of mind. I was told each time that she was doing just fine, came through the surgery with flying colors, and she was taking a little more time than usual to shake off the effect of anesthesia from sensitivity. So I believed them. Isn't that we are supposed to do?

Little did I know, it had nothing to do with still being slightly sedated and her sensitivity to anesthesia. In fact, she had been lost by the Veterinarians staff and facility and on the run for a full hour before I ever knew she was missing. Again, I only lived 6 short blocks away from where she was having her procedure.

The 3rd call from me took place at approximately 4:10 pm when I call their office and the young lady at the front desk of the office answers the phone and I tell her who I am and that I'm on my way to pick up Shiloh. I also asked that they have her paperwork processed with the total due on Shiloh's bill for her procedure and vet visit, so that I could have the money in hand when I got there. Quickly hand them the money, pay them in full and be on my way with my baby. I just wanted to get Shiloh home like any other puppy momma where she could rest peacefully in the comfort of her home to recuperate. We as a family had prepared an adorable little slumber party on the floor of the lower level of our house, for she and her other siblings to snuggle up together, so she could rest comfortably as we all surrounded her with love, and so she wouldn't be tempted to jump on the couch or the bed with fresh sutures. We were having what we call a quiet family movie night together.

I asked the girl who answered the phone at the Vet's front desk how my baby was doing. Explained that it was getting late and that I'd be right over to pick up Shiloh since it was nearing time for their facility to close for the night, and I wanted her home. For goodness' sake, I live such a short distance from their facility I wanted to get her home asap. I was beginning to think they had forgotten about Shiloh being there and was going to close the business for the night, and it would be morning before I could pick her up without my consent. Mind you, I found out she was missing from their care on this call that I'm about to share with you.

So the girl at the front desk said, "Ya know what?" I'm new here and haven't had a chance to check on Shiloh in the last couple of hours, but I'll go in the back and see how Shiloh's doing and have her ready for you to pick her up when you get here. I said, excellent since you're getting ready to close that would be great! She says, "Can you hold on for a minute, and I said sure." Now I'm on hold for a good 5 minutes that seemed like an eternity, as the same dreaded déjà vu feeling I had the night before suddenly came over me again, at that very moment. Suddenly the Veterinarian that treated Shiloh, gets on the phone and says, "Oh my, I was just getting ready to call you, with panic in her voice." I immediately said, "Why? What's wrong?" And she said, can you get over here as quickly as possible, Shiloh has gotten loose from us while taking her out to potty. I said, WHAT? She got loose? How does this even happen when you have a double fenced in area attached to your facility for the animals to do their business and potty? You were told to keep her in her run with pee pads until she was ready to come home.

I kept frantically asking her how this could happen. What does she do, but rudely keep talking over me and ignored my questions and said, "Just get here quick, we'll explain later." Explain later? I want to know now. Nothing made any sense at all about her statement or what I was hearing from her. At this point, I was frantic and in a state of shock trying to make sense of it all. I didn't know where to start or what to do, other than to grab my keys and get there as quick as I could, as I still had no specifics and only knew Shiloh was missing and on the loose.

The biggest thing that infuriated me most, is that this facility had NO protocol in place, as they say anyway, which I find very hard to believe. If that's indeed the truth, then I say, use common sense. They do have a huge enclosed puppy day care area and an enclosed double fenced in area attached to this building with NO gates nor openings of any kind, that has grass for all the pets in their care to go potty in this area for this very reason and to prevent anything like this to happen. It would eliminate this kind of tragedy from ever happening had they done what they were instructed to do from the start and used their designated potty area. But no, she still allowed Shiloh to go outside, against my will. Without my permission she took her outside to potty with fresh sutures, and still sedated by stepping on my feet doing so and making that deadly decision that I was totally against. I would have never agreed to her taking her out the door by a busy highway and would have said NO to the idea in a heartbeat, had she asked, and she knows it. She also knows how protective I am of my babies, and they were given strict orders several times to leave her in her run with puppy pads to do her business.

Okay back to the nightmare. My friend Chris jumps in the car, rushes over while the vet is giving me orders to phone Chris on her cell and tell her to come to the back door of her facility in the alley, so she could give her the location of Shiloh, so Chris and I could try to find Shiloh. Meanwhile, this heartless Vet wasn't even out looking for Shiloh the whole time she'd been missing, only a few staff members. The vet was still at her office standing there on her phone while seeing patients. Disheartening, unprofessional and ludicrous to say the least!

Any caring professional would have promptly closed the doors to their office or let the other Veterinarians that were there on duty and her remaining staff take care of her few clients waiting their turn. She should have been out looking for my girl that she had let loose and had been missing from her office for a minimum of 45 minutes to an hour.

I said to her, "Why didn't you call and notify me IMMEDIATELY to let me know that she was missing?" I still got no answer. She just kept saying I'll tell you where she was last spotted, and we'll talk later. I know in my heart of hearts, that they were hoping to find her before I even knew she had been missing from their office and that I'd never know that they negligently let her loose from their facility. Why else would they not call me, I'm her mother, immediately to inform me the minute she got loose? Purely the Vet thinking, if we find Shiloh we can once again sweep another negligent act under the rug like we do all the others. Not this time my friend, not this time. Now I'm on a mission.

No one will ever make me think differently and there is no doubt in my mind, if she had called me immediately that day when Shiloh went missing, that I could have found my girl and saved her life. Shiloh's life never mattered to she or her staff. Not ever. But it mattered to me!

She knew how close I lived, and she knew my phone number. It was in Shiloh's file and stored in her cell phone from prior calls. I only live two streets back and 6 blocks from her office, and she knew that too. It was a crucial time and time was of the essence. She is a heartless individual and in the wrong business that's for sure.

Now here's where it gets super CRAZY and everything would begin to spiral totally out of control from here! There were actually 2 dogs that were taken outside to potty at one time by the same person. One dog being Shiloh and the second being the Vet's dog. Her dog was huge compared to Shiloh, and towered my girl with height and weight by far. So why even attempt to do this, to begin with? Her dog was so much larger and outweighed mine, that the Vet's dog started tugging the employee's arm and hand and broke loose from the so-called vet tech that was in fact a vet assistant and took off running down that busy main, 4-lane road I just spoke about.

You NEVER take any animal outside by a busy four lane road of traffic, still sedated and on pain meds to pee and for a walk. You walk them in the daycare or fenced area that you have in place. And you NEVER drop a pet's leash to save another. This is one of the most important procedures that vet techs learn in training while being certified. The first thing they are taught, is the proper way of how to place their hand in the noose leash opening, while wrapping it around the wrist several times depending on the weight and size of the dog, to keep any pet from getting away from them and to keep from anything like this happening in the first place. Seriously?! How about some more staff training since there is lack of.

Now at this point, sadly the Vet's dog took precedence over mine, even though they said they didn't have a protocol in place. Well guess what? Yep, they saved her dog and let Shiloh take a back seat. I understand that the vet is their boss, and she determines their jobs and writes their paycheck, and they felt compelled to save her dog that got loose, but why not save mine too. Are you starting to get the picture here? Utterly PATHETIC and it makes me want to vomit just thinking about it and what they did to her!

Who in their right mind takes out 2 dogs together by the same vet staff member, when Shiloh weighed 18 lbs. and the vet's dog towered her, weighing approximately 75 lbs. Yes at the same time?! Absurd I know! Totally avoidable and unacceptable!! She should still be alive, sitting on my lap as I'm writing her untimely death. She was cheated out of her sweet little life, from a so-called professional that took an Oath to "Do NO Harm!"

This incompetent vet assistant purposely dropped Shiloh's leash, and she admitted to it, and started running after the Vet's dog to save her pup, while leaving Shiloh to wander off and fend for herself. Shiloh starts wandering off out of fear while waiting for someone to come back and get her, as I'm sure she was dazed, startled, disillusioned, and still drowsy in an unfamiliar place wondering where the heck am I and why am I out here all alone? My girl only 8 months old as she stood there by herself, while the staff had turned their backs on her and jump into action to run down the street after the Vet's dog during rush hour.

Remember, Shiloh had fresh sutures in her belly, still loopy and discombobulated from sedation and pain meds slowly wearing off. While dragging a noose collar as they say, around her neck from the leash that was dropped when she starts to wander off looking for help. After no one comes back to get her and take her back inside, she starts to wander off for at least 45 minutes to an hour and was already 2 miles from the vet's office, before I even knew she was missing, lost and on the run. Once I tried to wrap my head around this negligent act, the search was on. We (my family) were in total search mode and desperate to find "Shi."

We rushed down to UC College as we were told to do by the acting Vet, from her back door to help look for Shiloh where she was last spotted, and yes I just said UC College? Do you have any idea how far this is? It's a very looooong run for an 18 lb. baby that just had surgery. We are talking 2 miles from the Vet's office that Shiloh had already traveled.

Meanwhile, Chris goes one way and I go the other in separate vehicles. When Chris was passing McDonald's in our local area on the main street of McCorkle Avenue at a 4-way stop, she spotted the vet tech (which again was only an assistant) with a makeshift tourniquet shirt or jacket off of her own back wrapped around the vet's dog, to use as a restraint type leash to get her dog back to the clinic/office. So, the vet's dog at this point had again taken precedence over mine. And guess what? Yep, they saved her dog and let Shiloh take a back seat. I understand that the vet is their boss and all, and they felt compelled to save her dog that got loose, but why not save mine too. Shiloh's life mattered!

The tending Vet (owner) went home that night with her dog in her arms, safe and sound with not one blemish, because her dog was saved from running off and retrieved by her vet assistant and staff, while my Shiloh is running around the streets of Kanawha city in the dark, in the cold, it was raining, windy and with fresh sutures. So in short, I drop her off for a routine spay, and she is now coming home in a crematory urn. Nothing left of her but fragments of bones and ashes, all from being lost for 3 long days and 2 VERY LONG nights due to a horrible and negligent act from this heartless Vet and her staff that could have been prevented. Sadly because of their negligence and leaving her all alone to fend for herself, she was tragically hit head on in the face, by a fast moving train on the 3rd day of the search after being spotted just 20 minutes earlier by a worker at a local restaurant where she apparently smelled food and was hungry. I am beyond devastated and tears roll down my face as I type through the heartache reliving it all. No one ever stops grieving because the pain of losing a fur-child never goes away. As a grieving pet parent: "This is not something you get over; it's something you learn to live with." I'm still in utter disbelief and will never get over her loss.

Sadly, their exact words to me were, "that this was JUST an unfortunate thing that happened." Really?! Unfortunate thing was an understatement! Then why didn't they run after Shiloh until they caught her, if it was so unfortunate and since I trusted that she was in good hands at a so-called professional Veterinarian facility. Why didn't they just turn the table and let the Vet's dog run loose for 3 days and 2 nights and save Shiloh? If you could only imagine what was running through my roommates and my mind the entire time we were out searching after everyone left us, as she was running loose and lost in the cold, rainy, snowing, sleeting and wind of night. There were so many sightings in the same area off and on during the entire search, but we could never find her. It was sheer torture!

It was never about finding Shiloh on behalf of the vet and her staff, it was clearly all about saving the vets dog from the get go. I will NEVER and I mean NEVER get over what happened to my girl at the hands of this evil Veterinary facility, and this horrible nightmare that my family has had to endure and live through. I pray that no one ever has to go through what we have. It's been utter TORTURE! I will never get to see, hug, kiss or hold my angel baby "Shiloh" again. I have NO WORDS! All I am left with is a broken heart in a million pieces that will never be whole again. Oh, and an urn of ashes.

The vet and staff NEVER showed any remorse for their wrong doing, not one time. In fact, the acting and owner of the veterinary clinic called off the search just under 3 hours into the search. Yes, the Vet ordered her staff to go home and said they would resume the next day, which only two of her staff showed up the next morning after me calling and begging and pleading they come help. Where were their priorities? Obviously not Shiloh. Pathetic!!

Here are the exact words this heartless Vet had to say to me the first night that Shiloh was running the streets alone as she had just called off the search, that she and her staff had caused. She said she was going home for the night because she was tired from working all day, had kids to take care of and had to get up early the next morning to see clients because she had bills to pay? My head spun around and it felt like a Linda Blair moment, when they created the vomit scenes. My eyes were bulging out of my head, and I was hurt and fuming from the statement that just came out of her mouth. Here I am out searching with a severe case of bronchitis, sick as a dog and under doctor's care myself. But she's tired and going home to rest for the night, because she has bills to pay. And yes, she's going home with her dog that got loose earlier that day. Everything to do with this search that they caused was wrong on so many levels, but they were going home for the night. Nice, real nice.

She also had the nerve to say, Shiloh had to be tired from running and missing all evening. That she was sure that Shiloh would just go curl up on some strangers porch or crawl in their dark garage and sleep the rest of the night until morning from exhaustion. That is downright ruthless to say and coming from a so-called professional. How would you feel? Meanwhile, I'm getting phone calls all night from flyers Chris and I had posted, from caring individuals that live in Kanawha city and work at local businesses on midnights that spotted her walking around in the same area all the while she tells me that my girl would go curl up and sleep on somebody's cold concrete porch for the night. Come on. I mean really? What professional says that to a distraught, grieving pet parent? Never mind feeling that way about an animal she let loose earlier in the day from her practice and treats animals on a daily basis. Truth is, they should have NEVER left until my baby was found PERIOD. That first night was crucial, and she as well as her staff should have never left her out there running the streets. She should have stayed to help. That first hour that her leash was dropped, and I was never notified was actually the most crucial time of all. God only knew where she was by the time I found out the bad news. Despicable!! I'm speechless that any veterinarian would use this kind of behavior after their own negligence was involved, but I now consider the source.

Come on people, use common sense. Including all resources no matter the extent to find my baby. I don't care what it takes, or what you have to do or how you plan to do it, but it's up to you to help find her since you senselessly lost her.

Soon after I see there is going to be NO help from the veterinarian's office to get immediate help in the search and it was getting late and very dark quickly, my motherly instinct kicked in and I went straight to social media out of desperation and I begged for help from anyone that would hear my cry, listen, read my post, spread the word quickly and come help me and my family in the search for "Shi." Time was of the essence. There was no time to waste. There were so many of my friends, family and individuals that heard my crying plea for help, that they all came to help search out of love for Shiloh. For this I will forever be grateful.

These amazing folks that I now call my friends, came from near and far, and ranged from youths to adults and even family pets. Those who lived in the state and those who came from neighboring states searched day and night, on foot, on bikes and in cars. They came with food, treats, blankets, flashlights, handed out and posted flyers and even taking time off work, losing pay to help in any way they could in the search for my baby girl. Not once ever expecting anything in return for their help, and I mean nothing. I will be forever grateful and humbled by them all and there will never be enough words to express how thankful I am to each one of them. One thing I have learned through it all, is that it has very much restored my Faith in Humanity. Everyone with the same goal in mind and that was to search until we found Shiloh safe and out of harms way.

My dear friend that was in North Carolina at the time of Shiloh's missing and was on another search and rescue assignment, dropped everything when she heard about Shiloh running loose and offered to come help and search with her search and rescue dog. She drove well over 4+ hours, and she and her search and rescue dog searched for over 3 and a half long grueling hours. I owe her my life! She walked and searched steep wooded river banks with thick brush, while jumping river rats and opossums. She searched miles of dirt and paved roads, parking lots, and ravines, in the pitch black darkness and scary night in hopes to find Shiloh. Without her and her search and rescue dog, we'd gotten nowhere. She never gave up, and I am forever grateful to her that she dropped everything to come and help my family search. She was and is my saving grace in my darkest hour and I will forever be indebted to her. Yes she is an Angel!

It makes me angry and sick to my stomach when I think about how the Vet and her staff handled the whole situation. It was so unprofessional on so many levels. As my girl was pacing back and forth on those railroad tracks that night and scared to death. She was running and hiding in and out of holes while in the dark of the night, that were carved out on that cold river bank to feel safe and to stay warm. River rats, raccoons, snakes, opossums, and God knows what else ran past her and over her little feet and body just as they did us while searching, only she was alone while we had each other to lean on. It kills me of the thought. It was so frigid and cold and snowflakes swirling in the air, while the perpetrators took turns sitting in their cars for warmth and then decide to call off the search after only searching for those few hours the next night. Who does this?!

My Border Collie "Oliver" also helped in the search, along with Friends and VERY kind Strangers that all came together in the name of love. They kept coming from all over when word continued to travel and my friends read my post begging for help on social media. I even put out a $2000.00 reward for Shiloh's safe return. I was desperate to find her and grasping at straws no matter the cost. I would have literally done anything for her safe return. Even if it meant giving up my own life. I just wanted her home and back in my arms.

If it wasn't for everyone's help and the two men who found her dead shortly after she was struck by the train on day three, she would still be missing and would have never been found nor retrieved. There is no doubt in my mind. She would be laying on those railroad tracks for who knows how long, decomposing as the vultures and who knows what else pecking and eating her caucus and remains. It makes me so heart SICK when I often picture this in my mind.

Pet Parents, PLEASE make sure you do your homework before choosing a good Vet. It's so easily done. Research your local Veterinarian's for any complaints or disciplinary actions taken against them, by doing a background check with your State Board of Veterinary Medicine. It is public record. Ask as many questions as possible no matter what city or state you live in, to be sure that your animal is in the best care possible, so that they come home to you at the end of the day, safe and sound. Be in the know when leaving your pets in the care of any Veterinarian, or pet Professional who is actually caring for your beloved and know their capabilities and titles. If you are ever in question about any staff that calls themselves a vet tech under false pretenses, and like what happened to me, call your State Veterinary Board of Medicine, and verify their title. There is a HUGE difference between a vet tech and a vet assistant. This I had to learn the hard way!

Our pets depend on us as a parent. Make sure all your request are understood and written on paper and signed off by you, the attending Veterinarian or designated qualified staff member or personnel that they understand all your request for your beloved. You must dot all your "i's" and cross your "t's" to have the proper and legal binding paper trail that will hold any negligent Veterinary responsible for the care that your animals receive whether good or bad while in their care. Let me stress that not all Veterinarians are bad. In fact, there are more good ones than bad ones. Just do your homework ahead of time. As knowledge is power and can potentially save you from a lot of heartache in the long run.

It is a must that our pets are going to be in a safe environment and in safe hands when leaving them in the care of any Pet Professional. Learn from my experience, as my life will never be the same. It will save you from a lifetime of feeling guilt to no fault of your own. Intense anxiety, disbelief, anger, sadness, sleepless nights, and a shattered heart that will never mend due to a failed and broken system. My heart is beyond repair!!!!!!

What a Heart Wrenching Day it was. Nothing could have ever prepared me for this day or the outcome. I could have ever imagined it happening to me, not in a million years on those 3 dreadful days. I've read about these sad, horrid, scary, and nightmarish stories in books regarding Vet malpractice and negligence and heard of others going through them, but never thinking I was about to live and experience the very nightmares that I once read about myself. If I could only turn back the hands of time, I would do it in a heartbeat.

I was so scared and scattered when I heard she was missing. I went from my heart racing and pounding out of my chest to feeling like I needed to regurgitate. I was speechless, distraught, my mind racing. I fell down my flight of steps and hurt myself while crying to the top of my lungs and I couldn't focus. Then on to anger, nervousness, a million questions of how could this happen and every other emotion imaginable crossed my mind. I was numb, I couldn't speak - no words at all, as I was speechless. Nothing but a flood of tears, screaming to the top of my lungs, "Why Lord, Why?" Everyone in my home in disbelief, tears and heartbreak overwhelm my home that day and for the 3-day duration and search in hopes to find Shiloh and bring her home safe and sound, not dead.

I'll never forget as a mother, I jumped into search mode and nothing else mattered at that moment, but to find Shiloh before the darkness of the night set in. I was on a mission to do whatever it took to find her, never thinking this was going to turn into a 2 night 3 day search that would ultimately end with her death after being spotted 20 minutes before she was hit head on by a fast moving train that tore half of my beautiful girls head off her shoulders.

As I would lay awake at night screaming to the top of my lungs and crying uncontrollably while everyone fast asleep, asking God why my girl had to be a poster child for the negligence of a Veterinarian that took an oath to do NO HARM and asking why her life had to be cut so short. Why she had to die in such a tragic way. All I kept hearing from HIM, was I have a plan and you MUST trust me as you have always done your entire life. I have everything planned for You, Shiloh and her perpetrator regarding this tragic event that has taken place. Just believe in ME and keep your Faith. This is out of your hands my child, and I am in control. So, that's exactly what I've done.

Three and a half years later.... Does it get easier? I would be lying if I told you it does. I still can't wrap my head around nor comprehend the travesty of this event and why or how it would all play out. Sadly, I may never know all the facts regarding the death of Shiloh, thanks to Shiloh's perpetrator never having the guts to face me in person or in a court of law. Most likely it's because of her guilt. Hmm mm, could it just be another cover up, the hidden truth and lies that haunt her daily? Then thinking that they could once again sweep another horrible mistake under a rug as they've done before that kept the Vet from looking me in the eyes and explaining the truth as a loving licensed Veterinary should have done. Or in this Vet's case, is it just for the love and greed of money, that unfortunately takes precedence over most cases when it comes to our pets and a Pet Professional's services? Are they only a number, I ask? I feel in Shiloh's case it was both greed and guilt that overruled the acting Veterinarian's thoughts of honesty, and integrity. Otherwise, as a professional that is supposed to care for animals, she would want to voluntarily make it right by offering her sincere apologies and give sincere answers to what happened so that we as a family rightfully deserved in order to begin a healing process.

I will make sure that those responsible, never forget the face of my innocent baby girl Shiloh. I will be a constant reminder. Shiloh's perpetrator and staff will have to live the rest of their life with the blood of Shiloh on their hands and her tragic death on their conscious while showing NO REMORSE. They may have never had the courage to face me or give me an apology or an explanation of her death because she meant NOTHING to them.

I believe that one reaps what they sow. In the end, we ALL stand before Our Creator, and Shiloh's Creator. The ONE and only Judge with the highest power over anyone. It is then that we will all get our ultimate sentencing for our deeds on earth, whether good or bad and no one is exempt. They WILL all have no choice but to answer to her death and how they handled it. That will be their judgement in the end, that will be the only punishment and judgement that matters in Shiloh's case and in my eyes.

Have I ever gotten a professional or personal apology regarding Shiloh's death in person? By letter, by card, by email, by a phone call, by text or a private message, or by a smoke signal. My answer in TWO words: Unequivocally NO.

Fast-forward and here we are 3+ years later as her death still haunts me, on January 24, 2020, just after midnight the eve of Shiloh's death.

My goodness, her death is still so fresh in my mind and heart. I can't believe it has been 3 years since my SWEET baby girl was KILLED by this Veterinary Hospital. Where has time gone? Today 3 years ago was the start of the worst nightmare of mine and my baby girl's life.

So what else does one do on the eve of the negligent death-iversary of their unforgettable, sweet, and "Angelic" fur baby that was killed 3 years ago today?

I lay here and I can vividly see her flawless face tonight in my mind. A portrait that only God himself could have painted. When God created and painted every inch of her beautiful face and body, he drew a masterpiece that only HE is capable of doing. Every stroke, every line, every swirl and blends of color, and every mark on her face and body were flawless. She was PERFECT in every way!

I lay awake, reliving the entire nightmare that Shiloh went through those dreadful days and nights as she ran loose and scared to death, over and over in my head. Those 3 days... oh my gosh those 3 days (- as I cry -) and 2 very long nights were terrifying, and I was in an enormous state of shock and panic, on a mission to find her running scared. A feeling of helplessness that came over me, that's indescribable.

All I wanted to do was find my baby girl safe and sound, unharmed and cradle her in my arms. I wanted to tell her how sorry I was that she was running the streets of Kanawha city, WV by herself, only 18 lbs., eight months old, and a beautiful Miniature Red Merle Australian Shepherd while her pain meds continue to wear off and with fresh sutures in her stomach from her spay surgery earlier in the day. I wanted her to know how sorry I was that she was afraid and scared wondering where I was. She was my soulmate and my heart dog. I can't help but think she was thinking to herself, why can't I find my momma? I want my Momma! Please find me Momma. It's so dark and cold out here and I'm scared. I need you Momma and I want to come home. But I never got that chance. This nightmare would ultimately lead to the death of my sweet girl. What would this nightmare accomplish, after having so much hope of finding her? It would ONLY accomplish many sleepless nights. Nightmare, after nightmare. Questions and so many "Why's." It would cause me to cringe from the sound of every train whistle when I would hear one throughout the day and night. It caused depression for both my family and my other fur babies. And it caused anxiety, seclusion, anger, heartbreak, my mind in constant overdrive and it put me in a state that I would never wish on my worst enemy. Yes, it changed my life forever!!

I remember the last kiss I gave her on her little head, promising her that I'd be back to get her later that day and not to be afraid. My heart hurts. I feel sick to my stomach, and my gut is churning and burning from the inside out with grief. I've asked myself over and over why I ever took Shiloh to Good Shepherd Veterinary Hospital in the first place. Never thinking a place of business that you think your pet will be safe and cared for, and unharmed, would be killed while in their care, and come home in an urn of ashes. There desperately needs to be better staff training in EVERY facility regarding proper pet care and the care that they give our precious fur babies in the event that this or anything else of this magnitude would ever happen again. A good start would be to master all protocol that should be in place and learn the proper use of a noose when walking a dog.

I would have never imagined an outcome like this. Not in a million years. Not even if I was told beforehand. To me, it would have seemed so farfetched that anything of this magnitude could happen. Not in my wildest dreams. Not ever! To be honest, it was the furthest thing from my mind, but yet look at me now?! A pet parent's worst nightmare! Never again will I be able to hold her. Cuddle with her, kiss her little face off, nor tell her how much I love her. I do know in my heart that she would still be with me today if I had kept her coddled and safe in my arms that dreaded day. I should have kept her in the safety of our home, instead of putting her life in danger by taking her there. Again, why didn't I listen to my inner voice? Unfortunately, I trusted this Vet and her staff at her facility to take care of my girl. To keep her safe, not kill her! Who does that? I still can't and will NEVER know or understand how in the hell they could have allowed this to happen. I still and will always have a hard time wrapping my head around it all. It's still so fresh in my heart and mind. (As if it were yesterday) It never gets easier, not ever.

Luckily someone directed me as to how to file a complaint to the WV Board of Veterinary Medicine. Soon after filing I would receive a phone call that they DID find probable cause to investigate Shiloh's death after viewing the complaint filed against this vet and after going through Shiloh's file. From what I've learned, that is a huge accomplishment. Given that most Veterinary complaints from clients don't get the attention deserved and get nowhere once filed. Usually once read never get any further than the desk of the Vet Board in the world of Veterinary Medicine. So, for that, I am grateful they found probable cause.

The WV Veterinary Board of Medicine did put into place new policies while having their board meeting for the state of WV shortly after the investigation as you can read below.

In the State of West Virginia, our laws prevent disciplinary action against a Veterinarian and it becomes totally out of the hands of the Veterinary Board when an incident happens and I quote from the Veterinary Board, "outside of the brick-and-mortar walls of a veterinary facility." Even if a pet is still in their care. Go figure. I'm still in disbelief and it's a hard pill to swallow. A Veterinary Board can only hold an acting Veterinary responsible and give disciplinary action to a licensed Vet if the abuse, malpractice, or negligence happens within the walls of the building and/or practice under the old laws. I had no idea and I'm sure other Pet Parents aren't aware of this either. I was told by the two acting board members of the WV Veterinary Board of Medicine residing over Shiloh's case, that under our states old, outdated laws, that the Vet Boards hands were tied regarding Shiloh due to Shiloh's incident taking place outside the doors of this establishment. The Veterinary Board was sincerely disgusted, outraged and upset about Shiloh's death, her gruesome pictures with half of her head torn off and how it happened. Even saying, that this was one of the most disturbing, and tragic cases they had ever investigated in their many years of being on the Board of Veterinary Medicine and in their career of Veterinary Medicine.

So unfortunately, once the staff walked Shiloh out the facilities back door she was no longer protected by and under the laws in effect to date. The surveillance tape they provided to the Veterinary Board was conveniently spliced and stopped right at the back door of the office as the Vet's employee started to walk Shiloh outside that would lead to her death. It showed nothing on that tape from that point on. It was a dry, sloppy splice and cut too. So obvious they were trying to cover their tracks. The outside is where it ALL happened, not inside. I am entitled to know EVERYTHING that transpired from the owner herself and should have gotten to see the entirety of the surveillance tape as it snowball out of control, after they walked my girl out that back door. But no, I never got to see it.

Sadly, by law they didn't have to show any more of the tape than what they provided, because it all happened outside. If it had happened inside it would have been a very different outcome for this heartless Veterinarian, I can promise her that. The Vet Board cannot implement nor bring disciplinary action or remove a negligent Vet's license under the old law but can and are limited to an investigation only. Another lousy loophole for our fur children that needs to be fixed.

All I can say, is that the only thing that saved her license with the vet board and not getting her into a lot more trouble than she was already in, is due to the old laws regarding our animals that are still in effect today. Because this madness happened outside the building where she practices, rather than within the inside of those cold ruthless concrete walls. Otherwise, she would be out of business with no license. One's luck does eventually run out.

Quote unquote words from the vet board: Unfortunately, Robin we are only responsible for what happens within the walls of a Veterinarian's facility and/or walls of an existing building that they rent or own. Anything that happens outside their doors, the vet board's hands are tied. So when Shiloh walked out that door with her employee under the old laws that's the only thing that saved her hind end. Change is already coming. So from now on she better dot your i's and cross her t's in the upcoming future. I will lobby and continue to fight to improve and change the laws with the help of many people backing me and have had issues with this same Veterinarian and staff.

Vet Board Resolution as follows:

PUBLIC RECORD

Hurdle #1

EFFECTIVE JULY 1, 2017

Yes, we made progress on behalf of getting the Justice "Shiloh" very much deserves.

This is PUBLIC RECORD for EVERYONE to read.

Please go to their website

www.wvbvm.org

West Virginia Board of Veterinary Medicine

And at the top of the page, click on the About link. Then on the left of the page, click on Board Newsletters. Then click on July 2017 link and download the NEW Standards of Practice

EFFECTIVE JULY 1, 2017

Go to the bottom of Page 6 and read the NEW Board RECOMMENDED Facility EMERGENCY PROTOCOLS for the entire state of WV.

Yes, we made progress on behalf of my Angel Girl "Shiloh Skylar Rayne" and ALL animals, as we've promised regarding her negligent death. So that NO ONE else will ever have to go through this insanity.

It reads as follows:

BOARD RECOMMENDED FACILITY EMERGENCY PROTOCOLS

As part of its statutory duty, the Board registers and inspects veterinary facilities. As such and part of its outreach and mission, the Board may make suggested recommendations for veterinary practices.

The Board suggests the following recommendations for all veterinary practices that they have in place protocols and procedures along with the appropriate training for staff on what to do in the event of the following emergencies:

- - Walking Animals Outside of Secured Enclosures

- - Lost Animals

- - Loss of Electricity

- - Loss of Water

- - Fire /Hospital Evacuation - Not only important for the staff but for the housed animals

- - Workplace Violence

The Board recommended making a protocol prior to an actual emergency occurring in order to save time and possibly save lives. Remember, it's always important to document staff training.

These changes made by the WV Veterinary Board of Medicine were a wonderful step in the right direction and by law the most they could do. Not enough for what my girl endured and definitely NOT ENOUGH repercussion to the perpetrator who killed my girl through our failed justice system regarding our pets that ARE family members and not as they say, "It's just a Dog and Personal Property." I say, "Put the shoe on the other foot and walk a day in my shoes and then let's reevaluate the punishment and outcome of blatant pet and animal negligence resulting in death. Then we'll talk.

There are too many nights I cry myself to sleep, begging God to take away the pain and help me to understand his plan.

When the day God took Shiloh Home, I screamed out to Him from the deepest place of my heart and soul, knowing beyond a shadow of a doubt that I simply could not survive this loss without his help. I still wonder daily how a shattered heart continues beating, how even though a part of me died that day. I asked God to "supernaturally" hold and carry me, cause the natural just wasn't going to do. There were days I thought I'd never make it through and didn't even want to get out of bed from depression, yet He carried me through. After 3 years I really began to worry about my grief for Shiloh and how it was totally consuming me and had continued to affect my health and life. It was wrecking me to my core. Physically and emotionally. There were days I was really struggling. I can't thank God enough for my friends, my family, my sister friend Jenn, and the unconditional love that came from my other fur babies. For the most unselfish act of love everyone provided through prayer, uplifting messages, and through the search of my girl when she was lost. My friends and family have been my rock for these past 3 years, and I am so very thankful for them all and I know I couldn't have survived this journey without each one of them.

I still don't understand why God chose her to bear this horrible pain, but I do know that the good Lord chose the right puppy Momma for the challenge that lies ahead. He knew that I would never give in, nor give up. My promise is to continue to fight for Justice for all animals, and to make a difference in the lives of others who own pets and either felt intimidation or as if they never had a leg to stand on. I don't ever want anyone to have to endure this roller coaster ride of emotions, nor the nightmare that my family has lived through these past 3 years. Our pets are a part of our family, and they are like children to most of us. They're not just a Dog!!!

Days and months pass us by and to no avail, sadly there was no resolution between my family and the vet at fault. She avoided us at all costs.

That's when another course of action was taken as it was the only way we were going to get any answers or resolution to what had happened to Shiloh. My family had to make the decision to move forward regarding the negligence of Shiloh's death and file a civil suit. The WV Veterinary Board of Medicine assured us that by doing this, my family would get the much-needed answers and truth about the horrific reckless and negligent death of Shiloh that took place that tragic day, as their hands were tied by our old laws presently in effect in the state of WV. This is where the old laws that are in effect come in to play. In the state of West Virginia, a Vet board can only try a case and/or reprimand a licensed Veterinarian if an incident regarding an animal happens inside the walls of a brick-and-mortar building and/or facility. When neglect, happens outside the walls of said building, even if your pet family member is in their care, they (the Vet Board) can technically do nothing regarding a Vet's licensing, nor can they hold them accountable. They can only investigate the inside of the facility and everything that took place before Shiloh was walked out the back door and let loose from them. Sadly, there was not much to investigate, other than to ask specific questions to the vet at fault, check for protocol's and a basic investigation, because everything took place outside of the building pertaining to Shiloh.

Unfortunately, since our pets are considered personal property, we had no choice but to retain counsel to get answers to her death, to try and understand what took place and to try and find some sort of closure and resolution. It is an absolute shame that it had to result in this course of action because Shiloh's perpetrator would never comply to many requests of a simple sit down, and a one-on-one discussion. A real shame because it could have been resolved so easily and in a much simpler manner since it was an open and closed case of neglect by the vet on duty. Anyone who truly knows me, knows that I have a heart of gold. I'm very forgiving and would give the shirt off my back to anyone who needed it. I would have been very grateful to listen to what the negligent vet had to say to find some sort of closure and to better understand why and how this tragic event happened.

Her perpetrator as a professional should have been more than willing to have wanted to meet with me on a voluntary basis. But no way, she wanted to rudely play hard ball and it got her nowhere but drawing it out longer for both sides and causing my family more unneeded anguish. If indeed she were in the business for the love of animals and wanted to care for them to the best of her ability, and truly took Shiloh's death seriously wouldn't she have agreed to a voluntary sit down and not run from her negligence? It still blows me away with her behavior. I begged this Veterinarian on multiple occasions for answers, and she would avoid me at all costs. Never ever offering to give definitive answers to me or my family so that we could have the much-needed closure to start some sort of closure and a healing process. She didn't care about my girl at all. She is heartless to say the least!

This is why Shiloh's story must be shared as I truly want people to be informed, because I wasn't. And if I had been, she would still be here.

I never wanted to have to be forced to pay out of pocket to get answers and closure, and no parent should ever have to if they have a caring Vet. I had to and I would do it all over again no matter the cost and loss of money that I've had because of the way they took my girl's life that dreaded day. You can't put a price tag on the life of your child. If need be, I would have sold my house to retain counsel and lived in a tent. That's just what us mothers do for our children.

I was told in the beginning not to get discouraged, that there would be bumps in the road and roadblocks after filing a complaint, but to never back off and keep pushing forward. Never dreaming an incident of this sort would become so difficult to resolve as it's been, when it was cut and dry and written in black and white. I've promised from day one when Shiloh was put in harm's way that I would not stop, until I got the justice that she so rightfully deserved, and we did just that. I see why so many clients and potential cases are swept under a rug, because of the scare tactics and threats that the Vet's voice towards their clients. Not counting the expense one incurs to fight over their beloved pet and all the bumps in the road that one encounters along the way. But I will be the first to admit, it was all worth it!

I will NEVER stop, and I am NOT going away until there is change! I have never been so passionate about anything in my life as I am today. Apparently, the man above knew who to choose to help make these much-needed changes and to fight to put them into effect. He knew I would NEVER give up and I won't. He chose a strong Momma indeed, and he knows my heart.

This has been a real eye-opener, as well as an education. Personally I feel on behalf of this Vet, that due to her negligence against Shiloh, her running from the truth, and never an attempt to speak with me, and NO attempted contact at all speak volumes. To me, actions speak much louder than words in all cases.

She also knows in her heart of hearts how much I love Shiloh, and how much it would have meant to me for a simple explanation. But she chose to leave me in limbo and to continue losing more sleepless nights that I will never forgive her for. I'm a fighter and stand up for what I believe in. No professional in any kind of business and not just a veterinary business, would have handled this situation in the manner that she has. I'm sure a caring and any genuine remorseful business owner would have handled it much differently if they truly care about their clients and animals. And most importantly, a simple APOLOGY is sufficient at best.

Shiloh's siblings are still so Sad :(and Depressed over their sister Shiloh's tragic passing. They just don't understand why she left one day and never returned home, as none of us can come to terms. I've literally witnessed tears roll from my babies eyes and it kills me. Especially my boy Border Collie "Oliver Grayson" who had a purpose and was on a mission to find his sister. He knew exactly what he was doing, as he searched tirelessly for her. Running in and out of coves, and holes dug in the hills of the riverbank. He searched down in ravines and hill sides when he would smell her scent. I wish I would have never listened to the vet begging me to go get my personal dogs to help search. That is another HUGE regret of mine, and it saddens me every time I look in his eyes and relive that moment in time. I know Ollie feels defeated that he never found his sister Shiloh, because he feels like his mission was never accomplished. I never want my boy to feel defeat of any kind, because to me, he is my hero for trying so hard and for searching for so many tireless hours. He never wanted to stop searching. We literally had to make him stop due to exhaustion and against his will as he continued to tug and wanted to keep searching. He is devastated and his heart is broken. Oliver feels he's lost his purpose after not finding his sister. He has never forgotten that day and has never been the same since that day 3 years ago. He was cheated too, in my opinion.

So many days of extreme ups and downs for me and my family. I go from one extreme to the absolute other, and so would they. So my go to is to pray to the one who has all the answers. That's where I've truly found my peace and continue to keep my faith as he asked from me. It takes practice and patience to find the peace that resides in all of us. I always keep a grateful heart and my faith continues to strengthen and grow, as I see God working out all the details. Through ALL these emotions, I can honestly tell you that, my cup does and continues to run over with gratitude, love, and a sense of relief to have been able to finally conquer this terrible fear and sadness that continues to try and hold me hostage in my own mind and body. When I feel this feeling start to come over me, I pray even harder. My Father God and I have made a deal between us. NO more holds of fear, anxiety, sadness, and depression on me. As I continue to grow spiritually it has started the healing process that I have longed for and it has given me the freedom from those terrible emotions that once existed and tried to rule my life. It feels absolutely freeing and amazing when I finally laid all my troubles regarding Shiloh's death at my Father God's feet. What a loving father we have! Through HIM all things are possible.

My house is only two streets from the train tracks and runs perpendicular to the very train tracks that my girl was ultimately killed on. The sound of a train whistle throughout the day soon became the most haunted sound to me immediately following Shiloh's death. I would cringe multiple times a day from the sound and it would chill me to the bone while cutting me to my core. The same train whistle that once haunted me, through faith and trust from my Heavenly Father and once I decided to take a different approach, has quickly become my way of communicating with Shiloh. He has helped me turn a negative sound into a positive one.

The same train whistle that once haunted me from the sound multiply times a day for years and would chill me to the bone and cut me to my core, has now become a positive sound in my life by choice. When I now hear the same train whistle that once made me cringe and brought me to my knees in tears, I had to train my mind to change a negative to a positive for my own sanity. I now know it's Shiloh saying hello Momma, and I reply with a smile, "There's Momma's girl passing by to say hello, and say I love you Shi" as the train whistle blows and passes by. I can finally after much soul-searching, smile and say that's my girl and rejoice knowing she is well, she is whole, and she is now safe and in the arms of her Creator where she will never know harm again. His promise!

I am forever grateful that I can now hear and see a train in a whole new light. From a noise that once made me cringe has finally turned to triumph, through God's grace. My father God has helped me cope in miraculous ways that I could have never imagined.

Much progress is beginning to take place. Yes baby steps, but a lot of progression with his help. I'm still a work in progress but have come a long way, and there's nowhere but up from here.

Here's a little something I want to share, as I will never forget the morning this came over in a private message and it never left my heart. Wow, it couldn't have been more perfect timing. I was having a really hard morning, trying to somehow put everything into perspective regarding Shiloh and needed to hear this. God always has PERFECT timing and knows when you need to be lifted. To me this lovely, heartfelt message is and will always be priceless as this message very much sums up those three days that we all came together as one, to search for Shiloh.

For days after Shiloh's tragedy, I was trying to find words to express the thanks I was feeling for everyone who came to help and became a large part of her story. I was trying to write in a journal how I felt about the present circumstances and the love and thanks that I was feeling to the many who came out on their own free will to search for her, those long miserable days, and nights as she recklessly was running loose, but I kept getting completely overwhelmed and could never finish how I was feeling. My mind was so boggled and consumed as to what had just transpired, that I couldn't see through the tears to write and I couldn't find the words to pull it all together. Under normal circumstances, I am a very expressive writer but could NOT find the proper wording needed to put in my own words. I needed to show my thanks, gratitude, love, heartfelt and humbled feelings that I was feeling towards those individuals including (friends, family, and very kind strangers) that came together to help find Shiloh, in the name of love and it needed to be expressed but I tried and couldn't get it composed. I kept getting too overwhelmed as I was writing.

So I decided to stop and take a breather when I suddenly come across this message. I quickly opened it and this is what I found. I will keep her name private for privacy purposes but felt the need to share her message because at that very moment when I read it, she was spot on as to how I was feeling, and she had composed the very words that I couldn't pull together myself. It was my feelings in entirety and I could have never written it any better myself describing how I felt about Shiloh's sad death and how grateful I was to everyone.

It reads as follows:

I know you don't know me at all but my heart is breaking for you. I've spent my free time the last couple of days searching for your baby. I don't want your thanks, I actually just want to tell you I feel so sad about what happened. This may sound corny or whatever but through all this I've seen people come together. Something our country desperately needs! I stopped at the gas station and had a few words with a woman who had been out looking for your dog. Neither of us knew each other or you but just felt compelled to come together. I do a lot of advocacy work and my goal is to always bring people together as one. No one cared who you voted for, or what church you went to, or whether we listen to the same music. We are all just people who want the best for our families. So I want to thank you for that and offer my sincerest condolences on your little angel pooch. I hope you find a little comfort in knowing she brought so many people together in love for a common goal.

- "S" - (Who has now become a licensed Veterinary technician from this experience she witnessed while searching for Shiloh)

You'd think when taking your pets in for a simple routine visit, a major operation, or just leaving them in a Pet Professionals care period even for an overnight stay, that they would remain safe. Correct? That's what I thought. However, let me stress this statement to everyone, as I have many times!!

Never fear going to a Vet as I assure you that NOT all Vets are bad. In fact, there ARE many wonderful Veterinarians in every city and state. Even in WV. I'm lucky enough to have one of the best. We have some WONDERFUL vets in our area that love their job, are caring individuals, and are truly in the Veterinarian business for the LOVE of our animals and for all the right reasons.

The problem with my situation is that I just didn't educate myself with the proper knowledge needed, or do enough research before making such a quick, hasty, and unforgiving decision, by taking Shiloh to this particular facility when I shouldn't have. I never knew there was such a need to educate oneself before a vet visit takes place, but I now know that "Knowledge is Power." Let's just say, "Lesson Learned the Tragic Way."

This mistake was VERY preventable, and costly for me. Not only mentally and physically, but it took my baby girl's life and left me with a huge void and a broken heart! I can honestly say, the only decision in my life that I wish I could take back or change, is the day I took her there when I should have listened to my inner voice and gone with my gut feeling. My decision was based on convenience, living so close and it being just a simple routine spay. I never dreamed that I would drop her off alive and pick her up in a crematorium urn. Who would??

After talking to others like myself who are pet parents, they definitely had no idea that our animals can be in such danger such as this, by going to a vet's office for a routine visit or spay. But to add salt to injury, if they are hurt, abused, mistreated, killed, or even die while in the care of these professionals, our fur children are recognized in a court of law as nothing other than personal property and their lives mean NOTHING.

Really?! Well, for the deep hearted love and bond that I have and share with my fur children, I beg to differ. They are SOMETHING to me and NOT just a worthless piece of NOTHING!! I treat them just as I would if I was fortunate enough to have had a human child. I give them the best medical care, I guard them with my life, and give them the unconditional love that they deserve, and they give it a million times fold in return. They depend on us for everything, and I do anything humanly possible to ensure their safety. No matter the situation or cost.

I feel blessed to see that Shiloh's tragedy has made such a difference for many and has shed some light on a much-needed area that has apparently fallen through the judicial system cracks, somehow through the years. How imperative it is to get some long overdue ad outdated laws passed, and put in place quickly. Believe me, I had no idea either, of how lost all of our fur children really are when it comes to the laws and how they've slipped through our court system. But now that I do, after Shiloh's negligent death I plan to complete my mission.

We as pet parents must make sure that these Animal professionals are and will be held accountable for their actions in the near future and not just get a simple slap on the wrist. Totally unacceptable! It must STOP now, and together we will make it happen on a National and Global level.

Now back to the third day and the ending of this sad story.

After missing for 2 nights and 3 days when tragically Shiloh's search came to an abrupt halt and a tragic ending. She was hit head on by a train due to pure and utter negligence. No excuse, rhyme nor reason for this tragic and grotesque event that unfolded before our very eyes.

On that third day, she was spotted at a local restaurant because she was hungry from running and missing for those 3 nights and smelled their food cooking, which breaks my heart at the thought that she was hungry. While the sweet lady who worked there went in to get her some food to eat, Shiloh had walked away and the unthinkable happened. Yes the UNTHINKABLE!!

Shiloh was sadly found 20 minutes later after being spotted alive, lying on the train tracks dead, and covered in blood. She was morbidly hit head on by a fast-moving train and part of her head was torn off. An event that was totally preventable. No question about it. Oh, how it makes me angry and sad!

Just because a Veterinarian who took an OATH to protect my Pet and others and do no harm, did NOT do her job, as a result of PURE and RECKLESS NEGLIGENCE.

After Shiloh's body was recovered on that cold dreary day, January 27, 2017, 3 days later. while the wind so frigid and snow flurries whirling in the air, her life ending after that sudden hit and impact from an oncoming train, WE were ALL absolutely DEVASTATED, to say the very least!! After many hours of nonstop searching and still out searching the trail and railroad tracks by a local restaurant where she was just spotted 20 minutes prior in the freezing cold, we abruptly got the call on our cell phone from the Vet's office that she had been found. With the false hope, we were given by a phone call stating, come quick we have the dog. Not we have your dog, but we have THE dog. They never once said to take our time getting there, again they Verbatim said, "Come quick, we have THE dog." Flashers on Chris speeding and the breeder in the car and her husband in tow all covered with mud from searching. All this time rushing to get there, thinking Shiloh may still be alive and maybe they needed consent for treatment from where she had been on the run for so many days and nights, and by the way we were instructed to get there so quick. We had high hopes she was found alive. All the while she had been killed, but yet they yell, "Come quick!" They arrive at the vet's office and when entering the building the vet says, she's in there and pointed to the room. Jenn, who was the breeder, spoke up and said, "I will identify her." She opened the door to the room where Shiloh was dead and lying on a table, draped with a blanket to identify her.

I asked her for all the details as we all sat sobbing in my living room after leaving the vet's office. She told me in detail because I begged her. She began by saying how she removed the blanket that covered Shiloh and lifted her up off the metal table that they had her laying on and cuddled her little dead body in her arms. In her words, she checked, touched, and probed every part of her little bloody body, while running her hands over every bump, gash, cut and wound that Shiloh received from the impact of the train. Jenn kissed her and told her that her momma and so many of us love her very much and that we didn't for one minute stop looking for her. I will never forget nor will I ever be able to thank her enough for such a selfless act that through her strength of identifying Shiloh, I know crushed her heart to pieces. If you had the privilege of knowing her, she wouldn't have had it any other way. She is an amazing individual and through this tragedy I gained another sister. I love her dearly! I can NEVER thank her and Justin enough for ALL they did. After we all hugged and cried for hours and parted ways, they started their venture back home to try and find some normalcy too, to a nightmare that had just played out before our eyes as most of you there experienced alongside us.

It sickens me every time I relive the day that we dropped Shiloh off a BEAUTIFUL, playful, stunning fur-child, with the most PERFECT and PRECIOUS soul in a whole and perfect body. She walked through those doors whole and unharmed, coming from nothing but love from a family who loved her dearly. To BAM.... a slap in the face, and a dagger to the gut from this Veterinarians office!! She was killed from the reckless care they provided, and she comes home to me in a Cremation Urn as ashes. It's just not fair!

To the Vet that killed Shiloh:

You took an oath as a Veterinarian to do no harm. And how you represent yourself as a Professional and a Veterinarian, leaves a lot to be desired.

I'd like to take this opportunity to let you know that you are one of the most evil individuals that I have ever met, and I know a lot of people who feel the same.

You have a very cold, and mean heart and should consider working on your professional career and communication skills, when it comes to conversing with your clients about something negligent that has happened to their animals while in your care at your facility, in the future and years to come.

You are one heartless individual and you are in the wrong profession. Shiloh will always be a constant reminder for the rest of your life. Whether you see a dog that reminds you of her, or you see her in your dreams with half of her little bloody mangled head missing, from being hit head on by that scary fast-moving train after running for days, due to your negligent act.

I despise what you did to my baby girl and I HATE the fact that you turned my family and my world upside down. May God have mercy on you come judgement day.

It's obvious you are only in the business regarding our pets for the money and nothing more. They are only a number to you and there are many past clients that will agree. I will never let you forget about the death of Shiloh. I promise.

Be a person of integrity if you truly care about your clients and animals as a whole. Next time, try looking your client in the eyes and being honest about your faults. Stop being a coward and act like a professional should. Stop running from your mistakes and own them all, you would be more respected if you would. You are supposed to be a professional in the business for the love and care of animals and NOT to HARM them. So honesty is the best policy to build customer rapport. It's obvious you couldn't care less about Shiloh or any other animal that your facility has harmed in the past. True colors bleed through. It's sad that people like you would ever choose a profession that you dislike and give the profession that so many of us trust a bad name. Maybe a good place to start would be to take some continuing education courses, or some excellent self-development classes.

It's apparent that you have some serious intimidation issues going on and won't talk to your clients in person because of guilt and intimidation. Seems after talking to others that you handle all your disputes with a certified letter and refuse to give one on one time. That's what we as clients pay for and it's pathetic and a shame on your part that you won't oblige.

Shiloh's story has traveled all over the world and I've had people who never knew Shiloh nor me from many parts of the world send messages of love and have sent their condolences. They are in just as much disbelief as I am about what happened and have cried alongside me and with me. To them her Precious Life Mattered.

It's very important for those of us who have experienced such neglect and heartache, to pave the road for Pet Parents moving forward. To assure that our pets are indeed considered part of our families and NOT a worthless piece of personal property.

Since Shiloh's death three and a half years ago, I've heard so many sad stories of Vet Malpractice from other Pet Parents that share similar stories. Anything from malpractice to negligence, abuse, and unfortunately death. A lot of them happened at the same Veterinary facility where Shiloh was killed by an individual who took an oath to do no harm. Some were severely harmed and injured and complaints were filed. Not by all, but most. Many stories have come from all over the globe and not just limited to the United States. It seems there is an epidemic and too many flaws in areas of Veterinary medicine that need addressed. I can tell you the system is terribly broken somewhere, and our pets are unfairly falling through the cracks. The laws DO NOT protect our pets or the pet parents. Sadly, the Vet boards don't seem to hold the Vets accountable for bad behaviors, and the death of our pets, which is their job. This must change!

On the other hand, you have verbal war between some Vets and pet owners, and most vets that run from their behavioral issues out of guilt. Some Veterinarians blame pet parents for the lack of respect they get and being overworked in understaffed facilities. Then the bottom line is, they must hire more staff and stop making excuses. If they accept their faults and own their mistakes showing true remorse instead of lying and discrediting everyone else along the way, they would be more respected by pet owners and wouldn't have to worry about losing present or future business. Some Bad vets are their own worst enemy. #facts

I don't know what the answers are in this area of Veterinary medicine that lacks serious attention and causes our pets to fall through the political cracks. What I do know for certain at the end of the day, is that we have a failed system that must change now. We must be the voice for the voiceless. Shiloh's death WILL NOT be in vain and I will continue to fight for Justice that Shiloh, all pets, and pet parents very much deserve.

I've always asked God what area he needed me in the most, and I found it. This is my calling right here. To fight for the fur babies who have NO VOICE. This is my mission and I won't be stopping anytime soon. I am NOT going away, and I am here to stay. I hope you will join me.

If you have a story and you're holding it inside out of fear, please for the sake of your pets and your sanity do the right thing and file a complaint to your state Veterinary Board of Medicine. There is no statute of limitations regarding malpractice of Veterinarian. It works wonders and feels so good to release any sadness, sorrow, and anxiety that you carry and keep bottled up inside because if you don't, it will eat you alive. Stand with us about telling your story, and help be the voice for the voiceless. They depend on us.

ALL Veterinarians and Pet Professionals must be held accountable for their Negligence, Abuse, Cruelty, and Malpractice while our babies are in their care.

Over the years I have used this example many times to explain that there is no difference between the two.

If this had been a human child who sadly wandered off and got loose while under the care of an employee at a daycare center and was missing the same amount of time as Shiloh. Was hit head on by a train and part of his/or her head torn off on day three, would the outcome have been different? Of course, it would have. There is no difference between these two given scenarios. Absolutely none! She was MY CHILD!! I cry daily for my girl and the way she had to leave me, until I can hold her once again. I will tell anyone, that when my heart dog was killed and died, a part of me died with her.

I'm sorry, but she was my baby girl. And yes, I said baby girl! She was my child, not just a "THING or a dog" as they say. Those words are ludicrous!

My friends and family were my pillar of strength. My rock, my encouragers, and everything in between. For that I am forever grateful! They were there for me through some of my toughest days and nights and would never waiver. It was most humbling to know that I could lean on them and have such a wonderful support system. They were one of "MY BIGGEST BLESSINGS." I will be the first to tell you that a support system and group of friends is a very important part of one's life and healing process, during times such as these. I am blessed!

You must always, always, always continue to educate yourself as a pet parent and take nothing for granted. Read as much as you can consume and do your research on your potential practicing veterinarian, no matter your City or State. Education is key. Educate yourself on their facility protocols and ask lots, and lots of questions before you leave your babies in the hands of any Pet Professional. Ask to see and read their protocols, they must oblige. Ask if they walk them outside or have an enclosed area. Have them show you around their facility, most will be happy to. Make sure they keep them inside and get it in writing, as ALL facilities should have an enclosed area for potty purposes, especially while medicated. Oddly enough, this facility had an enclosed area that we took Shiloh to, but yet they still without our permission took Shiloh outside and as a result, she is now forever Gone and DEAD.

Put your mind at ease when dropping them off by getting answers to any questions you have with your vet and always listen to yourself if you have any doubt about a Pet Professionals facility or a terrible gut feeling. If it doesn't feel right, then it's usually not.

We have to band together and change these old and outdated laws together, to better protect our animals moving forward. So that when we drop them off anywhere in the care of a Pet Professional, that they will be held responsible for any wrong doings, and/or negligent acts. We as a Pet parents deserve to be able to rest easy and be at peace knowing that our fur babies WILL be well taken care of and in good hands during their visits or stays at any facility without any hesitation or questions.

Until then, "Through her death WILL come triumph!!" Even if she had to become the poster child of a negligent Veterinary, for Pet Parents and their pets moving forward.

God bless every one of you for ALL of your support and help, and to those of my Friends, Family and Strangers who came in droves to go above and beyond to search for my sweet girl Shiloh. I will never forget the outpouring of love from each one of you and how so many people came together in the name of Shiloh to help search to bring her home safely. None of us were prepared for this horrible outcome. Just know that I love you ALL!!!!

I've received at least a dozen stories from families I do not know, who has sadly been disrespected, has experienced negligence and abuse from this same Veterinary office, who wrongly killed Shiloh. I will NOT share their names for privacy purposes but would ask that you pray for these families and their fur-babies too. I'm not quite sure why Shiloh's perpetrator is allowed to continue to practice and harm other animals, before Shiloh and years after Shiloh's death, other than a failed system and old laws regarding our pets that must be changed. Sadly, Shiloh was not the first pet with a negligent act there, and it's apparent that she won't be the last from the complaints written to the WV Veterinary Board and pictures of the abuse and malpractice of others that I've seen with my own eyes. Please continue to pray for change. It's needed in a BIG way!

Shiloh's halo continues to shine a light for other animals each day that her story is shared and talked about. I've always said that she was too perfect from the day she was born. From the markings and spots placed strategically on every inch of her beautiful little face and body, to her angelic and sweet personality that she was blessed with. There is NO question in my mind thinking back way before this horrible tragedy and as I saw this story unfold, that she was indeed an angel in puppy form. I feel blessed that SHE is making a difference for so many other fur babies who have NO Voice. But most importantly, I feel the most blessed that she and my Father God chose me to be her Mother. What an honor it was, even if it was such a short time. I miss Shiloh, more than words could ever express. So much, at times it's unbearable and it literally takes my breath away.

The biggest lesson I have learned through her tragedy is to: Never give a negative thought an inch or it will take a mile as it has way too many times. We must stay strong! We will continue our fight as Pet Parents, and WE shall prevail and use our Voices for the Voiceless!

Many blessings to you and your fur children and if her death saves one life, hundreds, or even thousands, then we've accomplished our goal and what we've set out to do while on this mission. Goodbye for now My SWEET angel Girl. Momma will see you on the other side.

We love and miss you so much my girl. You may be gone, but YOU will never be forgotten.

I'll hold You In My Heart Until I Can Hold You In Heaven. What a Glorious Day it Will Be. One Sweet Day My Girl, One Soon Sweet Day.

Shiloh Skylar Rayne

"My Angel With A Purpose"

5/10/16 - 1/27/17

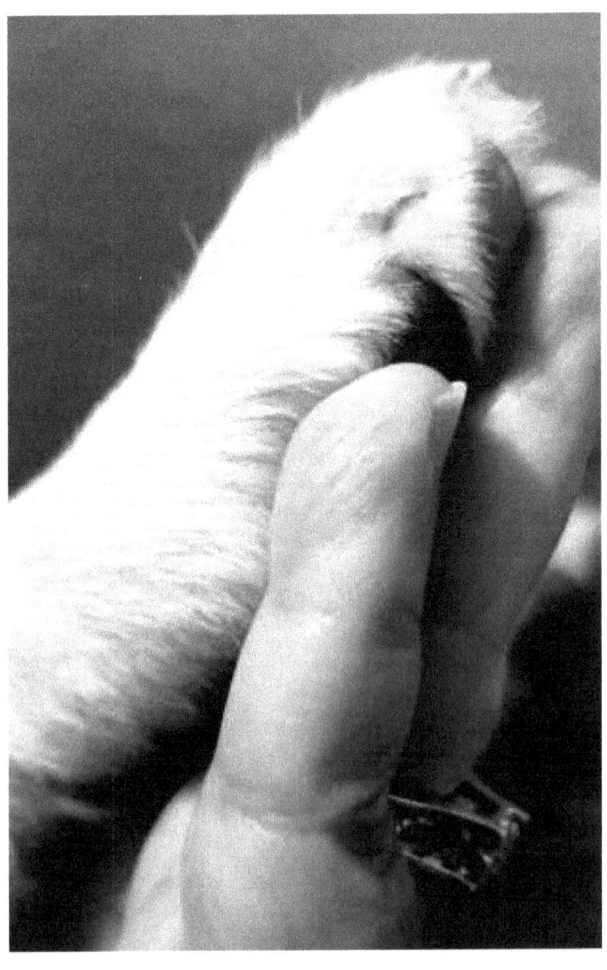

Chapter Thirty

Sir Winston Burkhart's Story

July 1, 2005 - May 10, 2017
Kristie Jackson

February 28, 2017 changed my life forever. My Miniature Schnauzer, Sir Winston Burkhart turned 11 years old on July 1, 2016. I had no idea this would be his last birthday on earth with me. God has blessed me in so many ways all my life and being Winston's Mom is among the top of the list. I've had many dogs growing up but Winston was truly special. He made me laugh daily with his antics of standing over his water bowl and barking to let me know it was empty and my very favorite memory was him sitting in our foyer staring at me and barking as I sat on the sofa. It would be around 10:00 pm and to Winston that was time to go to bed and he wanted me with him. I'd give anything to have that ritual for the rest of my life.

As a normal routine I would let Winston go outside so he could have a potty break around 3:00 p.m. He loved roaming around our fenced in pool area and I'm sure hoping to see a bunny or 2. I realized he had been out longer than normal so I walked outside on my deck and called for him. I knew there was no way for him to get out from the fenced are but he was nowhere to be seen. Finally, as I walked closer to a mulched area there he was. He was lying in the mulch and looking straight at me without attempting to get up. I noticed mulch stuck to his little nose and was puzzled because he was not a digger like some dogs. I immediately picked him up and rushed to call my husband who was at work. I explained what had happened and asked him to come home so we could get to the ER Vet. Winston seemed alert but not active. He had a strange stare look in his eyes.

The Vet immediately recognized the problem and quietly began to explain and also gently suggest my worst nightmare, euthanizing. I could not believe my ears. My baby was fine, he was not anywhere close to being sick and certainly not at this point. What I was hearing just could not be true. This has to be a mistake.

The Vet's only other option for us was a very expensive and very serious surgery with only one Vet skilled enough to perform it. This Vet only comes into our city a couple of weekends each month and this might not be one of them. I pleaded with him to make the call to see. I was not giving in to the other option.

Dr. Dennis Tim Crowe, DVM, DACVECC, DACVS, FCCM, DECC, FCCM, DACHM, NREMT-1, CFF, best surgeon/vet and was my Godsend and a devout Christian. I will always be his biggest fan. He was in town and he agreed to see my baby. His first concern was to make us understand that Winston could easily die during the CT scan, during the surgery or within a few hours, days, or weeks after the surgery. I didn't care to hear anything except that he would try to save my best friend. I honestly could not comprehend the likely outcome. This was my Winston and it would be different.

We began signing all the papers and Dr. Crowe held my hand and began to pray a powerful prayer. I loved that God had provided a Christian animal surgeon for Winston. I needed his strength and his faith. Winston was my life and God knew it.

Each day I would visit Winston while he was recovering. I put a prayer cloth bandanna around his neck. I read him healing scriptures, I served him communion and anointed him with oil. These were things I'd done with him all his life. People at my church said Winston came to church more often than some members, lol, (he always stayed in the car, weather permitting). He was prayed for by many people. Dr. Crowe and I had many discussions about our faith. I'll always cherish our friendship.

After several hours the surgery was finished and Dr. Crowe had removed a tumor the size of a softball from Winston's liver. He also removed his spleen and felt he had fairly clean margins although the tumor was alongside the main artery and difficult to get any closer to remove more questionable areas. Winston began the long hard recovery process and was doing better than expected. Dr. Crowe was almost certain the report would come back with his suspected HSA diagnosis. Hemangiosarcoma, the most EVIL of cancers. Absolutely no symptoms until the infamous collapse. This collapse normally results from the tumor bursting without any prior warning. The mulch stuck on my baby's nose was evidence he had collapsed at the pool earlier that day. My baby was going to die and there was absolutely nothing to do to change it. There was only the hope it would not be soon and it would cause my baby to suffer. A huge part of me died that day.

The next several weeks I lived in shock, denial, and fear. Winston remained in the hospital and Dr. Crowe changed his schedule and was by Winston's side almost daily. He spent his valuable time calling me at home even late at night to give me updates and offer prayer and hope for a longer time for me to prepare to say goodbye to my baby. How do you do that????? One time when Dr. Crowe suggested I take Winston home and "just let him be a dog" Dr. Crowe laughed and laughed when my response was "he'd never been a dog before". The times of laughter were sweet among all the tears.

We gave Winston the best of care, spared no expense, literally spent over $16,000 dollars, and used the latest technologies, hyperbaric, Assis Loop, turkey tail mushrooms, light therapy, 10.5 ph water, Yunnan Baiyao, etc. He had responded very well but was in need of a blood transfusion which boosted his recovery and seemed to give him more energy.

My concerns that Winston might not be getting the competent care he needed started to grow once I was told no when I asked to have a copy of the Ultrasound. Their reason was that they had no way to make a copy, not even to locate a disk to have a copy for me on my next appointment. This was the same Vet that had told me she saw the cancer spreading and that it appeared to have a "chewed up look". I remarked that that side was the side of his surgery. She then had this shocked, blank star look that told me she either didn't realize that or that she didn't actually do the Ultrasound. I really began to question my choices for leaving Winston in their care.

Another time after Winston had his hyperbaric treatment, he was handed to me and I could tell something was not right. I sat on the waiting room sofa thinking I'd wait and speak to the Vet about it. Winston decided he did not want me holding him and he left my lap and went to the opposite end of the sofa and began to stare at me. He looked like he was mad at me. I picked him back up and held him again to wait for the Vet but he did the same thing, wiggled out of my arms, and went back to sit alone. Soon the Vet was free and I explained his odd behavior. Her response was he had been sedated. I told her he had been sedated several other times for his hyperbaric treatment. She was bewildered and her response was "he's had this treatment before"? Now she states that possibly he had not been "reversed" so she took him with her. A few minutes later she returned with him and said that the Tech had forgot to "reverse" him but now they had "reversed him and he should be fine!

As time passed and as I began to have conversations with other Vets there, I had suggested that I'd like for Winston to have another blood transfusion to help bring him out of his anemia and help him feel better. This Vet responded to me that, "No, he couldn't have another transfusion because another dog might need the blood!!!!!"

At this point, I'm realizing I need to be working with someone I can trust to have Winston's best interest and reassure me he is getting the best of care. I make an appointment with his regular Vet and we discuss the transfusion. We decide to wait a couple of days and see how he is and then request the transfusion. My Vet doesn't do transfusions, they are only done at the ER hospital. Winston seems a lot better at her office and evens eats a few treats the tech offered. He hasn't eaten today or actually since breakfast yesterday so I ask the Tech about the ingredients and she assures they are very nutritional so I purchase a bag and let me have almost the full bag as a meal. I start reading the ingredients and see the fat content is way too high for Schnauzers because of their tendency to develop pancreatitis and point this out to the tech. She brings the Vet in and she suggests that since he had not eaten during the past day that he should be ok. OMG!!!!

We leave there and drive to the ER hospital to tell them our decision for waiting on the transfusion. They immediately say Winston has a high fever and that before the transfusion he needs to be admitted so they can begin antibiotics immediately in order to bring down his temp. Funny thing is he has been eating, barking at dogs at the regular Vets office, etc. but again I blindly trust them so Winston is admitted with the instructions of calling me so I can drive back and be there during the transfusio0 n. They acknowledge they will and we drive home.

It's around 9:30 P.M. and no word so I call the ER. They explain that Winston hasn't started the IV antibiotics yet because they are waiting for a particular Tech to arrive that is "more experienced" in placing the IV!!! I guess it wasn't such an emergency to get him started after all!!! Around midnight I get the call that they are about to start the transfusion. I've been told in the past that sometimes there can be a reaction to the new blood. I just wanted to be there if it happened. Winston did good and so we head home at around 4:00 A.M. with the understanding that to not expect this transfusions to raise his levels much but that we would be able to pick him up in the morning.

I haven't received any update so I call the ER and am told that they are really happy that his levels were raised over double the expected and that they would call me back after they were able to get him to eat.

About 2 hours later the tech called and told me that Winston had drank some water, how good his vitals were and that I could come pick him up.

Roller coaster feelings of trust for this group. As I start out the door my phone rings. It is the Director of the ER. She is frantically telling me Winston is coughing up blood and that she wants me to give her permission to euthanize him. WHAT??????? She begins telling me how he isn't going to live but a few minutes and that this way will prevent him suffering. I tell her of my phone conversation only a few minutes ago with the Tech and that I am walking out the door to bring him home. She proceeds telling me his vitals and I stop her and say they are NOT the vitals the Tech just gave me. Silence. Now she starts apologizing saying how sorry she is, she is reading the WRONG CHART!!!! She then continues wanting my permission to euthanize Winston but I SCREAM TO KEEP HIM ALIVE UNTIL I GET THERE!!!

A tech is waiting in the lobby to escort me to Winston. The shock of all I've just gone thru and now seeing him strapped down with a breathing tube and hooked up to a monitor is almost all I can bare. The Director immediately starts telling me how I am causing him to suffer needlessly and that he is scared and I should just let her give him the shot. I see the monitor and his heart rate and as I begin to talk to him, he calms down. I ask her to remove everything and she says he will not be able to breath. Again, on and on she tries to fill me with guilt of how I am causing him to be afraid and suffer. The tech now says that he is stable and I again ask her to remove the tubes. She does and he seems ok. Winston seems calm. I'm doing all I can to control my racing mind and heart and think clearly as I watch my baby and try to make sane decisions. Now Winston raises his head, cries, and turns to look at the Director. She is actually rubbing his surgical spot. He lays his head back down but then raises his head, cries out and looks back at her again. She is still rubbing his surgical spot which is obviously hurting him and causing him pain. I yell at her to stop because he is still sore there. She once again says I am causing his pain and I should just give up and let him go.

My husband is here now. Maybe it will be ok. Maybe we will just take Winston home and this will be over.

WHERE IS GOD??????? I DON'T KNOW WHAT TO DO!!!!! I don't want to cause my baby to hurt more, I don't want him to be afraid. I want him to come home with me. I want this nightmare to end. I just want to take him to the park and walk him and see his funny fuzzy face and let him make me laugh like he always does. I want her to stop saying I am causing him to be afraid and suffer. I just want it to be ok again.

I agree to give up. What if she is right??? She begins but I can't let her kill my Sir Winston. I stop her.

She again does what she does best. She feels me with guilt. I give in again. My heart is breaking into a million pieces. My mind is so confused. I am losing it. I'm dizzy and feel like I'm going to vomit. Maybe it is time to say goodbye. I shake my head yes. She starts again. NOOOOOO!!!!! I can't do this. Please STOP!! This is my baby. I want my baby. I can't live without him. He's my very best friend. He has been there for me during some of the most difficult times these past few years. He makes me laugh when I'm crying. He comforts me like no other. I look into his eyes and the world is ok and I'm ok. I need my baby; how can this be real???

I look at my husband. His eyes tell me we have done all we can do. I must be strong.

I whisper in Winston's ear how I'm going to take walking at the park. Just me and him. We're not going to take Baxter and Milo, his sons. Just Winston and Mommy. Over and over as I'm sure he tries to muster up the strength to get up and go with me. I say just Winston and Mommy are going to the park. I can't tell him bye; I can't tell him I'll be fine. I can't tell him it's ok.

They give me a print of Winston's foot on a sheet of paper.
Days later:

I totally believe the ER Director killed my dog when she shouldn't have. I totally believe God heard my prayer and was/had healed Winston. I totally believe I will live and spend eternity with Winston.

It now dawns on me all the mistakes that I overlooked. All the questions, all the wrong things that happened. All the negligence and cruelty. Reading the wrong chart. Redoing a test. For what reason? Was it wrong, was it the results of another dog and put into Winston's chart?

Less than adequately trained techs. Less than caring professional Vets. Not reversing him after a procedure, not knowing where his surgical site was? Telling me another dog might need the blood!!!!!

I was told Winston was coughing up blood. I didn't see any blood. Where was the blood?

The ER Director NEVER suggested a 2nd opinion.

Never suggested we wait till tomorrow.

Never suggested we take Winston home to do it.

Never asked if I'd like to hold Winston.

I called my regular Vet and told her what had happened. Her response was he didn't have a fever at her office just before going to the ER. She also said, "they euthanize way too soon there".

Later I learned her office doesn't refer to that ER anymore.
Dr. Crowe stopped coming to Chattanooga to work anymore.

NEVER BE PUSHED INTO DOING SOMETHING UNTIL YOU HAVE TIME TO THINK IT OVER.

NEVER TOTALLY TRUST A VET, TECH, OR EVEN A PERSONAL DR.

EUTHANIZIA IS PERMANENT.

IT SHOULD BE SERIOUSLY CONSIDERED WITH TIME TO THINK IT THRU. IT CAN NOT BE REVERSED.

My therapist told me to wait till I was ready to make the decisions I still need to make.

I may never be ready.

Each time I try to make the cremation arrangements I get so sick I have to go to bed for a few days.

This is still so hard to accept but Winston is still in my freezer and I need to get thru this last part but I'm just not strong enough to go thru the process and then only bring ashes back home.

I will do this, I'm just not sure when...........

And most importantly, I lost my faith temporarily and sank like Peter. Always trust God no matter the chaos surrounding you.

I spent 3 years drowning in a deep depression. Statutes ran out. I lost my rights for justice.

I can't express enough my thanks and gratitude to Scott Fine for his amazing accomplishment with Joey's Legacy in making the world aware of the horrid treatment of our special fur baby companions by many Vets. His tireless time and untold number of hours his work has produced is simply miraculous. It's sad that so many pets and their humans have suffered such cruel and needless pain. His love and loyalty to his own sweet Joey is changing the world. Thanks to him and his sweet wife, Debbie for not giving into the deep depression this loss causes and for not giving up when it would have been so easy to do.

I'd also like to thank John Robb for his wonderful contribution to making aware the need for change thru his writings. A true hero and special man with a heart for justice for animals everywhere. Thank you.

The ER Hospital I used was River but like many nationwide has recently been purchased by VCA.

Some of the pictures of Winston includes his 2 sons, Baxter, 11 years old and has the longer tail and Milo, 5 years old who I often refer to as my heart Dr. because he has tried so hard to help heal my shattered heart.

Companion pets should in NO WAY be referred to as only property!!!!

Sir Winston Burkhart

Chapter Thirty-One

Teagan
Penny Kazmierak (A Facebook Post)

Why is it that my capuchin monkey Teagan went in to be a spayed, a procedure that I was being cautious, turns into her death and mine of sorts? all I get are attorneys that don't have the time, too many cases, even been hateful and accused me of drinking and emailing at night. I had just found out that Teagan was cremated without my permission. Tears!! Called another name. "The email was sent in the morning". That morning.the attorney sends me contingency agreements twice, first telling me she would send a demand letter. I signed. The attorney sent the wrong paperwork. Giving the Veterinarian another 30 days to preserve what they did. The attorney quits. We're not a good fit .i did nothing to deserve this. Grieve. I sent an email giving to me to ask. Copied and pasted. The attorney tells me... don't bother writing the Veterinary Board they always side with the attorney.

I was insulted by the actions of the attorney. Now every other attorney will want to know why?? on top of losing her.

I believe negligence caused the death of Teagan. It wasn't an emergency surgery. She was 5 with a life span of 30yrs plus. She did excellent I was told .i was told by the Dr. her EKG was perfect throughout the surgery. The Dr left the surgery to wash and to tell me it went fine. Then after how long, a scream to come back to recovery. Teagan was unresponsive. No amount of life saving measures and no response whatsoever ,None. The Dr says she doesn't know what happened. First cardiac arrest then I don't know. We can do an autopsy. Ahh NO YOU WONT. I was distraught but I knew .I no longer trusted this Vet. I was going to find an independent Dr to do the autopsy. I made it clear I was not ready to make any decisions .It was wrong.

It is twice the amount to replace my Teagan. 18000 to buy another and it won't be Teagan.

I don't understand. Why it is so hard to get a compassionate attorney to take this case.

Here I sit. I don't know if she had surgery. I only have a bill. I didn't see Teagan. I have been told that she was probably sold or put her in a sanctuary. Why cover up. I asked by certified letter, multiple emails, text and they ignored me. How can a cremation take place without the consent of the owner? If you consider her property ?if it were an 18000 car and it disappeared and admittedly, they burned it. they would be arrested.

I am just sick over this.

Chapter Thirty-Two

Willow's Story
Dana Greene

On March 13,2012 I took my beautiful and perfectly healthy 18 month old Doberman to the Brewster Animal Hospital in Brewster Cape Cod MA to be spayed. I was told to be there at 8:30 am and I was. Dr. Louise Morgan who was my vet there was supposed to do the surgery. I later found out the surgery wasn't done until 3:30 pm.! My poor Willow had nothing to eat or drink since the evening before, and they just took her away from me and didn't let me go in and it was the first time we were ever apart.

From that day forward my Willow was a sick dog.! She didn't want to eat.. was vomiting bile. She tried to show me her tummy hurt pushing her ball to it..(photo). On March 16 2012 I went back to Brewster.. I was worried about her sutures(photo) cause they looked very sloppy.. and worried cause she didn't want to eat.. I was trying to hand feed her bits of chicken. I asked for Dr. Morgan and what did I find out? Dr. Morgan was on vacation!!! They should have told me!!! A Megan Krauth, a VET TECH ,that I never met before ,said nothing was wrong, her sutures were fine, and gave me tramadol.. BUT IT TURNS OUT MEGAN KRAUTH A VET TECH DID THE SURGERY!!!! Dr. Morgan was not there.!!! At a later time Dr. Morgan said "someday everyone will want her " referring to Krauth. A vet tech did the anesthesia too. By the time I got records, and I had to fight to get them, another vet there Dr. Kaser said he looked in and was there for the anesthesia..and there were no complications. The records were written by hand and very hard to read.. On March 18,2012 I took Willow to the emergency vet cause she still was hardly eating or drinking and throwing up bile. They said restrict her activity and continue tramadol, and they too were sure her issues had nothing to do with the surgery.

On April 16,2012 I took Willow to the Hyannis Animal hospital. A Vet I used in the past with another dog at a different hospital was now at Hyannis. Dr. Nancy Weintrob. By this time Willow had lost 10 pounds!!! And on this day she was also having loose stool as well as vomiting and not wanting to eat. She was kept overnight and got fluid infusions, Cerina and Famodine injections, tylan powder. and was scheduled for radiology, ultrasound and blood work, urinalysis, stool sample, etc. the next day with doctor I told them I was very concerned that Brewster Animal hosp. had botched her spay or did damage of some kind. i'm still beating myself up about this cause they said there was sand in intestine but when I looked at ultrasound with Dr. Weintrob she showed me something lying flat at the bottom of her empty stomach and also said it was sand.. I do live near the beach and we go to the beach . but don't see how she ate sand. I wish I did further testing..or something. I wish I objected to the sand idea. Willow was sent home with instructions for bland diet, pepcid and tylan if loose stool continues. and the conclusion that nothing could have happened during spay...

For the next year Willow continued to lose weight, another 10 pounds. Sometimes she had a good week.. but I kept a calendar and wrote down every time she vomited bile which was almost everyday. I started having Dr. Joan Goffi, a home vet, be her vet because she was already coming to the house to care for my elderly German Shepherd... It was a constant battle with bland diets and trying to get her to eat and trying to figure out what's wrong with her for almost a year. Willow's spine bones were now visible at the top of her back. She was so skinny..Then Dr. Goffi suggested I see Dr. McCartin at Hyannis Animal Hospital (Dr. Weintrob not there anymore) because he was good at doing endoscopy's. I had an appt for March 20, 2013.

On the morning of March 20, 2013 Willow looked VERY VERY bad. It's hard for me to describe her posture. I called Hyannis Hosp. and told them she looked very bad and I wanted to come in earlier than my appt. They said come right away. A Dr. Kevin Smith came out and palpated her belly and said there was something in there(I don't know why no other Doctor did this in the whole year!). After an examination, Dr. McCartin said she had sepsis and a high fever. She was basically at death's doorstep. He said she needed emergency surgery right away and that she had a chance because she was young. He said they could do it or I could take her an hour away to another hospital that had 24 hour care. I was hysterically crying. I didn't think I could drive. Then he said" let me decide for you". I think we should do the surgery now. It turns out he had another surgery and Dr. Kevin Smith was to do the surgery..He looked so young but then I thought well maybe his eyesight is better and his hands more steady.. I can't even list all the drugs she got as well as plasma. Willow was in the hospital for 4 days and 3 nights. She had "septic abdomen- perforation of small bowel, foreign body" Dr. Kevin removed her entire small intestine because the foreign object had broken thru it. I wish he could have repaired it.. but he said it was beyond repair and he took it all out and bypassed it. He showed me what was in there. It was in pieces ,but put together it would have been a black rubbery O SHAPED OBJECT ABOUT 4 INCHES IN DIAMETER . It was almost a half inch thick. I am convinced whatever it was, it was in her body for a year, since the botched spay! I don't know how she could have eaten it or how it got down her throat, but she was abandoned there for 8 hours before the spay by the VET TECH. I imagine it was in her stomach and at some point broke and went into her intestines and ultimately perforated them. I had to divide the payment between 3 credit cards that thankfully I had or else I can't even imagine...It was almost $5,000.

Of course even the surgeons implied it was my fault. I let her eat whatever it was .... and that it had nothing to do with the botched spay done by the VET TECH at the Brewster Animal Hosp. But then how come she was perfectly healthy before the spay and a sick dog for a year after? And how come after the 2013 surgery she regained her appetite and stopped vomiting, except for the occasional times that are pretty normal ? And how come after the object was removed she gained back 25 pounds? I'm thankful beyond words that she still lives, though I don't know how without her small intestines. I lost one dog in 2002 to rymadyl and another cause of a lousy cruel vet.. So with Willow I am so thankful to still have her and feel very sorry for all the others that have had their beloveds killed. I know what it feels like.

Willow just turned 10 years old. Dr. Kevin Smith is still her vet cause I believe he saved her life. It's ironic that the same hospital that didn't find the foreign object ultimately saved her. She has some lumps and is taking Denamarin because her liver enzymes are elevated. Her face is getting grey and teeth worn but her coat is beautiful, and Dr. Smith says she's all muscle and looks good for 10 .. She is my everything! I'm an old lady that lives alone. She even sleeps with me. I always had older rescues before. Willow was my first puppy, my baby .I studied so much about raising and training a puppy so to be sure everything was good .I can't forgive myself for going to the Brewster vet and not researching .. My poor baby suffered so much for a year. I still feel her life was shortened due to losing her small intestines because of the botched spay and I'm terrified of losing her. But for now Willow can still run! We go to the beach all the time and I don't think there is any sand in her stomach.

Willow

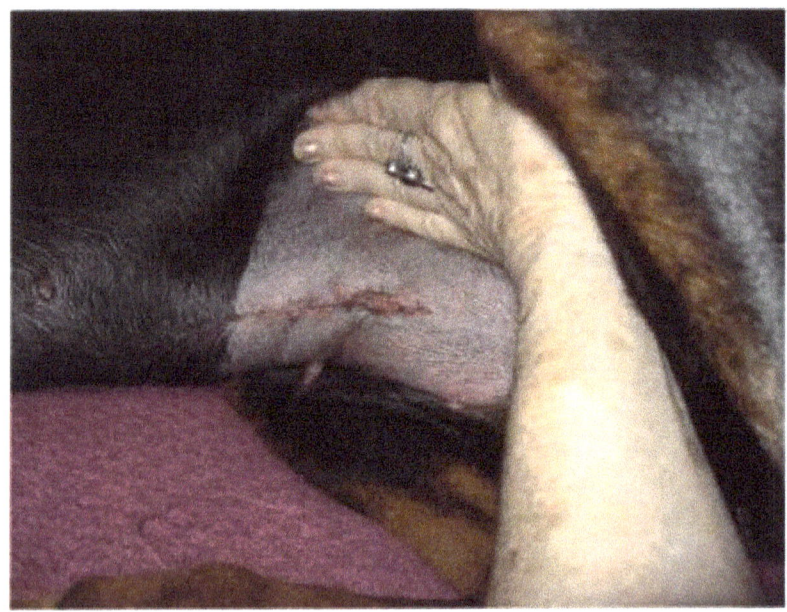

Chapter Thirty-Three

Wilson's Story

Sheryl and Timothy Blanford

Wilson (Dog) Adopted 1-18-2011 1.5 yr old rescue

My husband and I got Wilson as a 1.5 year old American Rottweiler dog from a rescue that I was working with from 2010 to 2012. Wilson was coming to our house as a foster in fall of 2010. He needed to be socialized and to be trained in basic obedience commands. We would then find a good home for Wilson. Well we found him a good home with us and he was trained and passed his CGC/Canine Good Citizen test with flying colors. Wilson became part of our family 4 months after he came to live with us. Wilson was "rescued" from a pet store in Naperville, IL. A customer heard the rottweiler was going "back to the farm" and a customer bought him and brought him in to the rescue to find a good home. Since the man already had 5 other dogs and knew the owner of the rescue it was a good idea for the rottweiler puppy. He was named Wilson from where he started out his life. WILSON = Was In Looser Store On Naper rd. Wilson was adopted out to a nice lady and her family but sadly Wilson did not like that situation and urinated on people when they came to visit. Not good. So back to the rescue. The 2nd family Wilson went to live with was the owner of the rescue neighbor across the street. Single guy with a female rottweiler. The dogs got along great but Wilson did not like the friends and he urinated on them too. So back across the street to the rescue owners house. So she asked my husband who worked part time at a dog trainer to take him and re-train him. So Wilson came to live with us and our 3 cats and 2 other dogs. A full house. Wilson got along with our cats and other dogs perfectly. Wilson also got along with us fine. Our neighbors all fell in love with him and even their kids too. Wilson never had any more issues with people again.

Now time for our healthy and happy 3 year old 110lb rottweiler for his vaccines. We take him to the vet and get all his vaccines to "keep him safe from everything" because that is what good pet parents do for the pets. Now we know better that this is the scare tactic used to sell vaccines and chemicals. We get a rabies vaccine and a combo vaccine too. We come home and he is fine but tired. He eats normal that night. In the morning he does not want his breakfast at the same time with our other 2 dogs. I did not think anything of it. He will eat when his daddy feeds him in the evening. He barely touched his food that night. Next morning and the next 3 days he barely eats anything. He is drinking normal. Next morning, he refused his food, so I called the vet. He has not eaten in 3.5 days any food of great quantity. He is losing weight and he sleeps a lot. I have taken the last 2 days of work to stay home and watch him and try to feed him throughout the day with no luck. Vet says bring him in and we will do blood work. I brought him in to the vet and he does not stand very long. Constantly laying down. This is not my happy dog. Vet draws blood and runs the tests and the tests come back perfectly healthy dog on paper. The vet says well since I am just a small clinic I can't run all of the blood work here so you will have to drive him 45 minutes to the animal hospital and they can do more blood tests and other tests too. So we drive to the hospital and he is so lethargic. It is hard to get him to walk into the building. We get him into a room and they draw more blood for different tests. The other vet sent the earlier tests to them so we can do different ones now. They do a weight on him and he is down to 95 lbs. He is so thin for a rottweiler. They do an ultrasound and other tests while the blood tests are running. We get the results back from all the tests. On paper he is healthy as a horse. WHAT??? They can find nothing wrong. My dog looks like he is so sad and miserable and dying. They say sorry we can't find anything. Maybe he is nauseous and does not want to eat. So they sent me home with anti-nausea pills and no other ideas. I get him home and comfortable and give him the meds. He pukes them up in 2 minutes. Well that is not going to work. So I have to figure out what to do to help him myself. I call friends and google and find Facebook pages for other vets names and advice. We decided to feed him whatever we can to get him to eat. This may be the end. So I got him baby food, canned cat food, canned dog food, sardines, canned chicken, anything I could think he would eat. I made a plate every few minutes of something different to get him to eat. After a day he found a few things he liked and ate tiny pieces here and there. Some room temperature and some I warmed up for him. He started to turn around. Each day he ate more and more options and he started to come back around to his old self again.

After 2 weeks he was pretty much back to normal. He was barking at the neighbors dogs through our wooden fence and running back and forth a little. We were so happy he was coming back around. Then he came in the house limping and we thought he hurt himself on the fence or the bushes near the fence. We saw his paw and his nail was coming out of the paw. We put ice on it and called the vet. Vet said come in and we will look at it.

We got there and the vet said it was probably the fence and running. Do we want to do surgery and amputate the toe? We were stunned but we declined. So we took the antibiotics and meds and let the vet know in 7 days. The nail fell off and he was sore for a few days but he was ok. A week later he came in again limping on his other front leg. He pulled 2 more nails out. We called the vet and he said to kennel him, give him these meds again and watch him for 7 days. We watched him like a hawk. He was ok. We were outside in our back yard pulling weeds and the dogs were all outside with us and Wilson came limping over with his back paw now. This is a 3rd leg/paw now. He has another nail coming out of his paw. He was not running the fence or anything. He was laying in the yard like the other 2 dogs were doing in the sun. We are stunned. We call the vet and go in and he says "Oh I guess he has SLO Disease" We are in shock. He has what? A disease? How did he get a disease? The vet says well this is an autoimmune disease where the body is attacking itself. In this case SLO is a nail disease where the nail pulls out of the nail bed all by itself. It is painful and bloody and he will have it for the rest of his life. WHAT? We take Wilson home and tell him sorry for scolding him for running the fence and keeping him kenneled and we feel it was the vets fault for not suggesting this sooner. We now have to find out and figure out what this disease is and how to manage it. I research for days and go to Facebook pages and call other vets and ask around for help. I find out that SLO is an autoimmune disease that can be triggered by over vaccinating. So I look into all kinds of help from all the holistic vets and friends I know to try to heal my baby. I switch all my dogs to raw and vow never to give another vaccine or chemical in their life.

Now this is the 2nd dog in my house with a possible over vaccinated disease or adverse vaccine reaction. A blind dog my Major and now an SLO dog my Wilson. I spend the next 12 months healing and detoxing my Wilson from vaccines and chemicals. He does not have another issue in those next 12 months. The next 5 years he has 2 small issues with his nails. We keep them short with a dremel grinder and never cut them. He is doing great with everything. Wilson will turn 11 years old in July 2021. He is a somewhat "healthy" dog for being over vaccinated. I have detoxed him off and on for 8 years since this initial incident when he was 3 yrs old. I do everything 100% natural with all my pets now. Almost killing the biggest dog in my house with vaccines woke me up quickly. If I had taken my 95 or 75 lb (previous dogs) or my 45 or 12 lb (current dogs) to get vaccinated that day too maybe they could have died.

I will not vaccinate another animal I get as a pet ever again. I am thankful for all I have learned from my animals. I am sorry that I did not know sooner to give them a better life. Mommy and daddy know now and will do better from here forward. Xoxoxo. Sheryl and Timothy Blanford Romeoville, Illinois

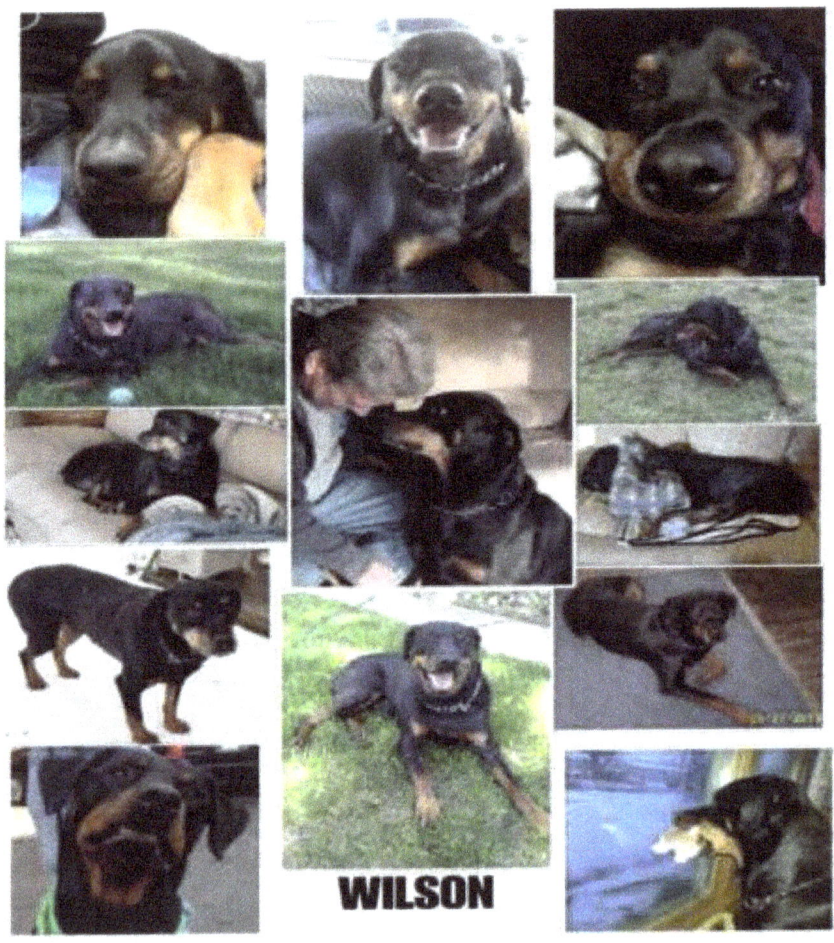

ROMEOVILLE, ILLINOIS

WILSON

Romeoville, Illinois

Chapter Thirty-Four

Zoe's Story

Melody Lively Langston

I am living a nightmare. I took my puppy April 2, 2021 to be spayed. She turned 1 year old April 6, 2021. I was contacted by the front desk of the vet there were complications with the beginning of her surgery and when they administered the anesthesia she went into cardiac arrest. The then gave her epinephrine and brought her back but decided they couldn't do the surgery. I was told that she was not awake yet and to pick her up around 3pm but call first. They wanted her to be fully awake. I wanted because I didn't know you couldn't trust your vet. At 3pm I called and said I was on my way to pick up Zoe. They put me on hold and when came back they said to please wait until about 4:45pm she was still sleeping it off.

In 1 hour received a phone call from the vet. She said Zoe had been allergic to the Anesthesia and it caused cardiac arrest. However they brought her back with the epinephrine shot in the heart. She said she had been going in and out all day but needs fluids to help flush out anesthesia from her liver. She also said she had been having seizures so she wanted me to come get her, take her to the Er Clinic, since it was Friday and leave her there so she could receive fluids for the weekend.

Ok, by this time I was devastated and having a nervous breakdown, I am a widow and Zoe saved my life getting her. My son in law took me there to pick her up. The vet never showed her face, but the front desk receptionist went and got her with fluids in her leg and back still attached. My baby looked so frail and her face was cut in places. I asked what happened to her face she said it was her flaying around in the cage having seizures. I was crying and took my baby whose eyes just rolled in her head. We got her to the car and I held her but before we could get out of the drive she started seizing again. I couldn't hold her. My son in law stopped the car and came to my door and took her and said I need to hold her and you drive to ER clinic. So as we were changing places the receptionist ran out there screaming and crying telling me she was so so sorry for what has happened to Zoe. I couldn't even talk to her. I just got in the car and drove away. We got to Er Clinic and left Zoe. Crying my eyes out. They told me I had to come pick her up at 7am Saturday because they closed from 7am - noon. I was in shock so I agreed. I went the next morning with my granddaughter and picked up my frail baby, brought her home for an hour until another vet opened and took her there for observation until ER Clinic reopened. Crazy it was just crazy. Zoe did not know any of us. Right before noon I went and picked Zoe back up and returned my baby to the ER Clinic. The Vet that was working there came outside and talked to me. She said if Zoe wasn't better by 48 hrs it would be best to put her to sleep. I was devastated. But I went home and waited. I called every 2 hrs to check on her. Sunday was Easter so we went to our Sunday Easter Service and after church they called me and told me I could come get Zoe when I got ready. After church we went and got her. She acted strange towards us but she could smell and she knew who we were. And was so happy. She was blind, she did not bark anymore, she sleeps under my bed instead of in the bed with me. She doesn't know to move when she's standing right under you. She has regained some of her sight but still has bad days. It comes and goes. She use to love riding with me in the car and going places but now she doesn't, she whines and cries the whole time.

I found a specialist vet about 30 minutes away but her tests are expensive. The Vet that did all of this gave me paperwork of everything they gave her and what they said happened I took to this specialist.

She did tests and said she will never regain her sight totally, she has brain damage and possibly liver damage. I am taking her back on May 5, 2021 to get a liver test done. I have to split it up because I am on a fixed income.

The State of Louisiana where I live will only make them pay me what I paid for my dog. They look at her as property. I am going to write a new law and hopefully it is admissible to our legislatures.

My Zoe has changed but I still love her and will work with her to help retrain her. She is learning day by day new things. She is a Shorkie. Nobody will help me, such as an attorney. They don't want to get involved. I am sorry this is so long. I have to see if someone can help me.

Zoe

Chapter Thirty-Five

Zorro's Story
Erin Greise

On Friday, July 24, 2020 at 9:00am, I had an appointment for Zorro with Dr. Kayode Garraway at Seattle Veterinary Specialists (SVS) in regard to his coughing and to address his trachea. Due to COVID restrictions I was unable to go inside and meet Dr. Garraway in person, so we spoke on the phone. The doctor performed X-rays and bloodwork, then called me on the phone as I waited outside to discuss treatment for him. He told me he was going to put Zorro on Prednisolone and Terbutaline. I told him *very firmly* that I had a lot of concerns about Prednisolone, especially due to it exacerbating congestive heart failure. *I also firmly told him I didn't want to do that and was uncomfortable giving it to him.* **The doctor assured me that he would be ok and that it wouldn't be a problem.** He said that studies from 2017 and 2018 proved that it wasn't the case, and that I should give it to him. **He again assured me it wouldn't be a problem.** *Again, I expressed my concerns* ... but he told me to give it to him and he would call me on Tuesday to see how Zorro was doing.

At 12:30am on Monday, July 27th, Zorro started to display signs of respiratory distress. I called them (SVS) at 12:41am and told them what was happening and that I was on my way to their hospital. When I arrived, I still couldn't go inside due to COVID restrictions, so I waited outside by the door as they took Zorro inside and put him into an oxygen tent. I called them for an update on his condition, and was told by the attending doctor, Dr. Karen Lin, DVM that Zorro was still in the oxygen tent and was breathing better. She wanted to stabilize him more and then repeat the X-rays they had been taken on Friday. After the X-rays, Dr. Lin called me and said Zorro was in extreme congestive heart failure and that his prognosis was poor.

I told Dr. Lin about the Prednisolone that Zorro had been prescribed and given, and **the doctor replied that it was the medicine given to him that caused Zorro's congestive heart failure! She said there was NO sign of congestive heart failure in Friday's X-rays.** She then told me my options were to euthanize him or to keep him in an oxygen tent for a few days while they administered medications to drain the fluid out of his lungs . . . and she said she *needed a decision and money immediately.* I told her I wanted to keep him in the oxygen tent and was ready to do treatment; and I also needed to call my mom. Within only a few minutes on the phone with my mom, Dr. Lin called me on the phone and said *I "had to euthanize him because he could die at any moment!"* She brought me in to see him; I pet him for only a few seconds when he fell over having a seizer. The doctor quickly and boldly told me "I had to do it, and do it RIGHT NOW" ... she gave me no other option but to euthanize Zorro **immediately.** She gave me no time to think or make a decision - no time to say goodbye, or even tell him I loved him. She administered the shot to him before I could even understand what was happening, and then my Zorro was gone. He went from breathing better and stabilizing . . . to dying before I knew it or even realized what happened.

While I was still in shock and gneving from his passing, and after finding out it was the medicine had killed him, Dr. Karen Lin demanded payment of $1,209.

So . . . not only did they kill my precious Zorro . . . but demanded payment to do so. It's their fault all this happened and Zorro would still be alive and with me if I had not taken him there. Zorro did not deserve this, and I **will mourn for the rest of my life.**

Zorro

Chapter Thirty-Six

SO NOW WE'RE COOKING...

Lots of changes happening here...I'm getting, on average, about one new inquiry per day seeking help with allegations of negligence or malpractice. This compares to the 10-15 per month that I used to quote. Is malpractice increasing? Probably not. Is Joey's Legacy becoming more widely known? Uh huh...yep. Look how our team has grown, and will continue to grow. All it took was the very tragic loss of a beloved companion animal at the hands of an arrogant narcissist (that's Joey's vet) and the resulting ongoing, unforgiving attitude of a companion animal parent (that's me, folks) to form an organization that grew from one to almost 2,600 in about 4 years.

In other words, Joey's vet pissed off the wrong guy.

Hell hath no fury like an irate, betrayed and broken-hearted companion animal parent. And we're just getting started...

Best-selling author JL Robb and I met through a mutual friend, and his series, "Joey's Legacy-Seeking Truth and Integrity in Veterinary Medicine-Volume 1" began in February 2021 when it hit Amazon.com and all the major booksellers. Volume 2 will be released in 30-60 days. Volume 2 will be a bit different and will expose Joey's vet.

The 9-time Emmy winning documentarian John Biffar has agreed to produce and direct "Joey's Legacy-The Documentary", which we hope will attract many television and other media channels. We are very excited that someone of John's caliber is on our team.

Lori Johnston, who many of you know from our Sunday night shows, is our marketing consultant and is in the early stages of creating meaningful change in our marketing efforts for Joey's Legacy. Lori will be a very positive force for Joey's Legacy.

Our media consultant, Colleen Beasley , is the newest member of our team. Colleen will deal strictly with the media, scheduling interviews with Jerry, John and me, and other types of interaction that will promote and expand the prominence of Joey's Legacy and our mission.

One of our new members heard about us, and asked me a very interesting question: she wanted to know what the world for companion animals would be like if I woke up from a dream about that subject.

That's pretty easy:

Every state in this country, every country in the world, any civilization where companion animals existed would be a place where all animals are revered, not discounted...are loved unconditionally, as they love us. All people would feel as we do about animals, and animal cruelty would be a thing of the past. Every state would have laws protecting animals. Every veterinary facility would be inspected biannually, with or without complaints. Bad actors in the profession would wake up and be truthful and transparent with their clients when a procedure or a surgery goes bad. Vet board members would stop the duplicity, the deception and the two-faced bravado and realize that there is no glory in being a member of a body that garners no respect, no trust and should be dismantled and restructured and that, by not disciplining their colleagues firmly and fairly, they perpetuate the careers of sloppy, sometimes incompetent, practitioners and, by doing so, they are indirectly responsible for the permanent injury and demise of many of our beloved family members. All staff members of veterinarians would be fully trained and certified. Only those with a profound love for animals would work in the profession, and all the others would have the wisdom and maturity to realize that their career path should be elsewhere.

My message to the moles in this group: take this message back to your bad actor bosses. If you're sneaking around here, that's fine with me. You probably need the education and humility that being a member of this group provides. Tell your bosses, and you might already feel it, that the landscape is slowly changing and definitely not in your favor. There are 85 million of us, parents of companion animals, and a much smaller number of veterinary practitioners that need attitude adjustments. Make your positive changes now. You'll have no choice, sooner or later.

The Jig is Up!

Final Disposition of Joey's Case

Gene Rinderknecht, DVM
Case number: 2017-044318
VM 6617

Dr. Rinderknecht was present and sworn in by the court reporter.

Dr. Powell was recused from this case due to her participation on the Probable Cause Panel.

Dr. Rinderknecht was charged with violation of 474.214 (1)(ee) "Failing to keep contemporaneously written medical records as required by rule of the board."

Dr. Rinderknecht was also charged with violation of 474.214 (1)(r) "Being guilty of incompetence or negligence by failing to practice medicine with that level of care, skill, and treatment which is recognized by a reasonably prudent veterinarian as being acceptable under similar conditions and circumstances."

After discussion by the board the following motions were made.

MOTION: Ms. Inzina made the motion to dismiss the 474.214(1)(r) charge.

SECOND: Ms. Johnson.

BOARD OF VETERINARY MEDICINE
General Business Meeting
December 14, 2018
Page | 9

Motion passed unanimously.

MOTION: Dr. Nelson made the motion to accept the settlement stipulation with $2,000.00 in fines and $357.01 in costs to be paid within 30 days of the filing of the final order, 1 year of probation with this meeting counting as the first appearance and the last appearance to be at the board meeting proceeding the end of probation. During the 1 year of probation, a records pull of 5 patients medical records shall be completed and sent to the board for review.

SECOND: Dr. Partridge.
Motion passed unanimously.

Number	Class	Incident Date	Status	Disposition	Disposition Date	Discipline Date - Description
2014032504	Licensed Activity	07/26/2012	Closed	Final Order	10/07/2015	10/06/2015 - Board Meeting Attendance Or Appearance 10/00/2015 • Cost 10/06/2015. Education 10/06/2015 • Fine 10/06/2015. Probaaon
2010035802	Licensed Activtty	05/10/2010	Closed	Final Order	03/23/2012	03/23/2012 • Cost 03/23/2012. Educaaon 03/23/2012 • Fine 03/23/2012. Probaaon
2017044318	Licensed Activity		Closed	Final Order	01/22/2019	01/18/2019 - Board Meeting Attendance Or Appearance 01/18/2019. Cost 01/18/2019. Fine 01/18/2019 - Inspections 01/18/2019. Probaaon

The End

joeyslegacy.org

www.ingramcontent.com/pod-product-compliance
Lightning Source LLC
LaVergne TN
LVHW072022060526
838200LV00058B/4646